Europe's Global Links

Europe's Global Links

The European Community and Inter-Regional Cooperation

Edited by
Geoffrey Edwards
and
Elfriede Regelsberger

Pinter Publishers
London

© Geoffrey Edwards and Elfriede Regelsberger 1990

First published in Great Britain in 1990 by
Pinter Publishers Limited
25 Floral Street, London WC2E 9DS

British Library Cataloguing in Publication Data

A CIP catalogue record for this book is available from the
British Library
ISBN 0 86187 878 7

Typeset by Communitype Communications Ltd, Leicester
Printed and bound in Great Britain by Biddles Ltd of Guilford and
King's Lynn

Contents

Preface

I warmly welcome the publication of this book on inter-regional dialogue between the European Community and other groups of states. It appears at a time when European integration has entered a decisive phase, indeed, perhaps one of the most important phases since the Treaties of Rome.

Far-reaching changes are taking place in the countries of Central and Eastern Europe in the quest for democracy, freedom, human rights and self-determination. The division of Europe and thus also of Germany, which has lasted several decades, is being overcome. At this juncture the European Community is proving to be an anchor of stability. As an example of democratic coexistence in peace and security as well as economic prosperity, it is an encouragement to other countries. The European Community and its member states are aware of their global responsibility. They strive for a coherent foreign policy and jointly maintain close relations with their neighbours in Europe as well as with states and groups of states on all other continents. The Community takes all possible steps to promote voluntary regional associations in other parts of the world. In these relations new thinking must be established in terms of openness, cooperation and dialogue. The path of political dialogue and economic cooperation embarked upon by the EC in a spirit of true partnership is proving to be the path of the future.

In particular the latest series of regional meetings between the EC and its partners, the ACP states, ASEAN, the countries of Central America, the Rio Group and the Arab Cooperation Council has demonstrated that Europe is viewed as an example worthy of imitation, and as a respected and sought-after partner. The path of a true balance of interests which the EC has always sought in shaping its external relations remains promising. This was by no means clear when the EC began its policy of cooperation with other groups of states.

The 1975 Lomé Convention, comprising 48 African, Caribbean and Pacific states (today Lomé IV includes 68 countries), was a pioneering development as regards cooperation between industrialized and developing countries based on partnership. Moreover, it provided the ACP countries with an important forum for their own dialogue with each other. Today the Lomé Convention is the only international instrument of cooperation in the North–South context which combines the areas of trade, raw materials and development.

The traditionally extensive trade and economic relations with

The ASEAN countries, as well as the need for close political dialogue on a long-term basis between both groups of states, led to the conclusion of the EC–ASEAN cooperation agreement of 1980. This new form of cooperation, involving major political and economic components, reassured the ASEAN countries that they also had a true partner for dialogue outside the region, who would function as an impartial counsellor and partner in times of regional tension. At the same time it has made the EC increasingly aware that, as the process of internal integration advances, its international dimension is growing. The agreement has set an example for similar arrangements of a political and economic nature.

In 1984 the series of annual ministerial meetings of the states on the Central American isthmus began in San José de Costa Rica. This process has made a decisive contribution to the stability of the region and can be described today as a successful example of cooperation between two regions in a spirit of partnership. Since 1987 an informal exchange of views has developed with the countries of Latin America which cooperate within the Rio Group.

The last new-style regional agreement for the time being was concluded with the countries of the Arab Cooperation Council, again in Luxembourg. Following the agreements between the EC and the Arab countries bordering on the Mediterranean, it establishes a link with a region which has close traditional ties with the EC and contributes to economic and political stability in the region.

The concept of inter-regional cooperation is developing further. New forms of cooperation are being discussed and realized. Talks have begun with the EFTA countries on the European economic area which will link the EC and EFTA through a kind of common market. But not only Europe, including Eastern Europe, is drawing closer together. Throughout the world new forms of regional cooperation are emerging, from the Arab Maghreb Union to the Arab Cooperation Council, from the South Asian Association for Regional Cooperation to Latin American cooperation between the Southern Cone countries and the Andean Pact. The EC will pay close attention to these and other associations, place its experience at their disposal and establish new cooperative relations. In so doing it will make an important contribution to the ever closer network of global economic relations and towards strengthening multilateral trade, but above all towards greater regional stability and more calculable international relations.

Thus I expect the EC's regional dialogue to continue to provide impetus for ever stronger global partnership and a true balance of interests benefiting the international community of nations.

Hans-Dietrich Genscher
Auswärtiges Amt
Bonn

Foreword

Group-to-group dialogue

The European Community (EC) and its member states not only claim to play an active role today in international politics, but they are also expected and sometimes pressured to do so by the outside world. The relationships of the EC/Twelve with other (mostly regional) groupings are a major part, and an outstanding feature, of Europe's endeavour jointly to formulate and implement a 'European foreign policy' (Article 30.1 of the Single European Act (SEA) of 1986).

This volume tries to catch the phenomenon of the EC/Twelve's group-to-group approach and its dynamism, especially over the decade of the 1980s. It also offers some explanations on the motives behind such an approach and other determining factors such as economic and political interests, and institutional prerequisites. The studies presented here focus on the European side rather than on the other groupings, and on, therefore, the EC institutions and European Political Cooperation (EPC). It examines above all how the two European institutional structures seek to define and implement a 'consistent' external posture as required under Article 30.6 of the SEA. Several contributions focus therefore on the interests and behaviour of the actors involved at the European level, while others analyse the most prominent features of the EC/Twelve's political dialogue and economic cooperation with other groupings in greater detail.

The book is based on the results of a research project conducted in 1988–9 at the Institut für Europäische Politik, Bonn, in collaboration with both academic experts and officials from a number of different bodies involved in European diplomacy. In July 1988 and in June 1989, two international workshops were held to discuss the findings of this research with other academic colleagues and other officials from the EC Commission and EC Governments as well as from the European Parliament and diplomats from among the EC/Twelve's dialogue partners.

This book could not have been published without the cooperation and support of many people and institutions, for which I extend our gratitude. I should like especially to thank my colleagues who readily accepted the invitation to contribute to the volume but who also accepted suggestions and criticism with considerable good grace.

Finally I have to thank the Fritz Thyssen Foundation, Cologne, for its generous grant to conduct the research project and the Auswärtiges Amt, Bonn, which gave financial support for the conferences.

Wolfgang Wessels, Project Director
Institut für Europäische Politik
Bonn

List of contributors

Geoffrey Edwards	Royal Institute of International Affairs, London/University of Southern California
Catherine Flaesch-Mougin	Centre for European Research, University of Rennes I
Wolf Grabendorff	Institute for European–Latin American Relations, Madrid
* Peter von Jagow	Political Division, Auswärtiges Amt, Bonn
Barbara Lippert	Institut für Europäische Politik
Manfred Mols	University of Mainz
* Karl-Heinz Neunreither	Secretariat General of the European Parliament
* Simon Nuttall	Directorate General I, Commission of the European Communities
Thomas Pedersen	Institute of Political Studies, University of Copenhagen
Elfriede Regelsberger	Institut für Europäische Politik, Bonn
* Eberhard Rhein	Directorate General I, Commission of the European Communities
Otto Schmuck	Institut für Europäische Politik, Bonn
* Andreas von Stechow	Economic Division, Auswärtiges Amt, Bonn

* Note: Messrs von Jagow, Neunreither, Nuttall, Rhein and von Stechow write in their personal capacities and in no way commit the institutions to which they are attached.

Part I
Introduction: concepts and instruments

1 The dialogue of the EC/Twelve with other regional groups: a new European identity in the international system?[1]

Elfriede Regelsberger

The pace and potential significance of the changes in Eastern Europe have become issues of almost overwhelming proportions in the European political and academic debate. Negotiations on other aspects of Europe's future, including the completion of the Internal Market and the establishment of Economic and Monetary Union, have taken on a new, and for some an urgent, quality. The issues raised by Eastern Europe also add an important new dimension to the existing external relationships of the Community and the often more discreet operations of European Political Cooperation (EPC). This volume develops a constituent part of these two threads of 'European foreign policy', the relations of the EC and its member states with other groups of states.

This 'dialogue' — based on economic cooperation in its broadest sense and political consultations of varying depths — is not an accidental development. It is determined by various factors including the internal dynamics of the EC and EPC, the role of the nation-state in an interdependent world and the behaviour of the superpowers. An examination of the phenomenon is not merely a pleasant academic exercise; its results could also bring about a better understanding of the EC/Twelve's present role in the world. It may, in addition, suggest appropriate steps to be taken towards the declared aim of 'consistency' in European foreign policy-making (Article 30.5 of the Single European Act (SEA)) and offer insights for the forthcoming debate in 1990–2 on further reforms in matters of foreign policy and external relations.

The significance of dialogue

A number of observations can be made about the significance of the EC's dialogue with other groups of states. These include the following:

*Group-to-group relations make up an impressive list of activities
undertaken by Europe towards the world*

Group-to-group relations today absorb a considerable amount of time
and energy on the part of those politicians and officials involved in the
management of the EC's external relations and of EPC. The network of
cooperation between the EC/Twelve and their partner groups is an
impressive one. To illustrate the number and range of activities that
take place, the calendar of ministerial meetings organized during the
German Presidency of January to June 1988[2] may serve as an example:

— the meeting of the EC and the EFTA Economic Ministers on 2
February 1988, the second in the history of this relationship;
— 'San José IV', the fourth conference since 1984 of Foreign Ministers
of the EC countries and those of the Contadora Group and the five
Central American states on 29 February–1 March 1988;
— the first meeting between the Twelve (represented by the Foreign
Ministers of the Troika) and 12 representatives from the ACP group
— explicitly and exclusively devoted to the political situation in
Southern Africa on 26 April 1988;
— an informal exchange of views at ministerial level between the
Twelve and the 'Group of Eight' or the 'Rio Group' (i.e. the
Contadora Group, Argentina, Brazil, Peru, Uruguay) to discuss the
political developments in the region — the second meeting since its
inception in 1987;
— the seventh meeting since 1978 between the EC/Twelve and
ASEAN at the level of Foreign Ministers on 2–3 May 1988;
— the annual Council of Ministers' session under the Lomé
Convention between the EC and the then 66 ACP countries, 10–11
May 1988;
— the meeting between the President of the Council and the
Commissioner in charge of North–South relations with
representatives from the Gulf Cooperation Council on the occasion
of signing a Cooperation Agreement and a Joint (political)
Declaration, 15 June 1988;
— the participation of Commissioner de Clercq (in charge of the EC's
external relations) at the Economics Ministers meeting of EFTA,
15 June 1988;
— the meeting between the Foreign Ministers (Troika) and
representatives from the Arab League, 24 June 1988 — the first in
the history of the Euro-Arab dialogue;
— the meeting between the President of the Council and
Commissioner de Clercq and the Secretary General from the CMEA
on the occasion of the signing of the General Declaration, 25 June
1988 — the beginning of a new relationship between Eastern and
Western Europe.

The list excludes all the contacts and negotiations undertaken at the official level, primarily by the Presidency staff and Commission personnel. In addition to all these activities at the ministerial and official levels, regular contacts took place between parliamentarians or businessmen from both sides, thus adding another dimension to the complex network.

The origins of the group-to-group approach can be traced back to the association agreements of Yaoundé I, II (1963 and 1969) and of Arusha (1968–9) linking a number of former colonies in Africa (and Madagascar) with the EC. But it began to take shape in the mid-1970s when the crises in the Mediterranean Basin and the Arab–Israeli conflict and also internal EC developments such as enlargement called for a more active international role of the then EC/Nine. The result was the Euro-Arab Dialogue and cooperation with the ACP Group within the Lomé Convention of 1975, followed later by agreements with the Mediterranean countries. Thereafter contacts were extended towards Asia. The first ministerial conference between ASEAN and the EC/Nine in 1978 is often referred to as the real date of birth of the group-to-group dialogue.

As Table 1.1 indicates, 'inter-regional' cooperation has entered a remarkable period of growth since the early 1980s. The group of the EC/Twelve's privileged partners was enlarged towards Latin America, thus broadening the existing (loose) arrangement between the EC Commission and the Group of Latin American Ambassadors in Brussels (GRULA). After the political change in the Soviet Union in 1985, the way was opened for renewal of contacts with Eastern Europe, culminating in 1988 with the signing of the General Declaration and an agreement on trade between the EC and Hungary. At the same time, existing links like those with the ACP Group and the Arab League were (for different reasons) supplemented by new ones with more restricted participation. The political dialogue with the African Front Line states was a response by the EC/Twelve to the increased external pressure to revise Europe's policy towards South Africa. Closer contacts with the Gulf Cooperation Council were strongly supported by the Twelve themselves as a sign of solidarity towards moderate Arabs threatened by the Iran/Iraq war and the Islamic fundamentalist movements. A European Community reinvigorated by the Single European Act also extended cooperation with the EFTA countries beyond the existing framework of bilateral agreements and opened political consultations with the non-EC members of the Council of Europe in 1983.

Table 1.1 - The growth of group-to-group relations

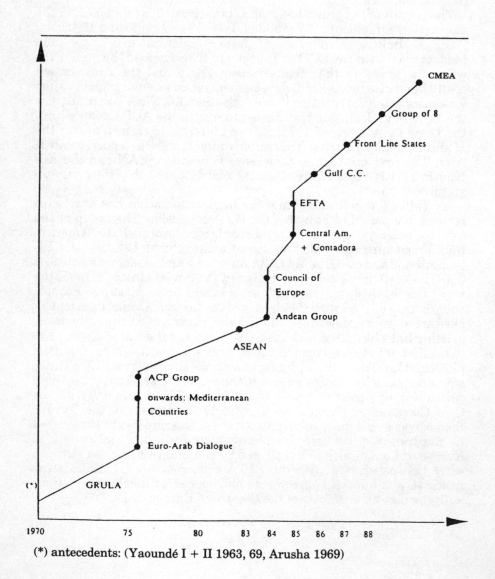

(*) antecedents: (Yaoundé I + II 1963, 69, Arusha 1969)

Table 1.2 EC trade with the dialogue partners and selected countries*

1986 total	Imports 334 563	%	1980	Exports 341 934	%	1980	Trades balance 7 371
ACP Group	19 575	5.8	3.6	16 019	4.7	3.3	−3 526
Andean Pact	4 579	1.3	0.7	3 953	1.1	0.6	−626
Arab League	34 273	10.2	11.3	38 663	11.3	7.4	4 390
ASEAN	9 108	2.7	1.3	8 217	2.4	1.1	−891
Contadora Group	5 987	1.7	0.9	5 487	1.6	1.1	−500
5 Central American States	1 103	0.3	0.2	643	0.1	0.1	−460
CMEA	24 884	7.4	3.8	20 254	6.0	3.4	−4 630
Council of Europe	75 268	22.4	6.7	86 925	25.4	9.7	11 657
EFTA	78 650	23.5	9.4	87 191	25.5	12.0	8 541
Front Line States	1 774	0.5	—	1 588	0.4	—	−186
Group of Eight	16 682	4.9	2.0	11 515	3.3	2.1	−5 167
GCC	12 396	3.7	6.7	14 781	4.3	2.5	2 385
Med. Basin†	28 311	8.5	6.2	36 326	10.6	8.1	8 015
Latin America	20 046	6.0	2.6	13 830	4.0	2.4	−6 216
USA	56 643	16.9	8.5	75 151	22.0	5.6	18 508
Japan	33 215	9.9	2.4	11 399	3.3	1.0	−21 816

* Table 1.2 indicates that in most cases the dialogue partners were able to improve their performance in trade during the period 1980–6. One could assume possible effects of the group-to-group agreements, but it is also clear from the figures that even those countries, like the CMEA, that do not enjoy preferential access to the EC market, increased their shares over the 1980s.

† includes the countries listed in Table 1.3 (plus Albania, Ceuta, Melilla, Gibraltar)
— no data available
Source: calculated according to: *Eurostat, External Trade, Monthly Statistics,* No. 4, Luxembourg, 1987, p. 104.

*Group-to-Group relations are a link between important trading
partners and those of less economic significance*

The figures of Table 1.2 show that group-to-group relations are not
limited to regions and countries that are Europe's biggest trading
partners. Those with only marginal shares in the EC's trade are also
included. This suggests that group-to-group dialogue is not exclusively
or even primarily based on economic interests from a European point of
view at least, but on political ones — as many of the subsequent chapters
show. The ratio of a low economic relevance, on the one hand, and the
high quality of inter-regional cooperation, on the other, may support the
view that political motives are the driving force of the EC/Twelve's
approach. It is precisely through the means they have at their disposal,
like the granting of privileges in the field of trade or offering diplomatic
support and political solidarity, that the EC/Twelve wish to make their
contribution to foster economic development and peace in the world.

If we measure group-to-group relations against the use of EC
instruments, a specific hierarchy of partners emerges imposed mainly
by political considerations. Most far-reaching trade concessions have
been extended to the ACP countries, followed by the countries of the
Mediterranean. The signatories of the Lomé Conventions also receive
the biggest share of the EC's development aid (around 60 per cent of the
total) while the rest is destined for the technical and financial aid
offered to the non-associated developing countries (primarily in Asia
and, to a lesser degree, in Latin America). The EFTA countries also
enjoy free access to the Common Market on the basis of complete
reciprocity. Other groups like the Gulf Cooperation Council and
ASEAN do not profit from preferential agreements but are treated only
according to the most-favoured-nation clause. If they are granted
developing country status, they are much better off and enjoy the
Generalized System of Preferences.

Group-to-group relations are a 'global phenomenon'

The examples given so far make clear that Europe's partners in inter-
regional cooperation come from both the 'Third World', the 'newly
industrialized countries', the 'West' and 'Eastern Europe'. They are also
located both in regions of crisis and peace. Group-to-group relations may
therefore be understood as a phenomenon of a global dimension. To be
sure, the existence and the policy of the EC can be seen as the major
stimulus for such a development. But if we widen our Eurocentric view,
we realize that other groups of states emerge as actors on the
international scene (for instance, the new Maghreb Union). It seems as
if this sort of collective approach is more effective in coping with the
global challenges than the individual steps of the nation-states can be.
They may fill the gap between traditional bilateralism and

universalism, thus stabilizing the network of international relations without, however, replacing those other forms either in the short run, or presumably in the long run.

The Phenomenon Explained

As we want to go beyond a mere quantifying exercise to explain the nature and basic elements of group-to-group dialogue, the following assumptions are considered as a useful point of reference.

Group-to-Group relations are the 'natural' answer of the EC/Twelve to managing global interdependence

Given the external challenges faced by the smaller and medium-sized countries of Western Europe, the EC/Twelve's will to 'endeavour jointly to formulate and implement a European foreign policy' (Article 30.1 of the SEA) may be regarded as a 'natural' reaction. Given also the uncertainties about political and economic developments elsewhere in a world of global interdependence, some kind of collective problem-solving would seem to be an appropriate strategy to preserve national interests. But this confronts the EC member states with a dilemma: cooperation with the European partners may increase the individual member state's influence on the international scene (and also the positions of the other members of the group); at the same time, national foreign policy becomes more 'vulnerable' to pressure from the rest of the group. Participating in such a collective approach means a 'give and take' and that limits the autonomy in foreign policy which ranks so high in the traditional perceptions of the sovereign nation-state in Western Europe.

The constant extension of the external relations of the EC and the growth of EPC activities suggest that cooperation is seen as a means of maintaining and perhaps even improving governments' room for manoeuvre and of providing a certain influence on international developments. Group-to-group relations are part of this collective approach, though they by no means replace existing forms of traditional bilateral or other kinds of multilateral cooperation. Through regular contacts between the EC/Twelve and their partner groups, the behaviour and policies of the latter become more transparent and calculable for EC governments.

Group-to-group relations are not an original concept, but the result of the EC/Twelve's 'internal logic'

Contrary to the assumptions of neo-functionalist theory, collective foreign policy-making at the European level does not imply an automatic transfer of competences from the national to the Community level. It may be better described as a 'pooling' and 'mixing' of national sovereignty with the powers assigned to the EC — sometimes also referred to as 'cooperative federalism' in analogy to the present collective share in responsibilities in national federal systems.[3]

In the field of the EC's external relations, this trend has expressed itself in the growing number of 'mixed agreements'[4] and in a complex system of outside representation, partly through the EC Commission alone, partly together with the Presidency of the Council — the so-called 'bicephalous' Presidency — or even in a 'multicephalous' way.[5] The character of the EC's 'interlocking system' (EG–Verflechtungssystem)[6] is also reflected in an increased interplay between the policies carried out in the Community framework and those originating from the cooperation of the EC member states within EPC.[7]

The dialogue of the EC/Twelve with other groups of states in its present shape confirms this general trend towards constantly enlarging the scope for activities carrying a 'European' label. It adds another dimension to the existing multi-faceted picture of a European foreign policy. It does not develop in a linear and precisely defined manner, but more in an accidental and pragmatic way. If, however, this assumption is correct, the group-to-group dialogue — or to be more precise the posture of the EC/Twelve in it — will be determined by similar factors inherent in the complex system of intra-European decision-making in general.

*Group-to-group relations are the product of a complex and
cumbersome intra-European bargaining process*

The growth rate of group-to-group cooperation since the early 1980s suggests a considerable convergence of views among the EC/Twelve about the importance of the approach. Those directly involved may pursue quite different goals, but positions seem to converge at a given stage without anyone obstructing the approach completely. Each party within the EC considers the 'benefit' of collective policy-making greater than its 'costs'. The member states involved do not fear or perceive a loss of national sovereignty or a greater degree of exposure to 'pressure' from the partners, nor do they limit themselves in their freedom of traditional diplomacy through participation in group-to-group relations. On the contrary, the multilateral level adds a new dimension to their external posture without replacing old ones.

Observers and officials alike, however, have commented on the cumbersome nature of the decision-making process in a system with a multitude of actors and based almost exclusively on the consensus principle. Whether the nature of foreign policy-making of the EC-Twelve is already close to what Fritz W.-Scharpf described when analysing the CAP and other EC sector policies as the 'joint-decision trap'[8] is open to debate. Scharpf argues that the institutional development of the EC system leads to a cumbersome bargaining process in which short-term national interests prevail over common values and goals. Each participant measures his consent to a common decision against the profits he can immediately draw from it. This behaviour is seen to be detrimental to adequate problem-solving, producing only sub-optimal solutions or — even worse — leading towards immobility of the whole system.

Some of Scharpf's observations may also apply to the group-to-group dialogue. Consensus on the 'political' elements of the approach dealt with in EPC seems to be easier to achieve than agreement on the 'economic' side of it. Depending on the nature and substance of this part, intra-European decision-making may be demanding. In view of the extension of competences given to the European Parliament through the SEA in the area of the EC's external relations (on Association Agreements, for example), it is more likely than not that the requirements of bargaining between the twelve governments and the EC institutions will even grow. MEPs will try to change the 'underdog' position of the EP in almost all group-to-group dialogues (except for the EC/Twelve–ACP case) to a more influential 'player' at the European level (see Chapter 12). This more active role will not necessarily be in line with the member states' policy, thus increasing the need for intra-European bargaining.

Group-to-group relations are a promising strategy to bring about 'consistency' in Europe's international profile

This contrasts somewhat with earlier points. It starts with the objective of efficiency in intra-European decision-making in matters of foreign policy. With such an aim, group-to-group relations may lead to a fulfilment of the SEA that 'the external policies of the European Community and the policies agreed in EPC must be consistent' (Article 30.5).

Of course, competences on matters of foreign policy remain formally split between the Community and the national level, with decision-making following the procedures developed in each system. The SEA, however, reflected the reality of an evergrowing interdependence of the issues of international politics. Inter-regional cooperation could become the 'model' for relations in that issues of both 'high' and 'low' politics are brought together and dealt with from an overall perspective. The 'mix' of policies, actors and instruments typical of this approach could approximate what has been called a 'composed' ('zusammengesetzte')[9] or a 'clustered' ('gebündelte')[10] European foreign policy. Such an interlocking EC system may be the best way to improve Europe's international profile.

Whether the EC/Twelve manage to translate their common will into the action of 'speaking with one voice' depends on their ability to find a common denominator. It also requires increased mutual interest and a better knowledge of the activities of the various actors. Tensions emerge particularly when precise 'offers' in terms of trade concessions and financial aid have to be made; simple diplomatic support and consultations are less contentious.

Group-to-group relations help to reduce uncertainties for third countries about the power of the EC/Twelve

What has been said about the EC/Twelve's interest in multilateral cooperation as a means of managing global interdependence also applies to the dialogue partners. Though the incentives to seek dialogues with Europe and the means to shape it may be different, third countries assign considerable weight to undertaking collective steps. To approach the EC/Twelve together offers a better bargaining position from which to gain economic benefits and political support. Collective action also helps to overcome the feeling of inferiority *vis-à-vis* the 'mighty' Europeans. But membership of a group, not only offers a promising strategy to safeguard interests and mobility in international politics. Multilateral relationships are also seen as a relatively stable framework that reduce uncertainties about the behaviour of other actors. It is also said that changes in the policy of a country are less directly felt and perhaps balanced through group membership. The 'civilian power' Europe seems to be a particularly attractive partner with which to cooperate since it claims to offer equal partnership and encourages the development of regional groupings and cooperation among the members.

Group-to-group relations are not free from 'power' politics

The motives for third countries to turn towards Europe may be of a very different nature. One factor to take into account is the overall political situation in a given region — for example, the Central American states wish to take their destiny into their own hands assisted by the EC/Twelve, to counterbalance the hegemonic presence of the United States. Others, like the ASEAN countries 'doing business' with the EC, at the same time hope to strengthen their own position through coalition-building with the EC/Twelve, thus mitigating the dominance of Japan in the region.

Another, and important, factor determining group-to-group relations is the economic performance of the group and its dependence on the European Market. This will increase as the single market is 'completed' in the 1992 process. The view is widely held already among third countries that access to the markets of a possible 'fortress Europe' will become very difficult.

Looking at the trade figures, remarkable asymmetries become obvious: while Europe's external trade is widely geographically spread, most of the dialogue partners depend heavily on trade with the EC. This is true for the ACP Group where the EC represents the biggest export market (more than 60 per cent). For EFTA, more than 50 per cent of exports go to the EC while several partners from the Mediterranean Basin depend even more on trade with the EC. Equally high are the EC's shares in the markets of the CMEA countries, while the trade performance of Europe in the ASEAN region only accounts for around 15 per cent. Compared to the other figures, it is also relatively low in Central America (23 per cent) where the EC ranks second to the United States.

Though inter-regional cooperation is officially designed to foster relations based on 'equality between sovereign states and mutual respect',[11] these economic factors may not only have an impact on the climate and atmosphere of the relations, but on the final shape of a dialogue as well.

Politically, the EC/Twelve's behaviour towards third countries and groupings is assessed quite differently. The official doctrine, as laid down in the 'solemn' declarations and speeches of those directly involved in European foreign policy-making, stresses the will of the EC/Twelve to answer international challenges by a strategy of 'speaking with one voice' and offers international cooperation instead of confrontation. They wish to become a 'centre of cooperation in the world ... founded on equality and partnership',[12] an approach in which group-to-group relations are to play a decisive role. It is an approach also referred to as Europe as a 'civilian power'[13] where Europe is capable of setting aside the use and threat of force both against its member states and against the outside world. It is not perhaps a question of the EC/Twelve seeking to export the European model of cooperation and integration, but of wishing to see others sharing the view that conflicts have to be resolved by peaceful means. The supporters of this view could interpret the growth of group-to-group relations as a sign of the attractiveness of the concept and argue that the phenomenon is without precedent in terms of its quantity and variety. Indeed, it has been described as unique, a 'landmark on the road to a new world order',[14] by the West German Foreign Minister, Hans-Dietrich Genscher.

Critics have tended to ignore the political values determining Europe's policy and, therefore, interpret the EC/Twelve's activities on the international stage as those of a 'superpower in the making'.[15] Group-to-group relations then have to be seen as some sort of neo-colonialism in disguised form, as a means of exerting control over third countries.

Even if one does not go so far, the question of who eventually 'sets the rules of the game' within the group-to-group dialogue has to be raised.

The use of 'power' in such 'regimes' of cooperation is different in nature compared to the traditional instruments such as military force or economic sanctions. It finds its expression more in the way the stronger side makes or refuses 'offers', like trade preferences, economic cooperation, development aid or political consultations. This has a direct impact on the institutional set-up and on the climate of a group-to-group dialogue.

Group-to-group relations are an interesting feature of international politics, but not a 'key element'

Given the constant growth of group-to-group relations in European foreign policy in the 1980s, together with the general trend towards a 'regionalization' of international politics, a new 'model' may have emerged for the conduct of international politics. Inter-regional cooperation could be understood as the appropriate answer at a time when the old superpower condominium is replaced by an emerging multi-polar system.

Collectivity helps to alleviate the feeling of inferiority in size and number that single states increasingly perceive. Group-to-group relations with a restricted number of participants seem to be more promising in terms of the 'costs and benefits' than institutions of a universal character like the United Nations. It is true that the group-to-group dialogue has become an important feature of modern diplomacy.[16] However, the network of 'traditional' diplomacy between individual states and other forms of multilateral cooperation still coexist with the inter-regional approach. It seems as if group-to-group relations have not replaced other forms but offer only additional means to manage international politics instead of becoming its 'key element'.

An attempt to set up a typology

In order to cover all variants of group-to-group relations and to draw the utmost benefits from this exercise, the analysis here is based deliberately on a wide definition of the notion. Certainly, the EC/Twelve represent the most advanced model of a 'group', different in quality from all its partner 'groups', whether they are deliberately organized to play an international role (e.g. the Gulf Cooperation Council or ASEAN), or if they are only loosely tied together for the sole purpose of dealing with the EC (like the ACP group). A presentation of such a broad spectrum of individual cases is seen as the best way to grasp the similarities and the differences of the individual cases of inter-regional cooperation and to assess the merits and weaknesses of the approach. Table 1.3 is designed to give an overview of the existing forms of the group-to-group dialogue. It presents 13 cases, each marked by a set of criteria pertaining to:

— the interests of the EC/Twelve and those of the dialogue partners;
— several formal elements (legal framework, institutional set-up, etc.).

The table can only give a rather static picture which neither reflects the dynamics nor the setbacks inherent in individual cases and the changes in quality over time. Given the low public interest in what happens in Europe's day-by-day diplomacy and the confidentiality of EPC, it may well be that other forms of the EC/Twelve's contacts with groups of countries (e.g. the SADCC — Southern African Development Coordination Conference[17] — or the SAARC — South Asian Association for Regional Cooperation)[18] are missing here. The extent to which our list is complete also depends on the definition of the point at which 'exploratory talks'[19] or 'expert consultations'[20] represent a starting point for systematic and structured cooperation in a given case. It is also clear that a period of negotiations usually precedes the official opening of a dialogue, particularly its economic dimension, which is not documented here. One may also wonder whether the Commission's contacts with the SELA secretariat represent some kind of dialogue worth noting here — or, on the contrary, ask if the EC's expressly 'informal' talks with GRULA after the Falklands/Malvinas crisis carry the elements of a group-to-group cooperation.

Starting from our basic assumptions, the present shape of the group-to-group relations can be understood as the result of various constellations of interests inside the EC/Twelve and of those on the other side, and at the same time as the extent to which those interests converge between the dialogue partners. The degree of common or divergent interests has a direct impact on the format of the relations which finds its expression in the individual set-up of each case.

Some general observations and preliminary conclusions

While detailed consideration of many of the groups follow in subsequent chapters there are some further generalizations that may usefully be made. Both the EC/Twelve and the dialogue partners show considerable interest in the cooperation. The motives to cooperate, however, differ. The interest of the EC/Twelve is mainly political and most obvious in the cooperation with the Contadora Group and the Central American states. The idea of political stability and solidarity for intra-regional cooperation is of considerable importance to Europe in its cooperation with ASEAN. However, one should not forget the economic dimension inherent in this dialogue, given the economic potential of the region. Cooperation with the GCC was undertaken out of economic considerations, i.e. to establish a treaty-based relationship with a region attractive for European export and vital for Europe's oil supplies

(Gulf oil still makes up around 20 per cent today). But in the course of the political disturbances in the region, the interest grew on both sides to counteract these tendencies through regional coalition-building.

The interests of most of the EC/Twelve's partners in any dialogue are clearly marked by the idea of improving their trade figures with the EC and of profiting from the EC's development policy. But here, the EC — meaning the member states — largely 'set the rules of the game'. If the concessions given to the ACP and Mediterranean countries set the pace, the EC offered only modest concessions to other groups. In the field of development aid, groups like ASEAN and the Central American states more or less have to accept the European proposal.

There are obvious similarities in the institutional frameworks of the dialogues. Economic cooperation is legally based while the political dialogue has its roots in a joint political statement (not for ASEAN). The latter, however, seems to be more a symbolic act than an indicator of its significance. Political consultations with ASEAN not only take place on various occasions (ministerial meetings, 'dialogue' meetings, UN), but cover the widest range of issues and are marked by a considerable convergence of views. At the level of economic cooperation ASEAN also has a sophisticated institutional network. The duration of a dialogue surely is a decisive factor in building up such an interest on both sides (as in the case of EC–ASEAN cooperation in fostering investments and contacts of the business world). The existence of respective intra-regional structures plays a role as well. Compared to other forms of inter-regional cooperation the institutional framework here is less legally based: while in the case of the Lomé Convention, the creation of a Council of Ministers and a Joint Assembly is expressly laid down in the treaty, similar provisions do not exist in the agreements signed with ASEAN and the Latin American states. The case of the EC–GCC Treaty is different, i.e. it provides for the creation of a Cooperation Council, thus becoming very similar to the institutional set-up prevalent in the cooperation with the Mediterranean countries. One might interpret this nuance in the wording as a 'concession' by the EC/Twelve towards their partners of the Gulf who have favoured a treatment equivalent to that of the Mediterranean group.

Another aspect worth considering refers to the strong or weak interplay between the various levels and actors involved in inter-regional cooperation. It is most direct in the framework of ACP–EC/Twelve cooperation, where the Council of Ministers has to submit an annual report to the Parliamentary Assembly, while in other cases the groups involved at ministerial and parliamentary levels enjoy considerable autonomy.

In several examples, shortcomings in the EC/Twelve's representation at the ministerial level became obvious. For whatever reasons (timetable, personal interests, etc.) 'ministerial' conferences are no longer 'ministerial' ones in the strict sense. The debate on how to reform existing habits is under way among the Twelve. The reduction of the ministerial presence to the troika alone offers one way out of the dilemma, as might limiting the location of meetings. Whatever the necessary changes in format, they will still have to be 'sold' to the partners, a somewhat delicate undertaking which carries risks for the credibility of Europe's international role as a viable coalition partner.

It has already been said elsewhere that inside the EC/Twelve the national governments play the dominant role in shaping the group-to-group dialogue. In none of the cases described here was there total resistance towards the approach, although there is little consensus on the ideal form of dialogue. Group-to-group relations tend to be cumbersome in nature, perhaps unavoidably given the efforts required in the intra-EC/Twelve decision-making system and the equally unfavourable infrastructure of the dialogue partners.

The 'concept' of inter-regional cooperation regularly receives strong support from the European Parliament and the EC Commission. The influence of the former depends largely on its competences in the field of the EC's relations and its participation in the budgetary procedure. The Single European Act opens new avenues that the EP is eager to enter. It has already used its right to consent to association agreements (Article 238) in the course of renewing the agreements with the Mediterranean countries. To the extent that the EP is part of the inter-regional network it may also play an important role; it has, for example, taken up issues such as human rights with the dialogue partners that governments have appeared to regard as too 'hot' to be tackled by themselves. The EC Commission is actively involved in all the variations of group-to-group cooperation, according to the competences assigned to it by the treaties. Whether during the process of negotiating a treaty, or afterwards during its implementation, governments have kept a close watch on the Commission's activities. In the case of the Twelve's political dialogue, the role of the Commission is more constrained, being able only to 'assist' the Presidency, not more.

The examples presented here confirm the attractiveness of the approach for both sides despite the time and effort required in general to translate it into concrete policy. The group-to-group dialogue has presented itself as a useful means of safeguarding interests and playing a role in an increasingly interdependent world. It helps the old system of the nation-states to adapt to the new situation of global challenges. However, group-to-group relations are not yet the only or the dominant 'safety net'. They have part of a pluralistic structure in which 'traditional alliances', be they bilateral or multilateral, have their place as well.

From the perspective of the EC/Twelve, the approach helps to maximize the local resources and to move on towards a consistent European foreign policy as well as fostering peaceful resolution of conflicts and greater cooperation. But the group-to-group approach remains only part of the broader spectrum of responsibilities and

Table 1.3 The group-to-group dialogue of the EC/Twelve: an overview

Dialogue partners	ACP countries at present 68 countries of Africa, the Caribbean and the Pacific	Andean Pact Bolivia, Colombia, Ecuador, Peru, Venezuela	Arab League 21 countries and PLO;	ASEAN Indonesia, Brunei, Malaysia, the Philippines, Thailand, Singapore	Contadora Group: Colombia, Mexico, Panama, Venezuela Central American States: Costa Rica Guatemala, El Salvador Nicaragua Honduras
Econ. cooperation	X	X	X	X	X
(legal) Basis	Lomé (III) Conventions (Art. 238)	Cooperation Agreement (Art. 113,235)	Memorandum 1975	Coop. Agreement (Art. 113,235)	Coop. Agreement (Art. 113,235)
Institutions	Council of Ministers; Cttee of Ambassadors Joint Assembly	— Joint Coop. Cttee EP–Andean Parl.	Meeting of Foreign Ministers (Troika) 1988 and 1989 (full representation) General Commission	Meeting of Foreign and Economic Ministers Joint Coop. Cttee EP-ASEAN Interparl.	Meeting of Foreign Ministers Joint Coop. Committee —

Table 1.3 cont

	Committees; Working groups	Sub-Cttees;	Working Parties (7) and ad hoc groups (16)	Committees	Sub-Cttees
Start	1975	1983	1975	1980	1985
Agenda	trade, industry techn and finance coop;; stabiliz. of exports	econ. trade and develop ment coop;; debt problem	econ. social and cultural coop. investments, trade technol.	trade, econ & development coop, GSP, investments, joint ventures	trade, econ & develop ment coop;, in fields of common interest to be defined
Others	Human rights Apartheid	Drugs, Central America	Arab–Israeli Conflict	Technology, training, tourism	
Pol. dialogue	X	X	X	X	X
(legal basis)	—	—	—	—	Final Act 1985
Institutions	Meeting of Foreign Ministers (Troika) and 12 APC countries (annually)	Meeting of Foreign Ministers (only once)	Meeting of Foreign Ministers (annually)	Meetings of Foreign Ministers (every 18 months)	Meeting of Foreign Ministers (annually)
Start	1988	1980	1988	1978/80	1984

Table 1.3 cont

Agenda	Southern Africa Apartheid	democracy Afghanistan, Andean region, Hostages	—	all major EPC issues	Central America, human rights
Interests of EC/Twelve	pol.	pol.	pol. & (econ.)	pol. & econ.	pol.
Interests of dialogue partner	econ. & pol.	econ.	pol.	pol. & econ.	pol. & econ.
Dialogue partners	CMEA, Soviet Union, Czechoslovakia, Cuba, Vietnam, Mongolia, Bulgaria, Hungary, Poland, GDR	Council of Europe (i.e. its non-EC member states) Austria, Sweden, Norway, Turkey, Cyprus, Malta, Liechtenstein, Iceland, Switzerland, Finland, San Marino	EFTA, Finland, Iceland, Norway, Austria, Sweden, Switzerland,	Front Line States, Botswana, Angola, Mozambique Zambia, Zimbabwe, Tanzania	'Group of Eight' Contadora countries, Argentina, Brazil, Peru Uruguay
Econ. cooperation	X	X	X	—	—
(legal) basis	Joint Declar. (Art 235)	Exchange of letters (Art 230)	Joint (Lux) Declaration	—	—

Table 1.3 cont

Institutions	—	Meeting of Presidents 1:1 (Foreign Ministers) & Sec. General/Commission President; Ministers Delegates–EC Sec. Gen.; High Level Contact Group; Expert groups	Meeting of Ministers (Foreign and other: econ., environment, education); High Level Contact Group; Expert groups
Start	1988	(1959) 1987	1984
Agenda	trade excluded; mutual recognition; coop. in fields of common interest to be defined	participation of EC in Council of Europe activities and common action	Trade: agricul. technology research, monetary, transport, environment and others, EES
Others		X	Fisheries, energy
Pol. dialogue	—		—
(legal) basis	—	—	—

Table 1.3 cont

		Meeting of Foreign Ministers Meeting of Political Directors/Permanent Representative (per Presidency)		Meetings of Foreign Ministers (irregular)	Meetings of Foreign Ministers (bi-annual)
Institutions	—		—		
Start		1983	—	1986	1987
Agenda		all major EPC issues	—	Southern Africa	Central America internat. conflicts, East–West disarm., debt problem
Interests of the EC/Twelve	pol.	pol.	econ. & pol.	pol.	pol.
Interests of dialogue partner	pol. & econ.	pol.	econ. & pol.	pol.	pol. & econ.
Dialogue partners	Gulf Cooperation Council Saudi Arabia,	Med. countries Algeria, Morocco, Tunisia, Cyprus	GRULA Group of Latin American Ambassadors to the EC		

Table 1.3 cont

	Qatar, UAE Oman, Bahrain	Turkey, Malta Israel, Jordan, Egypt, Yugoslavia Lebanon, Syria	
Econ. cooperation	X	X	X
(legal) Basis	Coop. Agreement (Art. 235)	bilat Coop./Assoc. Agreement & Finance Protocol (238 or 113)	—
Institutions	Coop. Council Joint Coop. Cttee —	Coop./Assoc. Councils; Coop. Cttees — Expert Groups	Commission–GRULA Coreper–GRULA EP–Latin Am. Parl.
Start	1988	1975 onwards	1971 onwards
Agenda	1st stage; trade excl. energy, agriculture, fishery, research/ technology, environment, investment	Trade, econ. coop. financial aid	Trade, GSP, debt finance & technical assistance

Table 1.3 cont

Others	2nd stage, trade incl.	—	—
Pol. dialogue (legal basis)	X	—	—
	Joint Dec. 1988	—	—
Institutions	Mtgs of Foreign Ministers (annually)	—	—
Start	1986	—	—
Agenda	Iran/Iraq War, Arab–Israeli conflict, terrorism		
Interests of the EC/Twelve	pol. & econ.	pol. & (econ.)	(if at all) econ.
Interests of dialogue partners	econ. & pol.	econ.	econ.

challenges the EC/Twelve have to face in the future, not least in their relations with the rest of Europe and especially Eastern Europe.

Notes

1 This is a revised version of a paper first published in *The International Spectator* (1988), Vol. 4.
2 The chosen period is largely representative of the state of group-to-group dialogues in the late 1980s, bearing in mind that the Federal Government traditionally attaches high priority to the EC/Twelve's international profile during its presidencies.
3 Simon Bulmer and Wolfgang Wessels, The European Council, *Decision-Making in European Politics*, Houndmills and London, 1987, p.10.
4 David O'Keefe and Henry G. Schermers (eds), *Mixed Agreements*, Nijhoff, Deventer, 1983.
5 Bengt Beutler *et al.*, *Die Europäische Gemeinschaft: Rechtsordnung und Politik*, 3rd edn, Nomos, Baden-Baden, 1987, p. 522.
6 Roswitha Bourguignon-Wittke *et al.*, 'Five Years of the Directly Elected European Parliament', *Journal of Common Market Studies*, 1985, No. 1, pp. 39–59, 40.
7 For further details see Alfred Pijpers *et al.* (eds), *European Political Cooperation in the 1980s: A Common Foreign Policy for Western Europe?* Dordrecht, Boston and London, 1988, and the articles of Simon Nuttall, 'European Political Cooperation', in Francis G. Jacobs (ed.) *Yearbook of European Law*, 1982 onwards, Nijhoff, Oxford.
8 Fritz W. Scharpf, *The Joint-Decision Trap: Lessons from German Federalism and European Integration*, Wissenschaftszentrum Berlin, Discussion Papers IIM/LMP 85-1, Berlin, 1985.
9 Reinhardt Rummel, *Zusammengesetzte Aussenpolitik, Westeuropa als internationaler Akteur*, Kehl, Strasbourg, 1982.
10 Otto von der Gablentz, 'Wege zu einer europäischen Aussenpolitik: Gebündelt statt "vergemeinschaftet"', in Heinrich Schneider and Wolfgang Wessels (eds), *Auf dem Weg zur Europäischen Union? Diskussionsbeiträge zum Tindemans-Bericht*, Europa-Union Verlag, Bonn, 1977, pp. 85–115.
11 As laid down in the Joint Political Communiqué of the EC, Portugal, Spain and the countries of Central America and of the Contadora Group, 12 November 1985.
12 Speech by the President-in-Office, H-D. Genscher, at the UN General Assembly, 26 September 1987.
13 François Duchêne, 'Die Rolle Europas im Weltsystem: Von der regionalen zur planetarischen Interdependenz', in Max Kohnstamm and Wolfgang Hager (eds), *Zivilmacht Europa: Supermacht oder Partner?*, Suhrkamp, Frankfurt, 1973, pp. 11–35. For a reassessment of the notion see Christopher Hill, 'European Foreign Policy: Power Bloc, Civilian Model — or Flop?', in Reinhardt Rummel *et al.*, *Konferenzbericht betr: Die Europäische Gemeinschaft zwischen nationaler Interessenbefriedigung und weltweiter Mitverantwortung*, Stiftung Wissenschaft und Politik Ebenhausen, 1987, pp. 29–57.
14 Speech by the President-in-Office, H.D. Genscher, at the UN General Assembly, 26 September 1987.

15 Johan Galtung, *The European Communities: A Superpower in the Making*, London, 1973.
16 Philippe de Schoutheete, 'The Future of the "External Relations" of European Political Cooperation', in Elfriede Regelsberger *et al.*, *The External Relations of European Political Cooperation and the Future of EPC*, EUI Working Paper 85/172.
17 Members are the five Front Line States, Lesotho, Malawi and Swaziland. SADCC was announced as one of the addressees in the course of the 'package' of measures the Ten, Spain and Portugal decided upon against South Africa in 1985. See Press Release on South Africa, 10 September 1985, published as Doc. No 85/172 in European University Institute and Institut für Europäische Politik (eds), *European Political Cooperation Documentation Bulletin*, 1985, Vol. 1, No. 2, Luxembourg, 1988, p. 47.
18 Members are Bangladesh, Bhutan, India, Maldives, Nepal, Pakistan, Sri Lanka. In 1986, the Twelve raised the question of relations with this group in EPC. Although these relations have not been developed, Europe's general support for the grouping has been reaffirmed several times, as in the EPC's political dialogue with India. *Agence Europe*, 8 March 1990.
19 Which took place as early as 1984 before the 'official' opening of contacts between the EC/Twelve and the countries of the Gulf Cooperation Council in October 1985. *Agence Europe*, 12 November 1984, 28 February and 4/5 March 1985.
20 See the report on 'expert consultations' between the Cartagena-Group and the EC Commission in *Bulletin of the EC*, 3/1986, p.67 (German edn). The following 11 countries belong to the Cartagena-Group: Argentina, Bolivia, Brasil, Chile, Dominican Republic, Ecuador, Colombia, Mexico, Peru, Uruguay, Venezuela.

2 Competing frameworks: the dialogue and its legal bases

Catherine Flaesch-Mougin

The multiplication of inter-regional relations is a phenomenon that undeniably characterises the 1980s. Earlier examples can be cited (such as Lomé), but it is only over the last ten years that such relationships have become an instrument systematically sought after by the EC/Twelve and preferred to their bilateral relationships with individual states. They represent a novel response to the evolution of the international community in which there has been a growing tendency for states to regroup themselves. These groups have a tendency to take the Community as a model in order to face up to the economic or political problems that for industrialised countries flow from the need to be competitive, or, for developing countries derive from the process of development, from relations with rich countries, or from regional conflicts.

The growing strength of the Community has also acted as a catalyst. Concern that the 1992 process may lead to a 'Fortress Europe' has led third countries to try to organise themselves better to have more weight in negotiations with Europe. But whether this regrouping is a reaction to or is incited by the Community process, the EC/Twelve have also encouraged it, especially in the Third World, because they not only have an intrinsic interest in economic growth and political stability,[1] but they also see value in becoming a 'third force' in certain areas.

The diversity of the contexts (geographical, political, historical, or economic) in which states find themselves as partners of Europe and the heterogeneity of the groupings with which the EC/Twelve maintain relations explain why there are almost as many types of inter-regional dialogue as there are partners.[2] Added to that is the very complexity of Europe's construction and the different facets of its external policies. In fact, the distinction between the Community's economic activities, where a transfer of authority to the Community takes place, and European Political Cooperation, where the Twelve cooperate on an inter-governmental basis, has repercussions on the framework given to the dialogue with partner groups. Despite the changes marked by the Single European Act, the two spheres remain separate and different. The highly organised nature of the EC's economic relations with third countries contrasts with the nature of political relations which, in the interests of greater flexibility and because of their greater sensitivity, are often less structured. In contrast to the palette of legal instruments that are at the disposal of the Community in its relations with regional groupings, EPC also lacks the means to achieve its aims, and tends to use EC instrumentation to do so.

The framework for group-to-group dialogues

The 'framework' in the singular should not mask the great variety of frameworks within which the dialogue between the EC/Twelve and the partner groups takes place. Beyond the political/economic cleavage, the character of the dialogues themselves are highly diverse, ranging from simple, informal and episodic contacts, which, arguably, do not constitute a real dialogue, to sustained institutionalised relations. However, economic dialogue is much more structured in principle and institutionalised in practice than the political dialogues. There is, for example, no constitutive treaty like the Treaty of Rome which allows the possibility of agreements to be concluded in the name of EPC. However, both the rigid division between politics and economics and the disconnected nature of the dialogues with partner groups have posed problems. Both have contributed to a 'globalisation' of the dialogues.

Unequal structures

THE ECONOMIC AND COMMERCIAL DIALOGUE

The Community has established contacts with the majority of countries in the world based on its commercial strength and its policy of aid for development: 120 out of the 180 states in the world are linked to the Community. Within this, four-fifths are linked by group-to-group agreements (66 ACP countries, six ASEAN countries, five Central American countries, six GCC countries, and five Andean Pact countries). This means that only a few regional economic organisations (including for example the SAARC [3] and the new union of Arab States[4] have not been incorporated within the Community's diplomatic framework.

Some agreements with the Community have been a response to those countries for whom the Community represents a significant market or a source of possible investment and technology transfer, as has been the case with many Latin American countries. But for the most part, it is the Community which has taken the initiative in proposing an agreement. Usually, it has done so because of the pressure put on it by one or more of its member states that has had a long established relationship or traditional ties with the countries concerned. Each enlargement of the Community has favoured new economic zones and partners; the accession of the United Kingdom led to the Lomé conventions and to agreements with ASEAN; the entry of Spain and Portugal encouraged the conclusion of the long-awaited agreements with the Andean Pact and the Central American states.

Some time can elapse between the proposal for an agreement and its conclusion as the propositions made by the EC or the partner group are not necessarily accepted immediately. Such was the case with the EC's proposals to ASEAN, and to the GCC where greater internal development was considered necessary before it opened up relations with the outside world. The proposals made by Central American countries were also put 'on hold' by the EC. In such cases, an informal pre-agreement dialogue has taken place, which has then gradually developed through, for example, regular meetings of specialists (as in the case of Central America since 1979), or the creation of a mixed study group (the case of ASEAN since 1975). The formalisation and institutionalisation of relations in an agreement constituted the conclusive stage of the dialogue.

The negotiations of the actual agreement are based on a highly regulated procedure. After preliminary contacts (which, as those with the CMEA have shown, can be protracted), negotiations are conducted by the Commission on behalf of the EC, based on a mandate agreed by the Council. After sometimes numerous sessions the agreement is initialled by the Commission and then at the end of a more or less formal procedure (which sometimes necessitates the intervention of the European Parliament) it is signed and concluded by the Council.

Once in force, the agreement constitutes the framework for the relationship, delimiting the aims and character of the dialogue either in relation to trade or to wider cooperation. It is, though, a framework; it allows for a certain flexibility and for evolution. The creation of a joint institution in particular, sometimes with significant powers,[5] allows the parties, if they wish, to widen their relationship. Such institutions have proved to be of fundamental importance. They represent a constant in the external policy of the Community in so far as all the global agreements and even certain important sectorial agreements, such as scientific cooperation with the EFTA countries, provide for them. The only and notable exception is the joint EC/CMEA Declaration[6] which establishes cooperation between the two organisations but no joint institution.

The joint institution has a variety of names and different modes of functioning (composition,[7] frequency of meetings, internal organisation) and powers, each set out under the agreements. These can also be extended or enlarged. In the case of Central America and ASEAN, various specialised sub-committees were established and objectives sometimes widened. In the agreement with the Gulf, a joint Council is assisted by a joint committee for cooperation. In the Lomé Convention,[8] there is not simply a Council of Ministers, but also a Committee of Ambassadors and a joint assembly.

The role played by these institutions is an important one. Beyond guaranteeing the smooth functioning of the agreement, their role is more and more one of promoting the widening or deepening of relations between the partners. In certain cases, the joint body enacts the 'evolutive' clause of the agreement thereby allowing the agreement itself to develop. However, it remains tied to the will of either party who can transform the structure of the dialogue into little more than an 'empty shell' of routine meetings at a technical rather than a political level.

THE NATURE OF POLITICAL DIALOGUE

In contrast to the economic relationship, political talks between the Twelve and groups of third countries appear to be much less organised. However, this characteristically pragmatic approach does not exclude the possibility of significant developments taking place. In keeping with the essentially responsive character of European Political Cooperation, political dialogue tends to result from a demand from outside the Community. In the ASEAN case, the economic dialogue called for a political dialogue. More often, an international crisis provides the occasion for the Twelve to formulate a political declaration that points to the role a regional group of states could play in maintaining or re-establishing peace and stability.

The dialogue can remain largely informal as in the Twelve's relations with the countries of the Front Line South African States (with only two meetings so far, in 1986 and 1989, and with no regular schedule or programme envisaged). But so recent are many of the dialogues that it is impossible to predict their future. Most examples suggest that if a crisis is the source of the political dialogue, it is the existence of institutionalised commercial and/or economic links with the group that tips the balance towards the formalisation of a political dialogue.

There is however no formal agreement behind political dialogue as there is in the Community framework. A declaration or communiqué published at the end of a meeting can suffice. While it may not be legally binding as a result, it constitutes a solemn political, moral and psychological engagement by the partners.

Moreover the institutionalisation of political dialogues remains undeveloped. Agreement is usually limited to a few commitments on the regularity of meetings (every 12 or 18 months), their location (alternating between the two groups) and their level (in general, at the level of foreign ministers with a representative from the Commission and sometimes from the European Parliament). But the subject matter of the discussions is rarely fixed, and can often extend to questions with much wider implications than the immediate security of the partner groups. The ASEAN dialogue was initially limited to regional questions (especially Kampuchea), but was gradually extended to East–West relations when the USSR invaded Afghanistan and now touches on all the important questions in international relations. More recent dialogues, however, with the ACP and Central America are still largely confined to the regional problems for which they were established.

The limited institutionalisation of political dialogue is not a handicap so long as meetings remain regular and take place at a high enough level, i.e. at ministerial level. But dialogues can of course still go awry. The rare meetings between the Twelve and the Andean Pact represent an appropriate example.

The links between the political dialogue of the Twelve and the Community's economic dialogue

The problem of linkages needs to be set against the overall coherence of the EC's and the Twelve's relations with third countries. Indeed, the two types of dialogue can sometimes overlap. There is a real tendency, for example, to intensify links with a more homogenous or more regionally limited sub-group, as in the case of Latin America or the GCC within the wider Euro-Arab dialogue. The multiplication of groups of states and the emergence of inter-group dialogues can create their own problems (as suggested in the GCC Cooperation Agreement)[9]. However, as the economic and political dialogues originate either within the jurisdiction of the member states or the EC, relations with regional groupings are not always conducted jointly, despite a clear tendency towards their globalisation. Moreover, the dialogues evolve from two distinct types of framework; the existence of the one does not automatically entail the other, and even if the dialogues are conducted in parallel, they are not always adjusted accordingly.

INDEPENDENT DIALOGUES

Having different authors, the dialogues are independent, the one not necessarily implying the other for the same group of countries. An economic dialogue is not necessarily accompanied by a political dialogue and conversely, though the latter is much less common in practice. Economic relations with the EFTA countries, for example, are not accompanied by a comparable political dialogue, though there are, of course, many contacts at different levels. However, this has been increasingly seen as deficient and proposals have been made to change the situation.

Although rare, it is not unknown for the Twelve to establish political contacts with a group of countries when there are no institutionalised economic links with the EC. The Twelve have been trying to establish a political dialogue with the Group of Eight (the Contadora group, Argentina, Brazil, Peru, Uruguay). While there is a considerable range of agreements between Latin America and the EC, from bilateral agreements with Brazil, Mexico, Uruguay, to a cooperation agreement with a group of states (Peru, Colombia, Venezuela, Panama), while Argentina has no contractual link with the EC at all, as a group, the Eight are not engaged in any economic dialogue with the EC.

GENUINE AND FALSE PARALLEL DIALOGUES

In practice, the EC's formalised economic relationship with a group of states takes place in parallel with the political dialogue conducted by the Twelve. Nevertheless, total parallelism exists only rarely. The only relevant example is that of the GCC where, at the same time and with the same partners, an economic dialogue (the conclusion of a cooperation agreement) and a political dialogue coexist. In other instances, such as that of ASEAN, political discussions which began in 1978 followed the economic dialogue established in 1975, though they were not formalised until 1980. In the ACP case, the political dialogue (with the ACP countries represented by a delegation of 13 members) dates only from 1988.

INTEGRATED DIALOGUES

The term 'integrated' denotes those dialogues where political and economic issues overlap within a single framework. The model, though it is not ideal, is the Conference on Security and Cooperation in Europe (CSCE) which groups all the European countries with Canada and the United States, and in which numerous political and economic aspects of East–West relations are examined. No such formula is being used for the EC/Twelve's relations with CMEA and/or its European member states. A second example is that of the Euro-Arab Dialogue (EAD). The EAD was begun in 1976 between EPC and the Arab League. Despite its ups and downs, many lessons can be drawn from it, not least the implicit inter-connectedness of political and economic issues, and the delicacy of the relationship between the activities of EPC and the Community. Indeed, in both the CSCE and the EAD, special structures were necessary in order to ensure the presence either of the Twelve or of the EC depending on the matter under review. In certain aspects, these two dialogues opened the way to the global dialogues that the Twelve and the EC are seeking to establish.

The tendency towards a globalisation of the dialogues

The fact that political and economic dialogues are often disconnected does not help the image of European foreign policy in the eyes of the rest of the world. The search for greater coherence, the 'globalisation' of the dialogues, would seem to be unavoidable, and developments in the EC/Twelve's relations with groups of third countries suggest that parallel dialogues are being sought more systematically. Where there was only an economic dialogue a complementary dialogue of a political nature was increasingly regarded as necessary by the Twelve. However, those dialogues recently established are the subject of further development, expressed in terms of becoming 'global'.

The 1984 San José Conference first employed the term 'global dialogue' and this was taken up in the Preamble to the Cooperation Agreement with the Central American states in 1985. It is also to be found in the Preamble to the 1988 agreement with the GCC states. Global dialogue seeks to avoid dissociating politics and economics in relations with third-country groups. It therefore goes beyond the 'global approach', which aims to treat partners within a coherent system of relations (as in the global Mediterranean approach) or which aims to show that individual bilateral relations are no longer appropriate (as in the global approach towards the Eastern bloc countries). The globalisation of the dialogues has been manifested in various ways. Those above were formalised at the same time in a political Declaration or Act and by the conclusion of the Cooperation Agreement. But this is not necessarily a condition of the existence of a global dialogue. More essential is that the meetings between Foreign Ministers involve questions of both a political and economic nature. The presence of the Community as well as Ministers of the Twelve maintains the division of powers which is further manifested in the publication of an economic and a political communiqué at the end of the meeting.

The Commission, supported by the European Parliament, had envisaged another mode of globalising the dialogues by proposing a global agreement with the Central American countries. Although it was a mixed agreement, the emphasis would have shifted the dialogue towards the Community's sphere of influence. The member states not surprisingly cast aside this 'audacious' initiative as a further attempt to undermine their freedom of movement in foreign policy terms. Nevertheless, it is possible that the Community had similar intentions (though executed more discreetly) in the agreement with the Gulf. The aim there was to reinforce the relationship between the parties (without being more precise) by means of a joint Council with unusually developed powers for a Cooperation Agreement. The Preamble made clear that agreement was to contribute to the promotion of 'global cooperation in all fields'.

The growing trend towards the globalisation of dialogues, or rather of their content, has been an inescapable answer to practical problems. First, it is pointless to separate the economic and political aspects of a problem. The two dimensions are inextricably intertwined whether in a crisis, such as that in Central America or Southern Africa, where economic factors are a fundamental element in the solution to the political problem, or in a less conflictual area, such as relations with ASEAN or Eastern bloc countries. Moreover, in practice, discussions often go beyond the scope of the initial framework of the dialogue. Thirdly, the EC/Twelve's partners, who in general tend to be grouped in organisations without a supranational character, do not always easily understand the division of responsibilities between the EC and its member states. Finally, the partner organisations themselves add a political dimension to their economic aims.

The opening up of the EC and later EPC to the world's problems constitutes a second factor in the globalisation of the dialogues. The EC quite quickly introduced some political 'touches' to its external economic policies, whether in the legal basis or the content of the agreements concluded with third countries. These forays beyond the Community's jurisdiction were largely limited to questions affecting human rights and democratic values. The European Parliament has generally encouraged the politicisation of the Community's external relations whether through its inter-parliamentary delegations (see Chapter 12) or its more active 'policy-making' in joint institutions such as the assembly of the Lomé Convention. The Single European Act, which gave the Parliament the power of co-decision on association agreements, has clearly added to its importance. However, it is the Twelve, and not the EC, who are in the position of conducting a genuine foreign policy though they have not been provided with the means necessary for the purpose. The Twelve have to rely on the Community to implement the declarations made, at least on matters within its competence.

These various elements favour the closer association of politics and economics and the globalisation of the dialogues with the Community's partners. The Single European Act, which declared that 'the external policies of the EC must be coherent' recognised the point. Putting aside the issue of any sanction, the pressing nature of the obligation is underlined by the use of the term 'must' — even if it contrasts with the frequent use elsewhere of formulae which suggest a certain legal laxity in the commitments of the Twelve. Respect for coherence in the Community's external policies should be ensured by the Presidency and the Commission depending on their respective competences, but it will be brought about largely through the practice of working together.

Beyond the texts, new practices are emerging that confirm the move towards coherence. The concertation between Political Directors and COREPER at the European Council in Madrid (June 1989) over East–West relations is a good example. It illustrates the influence and importance of the economic measures at the disposal of the EC in the conduct of a foreign policy by the Twelve.

The legal instruments for bloc-to-bloc dialogue

The instruments used for group-to-group dialogue are the same as those used in the EC's relations with individual states. Although the agreement with ASEAN has often been seen as a model used effectively with other groups, it is not the only possibility. Indeed, the whole palette of legal instruments at the disposal of the Community may be used. The lack of instruments available to EPC contrasts strongly with this diversity.

The foundation agreements

With a judicious use of the legal foundations present in the Rome Treaty (Articles 113, 235 and 238), the Community has endowed itself with various types of foundation agreements which serve as a basis for its relations with other groups.

Under Article 113, the EC is competent to conclude commercial agreements with third countries, which, if initially limited to tariffs and quotas, have evolved to take in new elements that affect international trade. The agreements with developing countries cover the vast province of commercial cooperation and the regulation of trade; those with industrialised countries cover all the obstacles to trade. Article 113 was used as the legal foundation for the 1972 and 1973 agreements with the EFTA countries.[10]

Under Article 238, the Community can also conclude with a third country, a union of states or an international organisation, Association Agreements 'characterised by reciprocal rights and obligations, common actions and particular procedures'. So far these have been confined to the EC's privileged relations such as those with the ACP states[11] but have not otherwise been signed with a union of states or an international organisation. The future relationship between the EC and EFTA countries or even EFTA itself, if it evolves, could therefore become a new departure. The UMA or the Council for Arab Cooperation, which includes states already linked to the EC through agreements based on Article 238, may also be long-term possibilities.

Article 235, which allows the Community to take action unforeseen in the Treaty, has, after an initial period of uncertainty, been widely used in the field of group-to-group relations. With Article 113, it has allowed the EC to sign all the commercial, economic and development cooperation agreements of the ASEAN type (such as those with Central American states, Andean Pact, and the first agreement with the GCC) where the scope goes beyond commercial issues but where the EC has the sole authority to act. These non-preferential agreements stimulate cooperation in numerous areas of common interest such as agricultural, industrial and energy development, regional cooperation and environmental protection. However, unlike the Association Agreements, there is no financial element in the agreements to finance such commitments.

Article 235 was also used in a group-to-group context in the joint EC–CMEA Declaration. This was justified by the particular aim expressed in the Declaration of the mutual recognition of the two organisations and the creation of a framework for future economic cooperation. Article 113 was inadequate because of the determination of the EC to refer commercial questions to bilateral agreements with the individual members of CMEA. However, since it was also a question of creating more than just opportune contacts with an international organisation, Article 229 was also insufficient.

The variety of existing formulae in the field of external relations offers the Community a wide choice in concluding (or modifying) an agreement with a group of states. In order to deepen or otherwise change the links established, the Community disposes of two types of action. In the first place, the content of an agreement indicates the importance of a group for the Community. The fundamental cleavage between preferential and non-preferential agreements itself masks different arrangements. The choice of a particular model proves sometimes to be difficult as in the GCC case. The resulting compromise was an initial agreement of the ASEAN-type as a prelude to a further agreement aimed at developing commercial exchanges, which, despite the general nature of the formula employed, was to be preferential (see Chapter 5). Secondly, the Community can, more or less, give reason to the Agreement through the choice of its legal basis, i.e. whether Article 113 or Article 238 in agreements with a comparable content. The use of Article 238 for the agreement with either EFTA countries or EFTA itself was judged too 'political' in the past. The debate on the content of the second agreement with the GCC countries included discussion on whether to use Article 238 as with the other privileged Mediterranean countries, or Article 113, which would minimise the importance of this extension of the EC's policy of preferences.

Building on foundation agreements

Foundation agreements with a group of states do not exclude the possibility of other agreements whether sectoral agreements dealing with a specific problem concerning one or more of its members (or even the group itself, although this remains academic so far) or, more exceptionally, global agreements with the members of the group themselves.

COMPLEMENTARY AGREEMENTS

The EC, on the basis of Article 113, or by virtue of the principle of the parallelism of competences derived by the European Court of Justice, has concluded numerous sectoral agreements with third countries. Some of these agreements can be seen as a bonus, reinforcing relations between the EC and a member of the group (or even several or all of them) within a given sector. Examples include the fishing agreements with some ACP States (suggested but not included in the Lomé Convention) or the numerous agreements with EFTA countries on, say, scientific and technological cooperation. Other agreements derive from rather different circumstances. Even though they aim to encourage the orderly and equitable development of commerce, they constitute limitations to such development; they reintroduce elements of discrimination between partners treated identically in the foundation agreement. This is the case with the numerous voluntary restraint agreements on textiles, which have been signed with many member states of the partner groups. Thailand, for example, which is a member of ASEAN, has signed voluntary restraint agreements with the EC on textiles (and also on cassava).

General bilateral agreements can also exist in certain cases, parallel with the agreement between the Community and another regional group. In theory, a prior group relationship should exclude the possibility of later global agreements. Nevertheless, in special cases, the EC wanted to promote bilateral relations with the member states of a group to the detriment of those maintained with the group itself. This was the case with the CMEA (see Chapter 9). On the other hand, superimposing an inter-bloc agreement on previous bilateral agreements with particular members of the other group tallies more closely with the Community's preoccupations; the Community has shown that it favours the emergence and strengthening of regional organisations. The possibility of an agreement with SAARC (the South Asian Association for Regional Cooperation), in which some members are linked to the EC by commercial agreements (Sri Lanka and Bangladesh) or by commercial and cooperation agreements (India and Pakistan), has been anticipated by the European Parliament.[12] However, this evolution poses several similar problems. Apart from associating with new countries as members of the group (for example, Libya in UAM), the imposition of a second level of agreement ought not to affect the advantages 'acquired' by the member states previously linked to the EC. The group-to-group agreement supposes, therefore, a deepening of the links already established.

MEASURES TAKEN WITHIN THE FRAMEWORK OF THE EC'S NON-CONTRACTUAL POLICY

At the commercial and financial level, a state or group of states can benefit from measures that result from a unilateral decision by the EC, independent of any contractual links. Several have done so even before an agreement has been signed with the Community; the Andean Pact, the Central American Common Market or ASEAN have benefited since 1977 or 1978 from financial and technical aid from the EC. But the signing of an agreement between the group and the Community has often led to an improvement in this non-contractual 'treatment', notably in the Generalized System of Preferences (GSP) and financial aid.

However, it has happened that a Cooperation Agreement refers back in an annex to an EC statement on the GSP. This was the case in the agreements with the Andean Pact and the Central American states. The double advantage in this disposition is that it allows countries to discuss 'their GSP' with the Community in the joint Commission, thereby making the initially non-contractual measure a contractual one, so guaranteeing the maintenance of the System and even its improvement. Such dispositions do not exist in the agreement with ASEAN, whose members are individual beneficiaries of the System. As a result, it is possible that they will suffer from the EC's policy of differentiation in the review of GSP for 1990–2000 and find themselves excluded from the GSP as dominant suppliers. This is also feared by the GCC countries, who have already been excluded from the American GSP for certain essential exports, which explains their vehemence in trying to obtain a preferential agreement with the EC.

Another 'bonus' to the concessions made by the agreements is provided by the EC's financial aid. This has various forms including financial and technical assistance, food aid, and commercial promotion, and is liable to benefit all the countries or groups of countries even if not linked by an agreement to the EC. Although it was initially envisaged[13] simply as a possibility, action in favour of regional cooperation has become more of a priority; it appears, for example, in the annual financial and technical aid policy orientations established by the Council.[14] The funds allocated to regional cooperation remain small (despite regular increases) and benefit ASEAN, the Andean Pact and Central America almost exclusively.[15]

The political dialogue and economic support

Under the SEA, the High Contracting Parties 'strive to formulate and to put into action in common accord a European foreign policy'. The different levels involved in the formulation and implementation of this European foreign policy need to be distinguished: the Twelve can easily meet to develop common positions, but they are limited largely to diplomatic moves through the intermediary of the Presidency if they wish to take common action. Any more concrete action presupposes the use of both the EC and the member states. However, recourse to the Community is not without its problems, whether for the member states or for the EC itself.

THE OPPORTUNITIES

The Community provides EPC with a solid framework by virtue of the vast panoply of commercial, economic and financial means at its disposal. If the Twelve wish to support the political action of a regional group, they can ask the Community to go beyond the concessions it would normally make. However subjective 'normality' might be, the

Community has increased economic and commercial concessions or financial aid to serve the Twelve's political commitments.

The example of relations with the GCC is revealing. Some of the Commission had favoured an ASEAN-type Cooperation Agreement, while others, more attentive to the political impact of such an agreement, favoured a preferential agreement. The latter solution went beyond what one could 'normal' expectations, as preferential agreements had until then been strictly reserved for well-defined partners. In the agreements with the Eastern bloc countries, where a correlation exists between commercial concessions and the degree of political liberalisation by the regimes, the Community went beyond its initial intentions in its relations with Hungary. Similarly, the Commission's mandate for negotiations with Poland was widened at the beginning of 1989, to take into account the changes then taking place in the country. Elements such as association with Community scientific programmes that had been exclusively reserved for relations with EFTA were included. In both cases the EC also took note of progress towards democratisation, by incorporating them into its GSP.

The Community's efforts in the financial sphere have been even more significant, with financial aid, through the Budget or the EDF, used to support political policy positions. It is often a more refined instrument than commercial concessions in translating the political will of the Twelve into reality. Various types of special aid were granted to the SADCC, for example, in connection with the Twelve's anti-apartheid policy. The aim, in parallel with the sanctions imposed on South Africa, was to help states subject to the negative effects of South Africa's policy. Aid to the SADCC countries was provided through Community-funded assistance programmes for victims of apartheid (25 out of 56 million ECUs for 1989), or victims of the fight against the destabilising politics of South Africa (a new line in the Budget in 1988 which foresaw 7 million ECUs for 1989). EDF resources also provided 31 million Ecus of aid for 1989 to favour regional cooperation, especially the development of transport designed to reduce economic dependence on their South African neighbour.

Another example of the important role played by 'Community' aid in support of the Twelve's policies has been the aid given to Central American countries. Following the first San José Conference in 1984, the financial and technical aid granted by the Community increased from 41 million ECUs in 1984 to 71 million in 1985. These and subsequent sums have come from 'normal' financial and technical aid funds for the non-Associated developing countries of Latin America and Asia, to which special 'flexible' reserve funds for Central America have been added. This has questioned the traditional 75 : 25 ratio between Asian and Latin American countries. It has also provoked questions about the limits to, and the impact of, Community choices in response to political motives.

THE PRACTICAL LIMITS

Technically, granting economic or financial aid in support of political dialogue poses no problem. In practice the margin for action is much more limited; the multiplication of such concessions often conflicts with strictly Community or even national interests.

The near doubling of aid for Central America led to a questioning of the allocation of funds between Asian and Latin America, just as the preferential agreement with the GCC modified the traditional privileged/non-privileged cleavage. Reactions have varied, though all the Community's partners have been attentive (as usual) to any new concessions given to others, especially if the concessions adversely affect their own advantages. But more fundamental perhaps is the questioning of changes to the basic philosophy behind Community aid. Contrary to the aid policies of United States or Japan, Community aid has not had a conditional character. Does this new 'flexibility' now modify the nature of the aid? A tendency to tie aid to democratisation is discernible in the increase in aid to Central America and in the EC's approach to relations with CMEA countries.[16]

Another limit to any recourse to Community instruments to support a political dialogue is their cost. Each trade concession constitutes a shortfall that needs to be made up in the Community budget. Each supplementary financial aid measure absorbs funds, the total value of which is relatively small and inelastic. The inter-institutional agreement of 1988 imposes budgetary discipline, which affects funds allocated to cooperation, until 1992. The margin for manoeuvre is thereby reduced to an internal redistribution of resources unless one envisages random and exceptional claims on reserve funds.

While the aim of EPC may be to achieve a common European foreign policy, it is not altogether certain that all member states always want the Community to be its 'secular arm'. Once they have appealed to the Community, member states lose an element of their freedom to act because they are then bound by the legal acts adopted; the mechanisms to ensure respect for Community law apply.

On several occasions when it might have been possible to give the Community authority to act (on the basis of Article 235), the member states were too anxious to keep their foreign policy prerogatives and so opposed the move. This reticence has been particularly evident where sanctions have been concerned, but it has also been present in more positive actions. At the Conference of San Pedro de Sula, it was decided that the aid deployed in favour of the Central American Bank of Economic Integration would be agreed by the Twelve, who decided individually on the amount to pay. In the same way, the global Cooperation Agreements of the EC do not exclude the possibility of bilateral cooperation agreements by member states within their sphere of competence. As such bilateral measures often allow for a clearer political purpose, the member states have been reluctant to part with them. Over and above this reluctance, pervading economic interests can still impede the use of Community instruments. Certainly pressure has been exerted by sectoral interests fearing increased competition from further trade concessions during negotiations on a possibly substantial agreement dictated by political reasons. This was the case with the United Kingdom, Italy and the Netherlands, whose reluctance to agree to free trade provisions with the GCC reflected their concern over their domestic petrochemical and refinery industries.

The problem can also occur when setting up an agreement important to the support of a political dialogue. This is particularly the case with Cooperation Agreements, for they create only frameworks; the actual working of the agreement is the responsibility of economic actors. In the ASEAN case, there has been a marked difference between the success of political exchange and the languid character of the economic relationship, despite the efforts of the EC to boost the latter through incentive-based measures such as the Cheysson Fund to encourage investments.

Notes

1 See as illustration the wording of the Preamble to the cooperation agreement between the EC and the GCC (OJEC L 54/1, 25.2.1989): 'Underlining the fundamental importance that the two Parties assign to the consolidation and strengthening of regional integration, which is an essential factor of the development of the GCC countries and a factor of stability in the Gulf region.' Even though enacted with different formulations, the cooperation agreements with the ASEAN states (OJEC L 144/1, 10 June 1980), with the Carthagen Agreement and its member states (OJEC L 153/1, 8 June 1984), and with the countries party to the general treaty for Central American Economic Integration such as Panama (OJEC L 172/1, 30 June 1986) use the same ideas. It is significant that the SEA (Article 30, para 8) in its dispositions on European Political Cooperation, expressly evokes political dialogues with regional dialogues: 'The High Contracting Parties organise, whenever they judge necessary, political dialogues with third countries and regional groups.'

2 The heterogeneity of the group obliges us to envisage the EC/Twelve's relations with other groups in a wide sense: i.e. relations with the organisation itself (rare, as it presupposes a transfer of competence analagous to the Community process), relations with all of the states as members of a grouping (a more frequent case), or even individual relations with each member state of a group (the case of relations with EFTA countries). Relations with groups of states without an organisational structure but considered as such in their relations with the EC or the Twelve should also be added. This is the case with ACP countries, whereby their group character has been established by the Lomé Convention. This is not, on the contrary, the case with the Mediterrranean countries, never considered 'en bloc' even if the EC has developed a global approach to them.

3 The South Asian Association for regional cooperation, founded in 1985, is composed of India, Pakistan, Bangladesh, Bhutan, Nepal, Sri Lanka and the Maldive Islands.
4 UAM (the Union of the Arab Maghreb) and the Council for Arab Cooperation, founded in 1989, are respectively composed of: Morocco, Algeria, Mauritius, Libya and Tunisia for UAM and Iraq, Jordan, Egypt and the Arab Republic of Yemen for the latter.
5 Some of them are invested with power of decision.
6 OJEC L 157/34, 24 June 1988.
7 Envisaged in a very general manner in the agreement, the composition of the Community delegation is made clear in the concluding act by the Council, and still consists of the Commission assisted by representatives from the member states.
8 Lomé Convention (OJEC L86/1, 31 March 1986).
9 Point 6 of the Preamble: 'Reaffirming that the cooperation between the GCC States does not replace, but completes, the Euro-Arab dialogue.'
10 The agreements of 22 July 1972 with Sweden, Switzerland, Austria, Iceland and Portugal (OJEC L 300/97, 189/42, 301/2 and 165, 31 December 1973) and the agreements of 14 May and 5 October 1973 with Norway and Finland (OJEC 171/1 of 17 June and L 238/1 of 28 November 1973).
11 It should be noted that the Lomé Convention is a so-called mixed agreement, that is to say, one concluded by the Community and its member states due to financial dispositions within the agreements (non-budgetised EDF).
12 Hitzigarth Report on the economic relations between the EC and the SAARC, Document A2-212/88, 6 October 1988.
13 Article 3, para 2 of Regulation no. 441/81, concerning the financial and technical aid for non-associated developing countries (OJEC 48/8, 21 February 1981).
14 Article 1 of the last paragraph for 1987: 'The support given to the efforts towards regional integration is elsewhere maintained and strengthened in all sectors where the influence of the Community can make a positive contribution.'
15 See the 17th Report by the Commission to the Council and the European Parliament on the setting up of the financial and technical aid for non-associated developing countries (COM (87) 588 final, 27 November 1987) dealing with regional cooperation (p. 29).
16 F. Mitterrand spoke about 'condition *sine qua non*' for aid.

Part II
Case studies: the dialogue in action

3 The Lomé Convention: a model for partnership

Otto Schmuck

Lomé est bien devenu le symbole de la coopération internationale ... pratiquement seul phare sur une mer obscure, tombeau de tant d'espoirs décus.
(President of the ACP Council of Ministers, R. Namaliu, on the occasion of the signing of Lomé III, October 1984)

Since 1975 the European Community and its member states have had a close contractual relationship with the now 68 ACP countries in Africa, the Caribbean and the Pacific. There have been three previous Lomé agreements between the ACP–EC partners; the Lomé title comes from the fact that they were all signed in the capital of Togo. On 15 December 1989 the fourth ACP–EC Treaty was also signed in Lomé. It will enter into force when all the countries of the European Community and more than two-thirds of the ACP states have completed the ratification procedure and — for the first time — when the European Parliament has given its assent to the Convention.

Now, as before, the assessment of the relationship between the European Community and the ACP countries varies enormously. The Lomé Conventions have been glorified by some as important markers on the road to a new international economic order, and described by others as tools of Western imperialism and neo-colonialism. Between these extremes, there are many who see ACP–EC cooperation as a successful model for North–South relations in general.

This chapter considers if, and to what extent, cooperation under Lomé can be seen as a model for EC relations with other regional groupings. It focuses on the following questions: can the Lomé ACP participants be considered as a regional grouping at all? What are the main aims, features and problems of cooperation in Lomé? What are the results so far? What are the institutional provisions? Is the fostering of regional cooperation within the ACP states generally accepted as one of the major aims? And in the final section, is cooperation in Lomé just a unique relationship between heterogeneous partners or can it be seen as a model for improving other group-to-group dialogues?

Fifteen years of Lomé Convention: a positive balance sheet?

In retrospect, expectations at the beginning of the Lomé partnership in 1975 were clearly much too high and too ambitious. It was inevitable that many observers would subsequently be disappointed and disillusioned.

Membership of the exclusive ACP–EC club is, however, as attractive now as it was fifteen years ago. Both sides work together on the basis of mutual respect for each other's sovereignty. Each has a strong interest in the continuation of this kind of cooperation within the Lomé framework, which covers economic matters as well as political, social and cultural aspects. The Treaties provide a sophisticated institutional framework which facilitates a much denser network of contacts than is the case in other group-to-group relationships of the EC such as EC–ASEAN or EC–Andean Pact. The number of ACP countries involved has increased from the 46 signatories of Lomé I in 1975 to 68 with the accession of an independent Namibia.

The solemn opening session of the negotiation of Lomé IV in Luxembourg in October 1988 revealed once again the great interest of all participants in the continuation of the common endeavour. On this occasion the Finance Minister of Guyana, Carl B. Greenidge, in his capacity as President of the ACP Ministers, articulated much of the criticism as to the unsatisfactory results of economic cooperation. But, at the same time, he emphasised the unique political quality of Lomé:

May I say first of all that if the nature of the relationship, as reflected in the Conventions and their implementation, is unique it is first and foremost because of the range and quality of the instruments and modalities that we have agreed to employ. Many other North–South relationships have existed and publicly endorsed the spirit of Lomé I. None have matched Lomé in terms of resources, flexibility and concrete efforts to enhance the human condition of citizens. We should be justly proud of this reality. We are not reticent about publicly acknowledging it.[1]

From the Community side, the Lomé policy is also generally rated as a success. On the same occasion, the President of the EC Council, Theodoros Pangalos, explained:

We all know that ACP–EC cooperation represents, without doubt, an as yet unparalleled endeavour to set a new pattern in North–South relations. Through more than a decade of joint experience, we have achieved in our successive Conventions the fullest and most innovative embodiment of our shared ambition to frame, through an ongoing dialogue of trust of equal partners, a contractual aid policy increasingly attuned to the specific and varied requirements of our ACP partners. For this ambitious exercise in solidarity, we can now draw on a common heritage which is regarded as a model by the international community.[2]

In addition to such positive statements, one can also find criticism and scepticism among both politicians and observers.[3] Many of the ACP countries belong now, as fifteen years ago, to the group of the least developed countries.[4] Even basic human needs, such as food, housing and medical care, are not guaranteed in all ACP countries. In that framework, the development of trade between the EC and the ACP remains unsatisfactory. The contradictions between the various assessments of cooperation in Lomé can partly be explained by the use of different criteria:

(i)   For some observers and politicans, the mere fact that 80 countries, nearly half the independent countries of the world, are working peacefully together on a contractual base is rated as an important step forward.

(ii)   For others, ACP–EC relations need to be measured in terms of economic and social development, using criteria such as income per capita, trade balances, schooling, etc.

(iii) For a third group, the results of the Lomé Convention are compared with its own aims and basic principles, namely inter-dependence, mutual interest, respect for the sovereignty and the social, economic and political choices of each party, non-discrimination between beneficiaries and guaranteed and reliable aid.

The question was often raised, especially in the early years of the Lomé Convention, of whether and to what extent the ACP–EC Treaty provisions could be seen as a blueprint for general North–South relations. A comparison between cooperation under Lomé and other group-to-group contacts between the Community and others has not been a major subject of political or academic debate, despite the idea expressed in some political circles that Lomé-type benefits should be granted to certain developing countries in Latin–America and Asia.

From Yaoundé to Lomé: the formation of the ACP and its image of itself

The ACP group is composed of 46 African, 15 Caribbean and eight Pacific countries.[5] They represent about 40 per cent of all UN members and about half of all the developing countries.

The foundation of the ACP was neither a voluntary decision of its members nor a 'logical' choice of the EC for development policy reasons. Part IV (Articles 131–136) of the EEC Treaty of 1958 included the association of the then colonies of the founding members, especially France. When most of these became independent in the late 1950s and early 1960s, the EC offered association treaties on the basis of equal rights. In 1963 and 1969, 18, largely West African, countries and Madagascar signed the Yaoundé Conventions.

When Great Britain joined the Community in 1973, it was unwilling to accept a common development policy that served, from its point of view, primarily French interests. Two options were discussed during the UK accession negotiations: the EC could either conduct a world-wide development policy without any regional preference; or the former British colonies would have to be included in the Yaoundé Convention. The outcome was a compromise. The EC agreed, in Protocol 22 of the Treaty of Accession, to offer the independent Commonwealth countries in Africa, in the Pacific and in the Caribbean the choice of either joining the Yaoundé Convention or negotiating a comparable preferential agreement.[6]

All the countries concerned decided to accept the invitation to join and thus the number of the associated countries rose from 19 to 46.[7] This enlargement created enormous problems for the coherence of the EC's association partners. Those who had been directly involved in the negotiations recognised that the new ACP Group had obvious difficulties in articulating common positions. This was especially so on the part of the 'Anglophone' developing countries, who feared that the EC would try to extend the neo-colonial relationship which they believed it had with the 'Francophone' Yaoundé countries.

Between 1973 and 1975, no less than 493 meetings of ambassadors and experts were necessary before an agreed position could be reached in this negotiation.[8] Nigeria played a leading role in this process and many observers saw the *rapprochement* between the former French colonies in West Africa and the former British colonies as one — perhaps the most important — impact of the negotiation of Lomé I. However, the coherence of the group was again adversely affected by the advent of the former Portuguese colonies Angola, Mozambique and Cape Verde in the early 1980s.

It is an open question as to whether the ACP countries today really form a regional grouping. The number of states (68) and size of population (about 380 million) involved and especially the geographical spread of these countries obviously hamper the articulation and implementation of common goals and the formation of traditional forms of regional integration like the EC, ASEAN or the Andean Pact. On the other hand, there are grounds for believing that the ACP constitutes a strong and vital grouping. All the ACP countries have signed the 'Georgetown Accord' of 6 June 1975 and the 'Suva Declaration' of 14 April 1977.[9] While the former deals primarily with technical and organisational matters, the Suva Declaration contains a political programme on such topics as intra-ACP cooperation, trade policy, finance, transfer of know-how and cultural cooperation. The ACP states have established a Secretariat-General in Brussels, specifically for the day-to-day functioning of the ACP, with a budget of its own derived partly from the

European Development Fund and partly from ACP contributions. The ACP states try to coordinate their positions in international fora such as the United Nations, the World Bank, UNESCO, etc. The group has official observer status in the UN.[10]

Despite these strengths, the heterogeneity of the ACP group and its difficulty in articulating and implementing far-reaching common goals clearly create problems. In the negotiations for Lomé IV, for example, it was extremely difficult for the ACP delegation to articulate clear-cut priorities in the trade sector because of the obvious rivalry between them and their specific aims and problems. Up to now, neither the mechanisms nor group solidarity have been strong enough to formulate clear group positions. The problems extends, too, to the recruitment of the ACP Secretariat's staff of about 75 persons. The appointment of the Secretary-General especially has caused serious quarrels between the various countries in the past. A number of observers criticised both the unsatisfactory functioning and efficiency of the ACP Secretariat.[11]

Had it not been for the Lomé Convention, the ACP group would certainly not exist. However, the member countries now do try to make the most of their 'marriage of convenience' with the EC and have come to recognise and accept the advantages of regional cooperation amongst themselves. But there are also, of course, several regional groupings within the ACP group.[12] The Organisation of African Unity (OAU) was founded in 1963. Other regional groupings, like the Economic Community of West African States (ECOWAS), the Southern African Development and Coordination Conference (SADCC), the Comité Permanent Interetats de Lutte contre la Séchéresse dans le Sahel (CILLSS), and the Caribbean Community (CARICOM), have also been set up, albeit sometimes with very limited success. In Africa, the fight against apartheid has usually been a major factor in the formation of solidarity within such organisations, but common problems such as transport and communications have been important factors as well. Obviously the African Lomé countries have developed a certain 'we-feeling', which is certainly stronger than any sense of belonging to the somewhat artificial ACP club.

There is, however, a high density of contacts and meetings in the ACP framework, and its meetings are prestigious. One must therefore conclude that belonging to the ACP group is an important element in the political life in these countries — even if their citizens are not necessarily very aware of the importance of the ACP. Among the political and economic élite, however, 'Lomé' is certainly seen as being of great salience.

More than trade promotion and financial support: the scope of Lomé

The ACP–EC relationship has always been more than just a matter of trade promotion and financial support. Both elements are, of course, as of crucial importance today as in the 1970s, but in the long history of cooperation, first in Yaoundé and then in Lomé, other issues have arisen and been dealt with, in some cases with considerable success. The Parliamentary bodies set up by the Yaoundé/Lomé Conventions have proved to be especially useful as a forum for innovative ideas.[13]

Using Lomé III, for example, the Convention included the following elements:

(a) *Trade regulations:* free access of 99.5 per cent of all ACP exports to the EC market without reciprocal obligation. Only the agricultural products within the CAP are excluded.

(b) *STABEX and SYSMIN*: new instruments devised and implemented to help stabilize export earnings for certain groups of commodities.

(c) *Regional cooperation*: special financial assistance measures to support regional cooperation among ACP states (Lomé III: 1,000 million ECU).

(d) *Principles of cooperation and political cooperation:* Articles 1–25 set out the fundamental principles of cooperation. ACP–EC cooperation is based on the equality of all partners and the mutual recognition of sovereignty. At the same time Lomé III refers to human rights and the fight against apartheid.[14]

(e) *Institutional arrangements*: discussions take place in joint ACP–EC bodies at ministerial, ambassadorial and parliamentary levels.

The balance sheet of these provisions is ambiguous. The effects of the Lomé Conventions on trade between the ACP earlier and the EC has remained unsatisfactory (see Table 3.1). It is true that there has been a remarkable increase in absolute figures, but over the years the ACP share of the EC trade has fallen slightly. The EC continues to supply

Table 3.1: The EC's trade relations with the ACP countries (values in million ECU)

	1960	1970	1975	1980	1982	1985	1987
exports	2 392	4 068	8 772	17 048	20 222	19 336	13 843
(in %)	(9.4)	(7.5)	(7.4)	(7.7)	(7.1)	(5.1)	(4.1)
imports	2 826	5 472	9 715	20 744	20 140	30 310	16 374
(in %)	(9.7)	(8.6)	(7.3)	(7.3)	(6.0)	(7.5)	(4.8)
trade balance	−434	−1 405	−943	−3 696	+82	−10 974	−2 531

Source: Eurostat, External Trade, 1988.

primarily finished industrial goods, while the ACPs continue to provide raw materials. Despite this structural problem, however, the ACP states have had a trade surplus with the EC in most years.

The STABEX and SYSMIN systems have provided a generally limited but helpful insurance against specific problems. In 1978, 1980, 1981 and 1987, STABEX and SYSMIN resources proved, however, inadequate to satisfy all demands, obliging the Commission to make some difficult decisions on how to manage the systems.[15] Despite such problems, STABEX and SYSMIN are still rated as the benefits of Lomé.

The institutional provisions

It is clear that the institutional provisions of the Lomé Convention are a major reason for its success. Two groups of countries at different levels of development have been working together in institutions on, at least formally, the basis of equality, partnership and joint decision-making. Both sides have seen an opportunity openly to discuss existing problems such as human rights, the fight against apartheid, security in air traffic, environmental questions, the role of women in society, and the aims and instruments of the development process. These discussions contribute to a greater mutual understanding and thus to global peace and stability.

Articles 22–25 of Lomé III established the following institutions:

(i)   The *ACP–EC Council of Ministers*, which sets guidelines and decides on all matters affecting the framework of cooperation. The Council meets normally once a year alternately in the EC and in one of the ACP countries. According to Article 269.6, it can institute committees or *ad hoc* working groups. Of particular relevance is the so-called Article 193 Committee (formerly Article 108 Committee) which advises the Council on the general conditions to be applied to works, supplies, and service contracts financed by the EDF.

(ii) The *ACP–EC Committee of Ambassadors*, which meets at least twice a year, normally in Brussels. The Committee of Ambassadors supports the Council of Ministers and deals with the day-to-day work.

(iii) The *ACP–EC Joint Assembly*, which is composed of one Parliamentarian or other representative from each ACP country and the same number of members of the European Parliament. Its functions can be described as those of a watchdog looking over the progress of the agreements and a forum for the discussion of new ideas. Moreover, the Joint Assembly organises regular contacts between the social and economic circles of both sides. The Joint Assembly meets twice a year, alternately in the EC and in the ACP.

An important element of the ACP–EC institutional relationship is its bilateral character. It is not 12 plus 69 independent states which negotiate, but two groups of states. Decisions are only accepted when there exists a majority on both sides. The annual meetings of the ACP–EC Council of Ministers are devoted to the approval of a detailed report on interim results. While the discussions in the Council are, in general, strictly limited to the substance of the Lomé Convention, the work of the ACP–EC Joint Assembly is more open and more 'political'. Questions such as the fight against apartheid, the debt problem and the protection of human rights are regularly to be found on the agenda of this body.

Experience since 1975 shows that the ACP side is following a certain 'institutional strategy'. In the beginning, new questions such as the fight against apartheid, cultural cooperation or the debt problem, were introduced into the parliamentary forum. If a common position can be reached there, and the subject seems to be 'ripe', the ACP side tries to put it on the agenda of the ACP–EC Council of Ministers. In some cases this approach takes a long time, but in most cases it functions in the end.

Since the beginning of Lomé cooperation, the fight against apartheid has been a major topic in the work of the Joint Assembly. Parliamentarians have regularly called for economic sanctions against the Republic of South Africa. For a long time the EC Ministers refused to discuss the question at all because this 'political problem' was not covered explicitly by the Lomé Convention. It was a success of the Joint Assembly that a reference to the problem was made in the Joint declaration on Article 4 in Lomé III. In the circumstances, the Council of Ministers could no longer refuse the ACP demand for an in-depth discussion on the issue. It was, though, an innovation when, on 26 April 1988, in the framework of the EPC the Troika (Federal Republic of Germany, Denmark and Greece) met 13 representatives of the ACP countries (Niger, Jamaica, Angola, Zaïre, Mauritius, Belize, Burkina Faso, Nigeria, Zambia, Sudan, Fiji, Burundi and Papua New Guinea). The partners agreed to meet again in the same format.

There are, of course, some criticisms of the ACP–EC institutional provisions and some unanswered questions. Among the latter are the following: why, for example, are the financial decisions always taken in the end by Europeans and not by joint institutions? Is it really worthwhile for freely elected MEPs to meet twice a year with ACP representatives who are for the most part ambassadors or other civil servants? Do Community Ministers themselves attend meetings of the ACP–EC Council or do they regularly send their substitutes?[16] But apart from such open questions, the institutional provisions of the Lomé cooperation are rated as being positive by both sides. The meetings are regularly characterised as constructive and open-minded.

European integration: a blueprint for intra-ACP cooperation?

For many Europeans, a major aim of ACP–EC cooperation is to support regional cooperation among the associated countries themselves. Their argument is that the European Community has benefited from a regional approach and so would the developing countries. To this end a certain amount of the financial support was reserved for promoting regional cooperation among the ACP states from the very beginning. This was regularly increased and, in Lomé III, 1 000 million ECU were provided for the purpose.[17]

The record of regional cooperation in the ACP countries is, however, patchy.[18] In the Suva Declaration of April 1977, all ACP countries accepted an action programme for intra-ACP cooperation, including sectors such as transport, communications, trade cooperation and finance.[19]

An example that may explain the aims of the Lomé programme on regional cooperation is that of the so-called 'Northern Corridor Transit Agreement'.[20] The term was used to designate the transport infrastructure and facilities located in Eastern Africa, served by the port of Mombasa in Kenya. The Corridor provides the essential outlet to and from world markets for the landlocked countries of Rwanda, Burundi and Uganda, and even for Eastern Zaïre. The Corridor consists of three elements:

(i)   a railway running nearly 1500 km from Mombasa to Nairobi, into Uganda and ending at Kasese close to the Uganda–Zaïre border;
(ii)   a road system of about 2000 km which joins Mombasa to Nairobi continuing to Kampala, then on to Kigali (Rwanda) and Bujumbara (Burundi);
(iii)   an oil pipeline which is 449 km long and runs from Mombasa to Nairobi.

Trade liberalisation between those and other ACP countries was envisaged, but obviously the creation of a free trade area or 'ACP Internal Market' is a long way off. Some attempts have been made in geographically more limited groupings (SADCC, ECOWAS, etc.), but their impact has been very limited so far. Nevertheless, the EC has contributed to many trans-frontier projects such as the construction of roads and telephone links. One must bear in mind that in 1975, when cooperation in the ACP states began, there was a far-reaching cleavage between the former French and British colonies and their respective 'mother-countries'. Compared with this situation, intra-African communication has developed considerably.

The Lomé approach: a model not for EC group-to-group relations, but for its structural quality

Obviously the Lomé approach as such is neither a transferable model for the North–South relationship in general nor for EC relations with other regional groupings. The Community has established a unique form of cooperation with a large number of developing countries, which are mostly former colonies of the EC member states. The vast majority of them also belong to the group of the poorest countries in the world. The EC has therefore been able to offer far-reaching trade concessions. The risk of these resulting in real problems for the EC has been small and — even if they had — the Lomé Conventions have included safeguard clauses, which would have helped to resolve them.

It remains an open question whether the ACP countries should be considered as a regional grouping at all. Obviously they are obliged to work together in the Lomé framework, without which the group certainly would not exist. But, at the same time, binding structures have been created and intra-ACP cooperation has developed a life of its own. But it is debatable as to whether a blueprint for regional groupings really does exist. A closer look at the various examples is likely to show that each of them is a unique product of a particular set of circumstances. Is not EFTA, for example, as much a direct result of the existence of the EC? Can the Mediterranean countries really be considered as a group of countries coming together as a matter of free choice? One could raise similar questions about all such cooperation groupings.

This study, however, has clearly shown the unique quality and density of the ACP–EC institutional contacts and especially the way in which problems are solved jointly in a well-defined way. This is, perhaps, the most important innovative element of Lomé which might find application in North–South relations as a whole, as well as in EC relations with other groups of countries.

In concluding, we can find at least three major reasons for the relative success of the ACP–EC cooperation during the last 15 years. First of all there is on both sides a strong interest in the continuation for economic and political reasons, and secondly the negotiations are organised in a bilateral way based — at least formally — on equality, and the third reason is that it is not a question of 80 independent countries putting forward diverging positions, but two groups of more or less homogeneous states. Due to the underdeveloped character of most ACP countries, the risks for the Community are limited. Therefore it is able to offer some relatively far-reaching provisions.

Despite these positive arguments, there are also deficits. The overall results of the ACP–EC cooperation in economic terms have been insufficient. The ACP side have been highly critical of the EC's concessions as falling far too short of existing needs. During the signing ceremony of Lomé IV in December 1989, the ACP representative, General Eyadema, stressed the fact that the recent historic events in Eastern Europe caused 'anxiety and concern' in ACP countries. He launched an appeal therefore to the EC countries that they should not abandon their friends in the South because of their brothers in the North.[21]

Notes

1 Groupe des états ACP, ACP/00/033/88 Rev. 2, Brussels, 12 October 1988, p. 4.
2 Opening of the negotiations for the new ACP–EC Convention, speech by the President of the Council, SN 3519/1/88, Luxembourg, 12 October 1988, p. 2.
3 A critical analysis of the results of the ACP–EC cooperation can be found in the annual reports of the ACP–EC Council of Ministers and the Joint Assembly ACP-EC.
4 See *World Bank Report 1988*.
5 For details see Edgar W. Carrington, 'Le Groupe ACP et son avenir dans le contexte international', *Le Courrier*, No. 93, Sept./Oct. 1985, pp. 73–5, and Dieter Frisch, 'Genèse et réalité du Groupe ACP: Le témoignage d'un Européen', ibid., pp. 76–8.
6 O J L73/1972, pp. 177–78.
7 Since 1969/1971 the Arusha Treaty linked the East African countries Kenya, Tanzania and Uganda with the EC.
8 For details see the article by the then responsible Director-General within the DG VIII, Hans-Broder Krohn, 'Das Abkommen von Lomé zwischen der Europäischen Gemeinschaft und den AKP-Staaten', *Europa-Archiv* (1975), Vol. 6, p. 180.
9 See *Le Courrier*, No. 93, Sept./Oct. 1985, pp. 55–6.
10 Edgar W. Carrington, *Le Courrier*, op cit.
11 For details see Marjorie Lister, *The European Community and the Developing World: The Role of the Lomé Convention*, Aldershot, 1988, pp. 167–85, esp. pp. 175.
12 For details see Dossier 'Regional Groupings' in *The Courier*, No. 112, Nov./Dec. 1988, pp. 47–85.
13 Otto Schmuck, *Vermittler zwischen Nord und Süd: Das Europäische Parlament und die Entwicklungspolitik*, Europa-Union Verlag, Bonn, 1988, pp. 72–82.
14 Article 4, Lomé III and the joint declaration on this article.
15 Kommission der EG (ed.), *Das STABEX-System*, Europa Information Entwicklung DE 59, May 1988.
16 For example, the 13th meeting of the ACP–EC Council of Ministers (11 May 1988 in Mauritius) was not chaired by the then President of the EEC Council Minister Genscher, but by Minister of State in the Foreign Ministry Schäfer, see *Bulletin of the EC*, 5-1988, para 2.2.51.
17 Article 112, Lomé III.
18 For details see the Dossier 'Regional Cooperation', *The Courier*, No. 112, Nov./Dec. 1988, pp. 47–85.
19 *Le Courrier*, No. 93, Sept./Oct. 1985, p. 55.

20 For details see *The Courier*, No. 112, Nov./Dec. 1988, pp. 80–1.
21 See *Agence Europe*, No. 5155, 16 December 1989, p. 5.

References

Commission of the EC, *The Europe–South Dialogue in Practice*, Luxembourg, 1988.

Cosgrove, Carol and Joseph Jamar (eds), *The European Community's Development Policy: The Strategies Ahead*, de Tempel, Brugge, 1986.

Dossier, 'Regional Cooperation', *The Courier*, No. 112, Nov./Dec. 1988, pp. 47–85.

Focke, Katharina, 'Das dritte Abkommen von Lomé, Fortschritte mit Fragezeichen', *Integration*, Vol. 4, 1985, pp. 143–7.

Gautron, Jean-Claude, 'La Convention de Lomé III', *Revue du Marché Commun*, No. 296, April 1986, pp. 184–93.

Gerth-Wellmann, Hella, 'Die Lomé-Politik der Europäischen Gemeinschaft', *Europa-Archiv*, No. 24/87, pp. 709–14.

Lister, Marjorie, *The European Community and the Developing World: The Role of the Lomé Convention*, Aldershot *et al.*, 1988.

Meyer zu Natrup, Friedhelm B., 'Die handels- und entwicklungspolitische Zusammenarbeit der Europäischen Gemeinschaft mit Schwarzafrika', *Aus Politik und Zeitgeschichte*, Beilage zu 'Das Parlament', B 7-8/88, pp. 43–53.

Pisani, Edgard, *La Main et l'Outil, Le développement du Tiers Monde et l'Europe*, Paris, 1984.

Regelsberger, Elfriede, 'Der Dialog der EG/Zwölf mit anderen Staatengruppen', *Integration*, No. 2/88, pp. 81–7.

Rummel, Reinhardt, *Zusammengesetzte Aussenpolitik, Westeuropa als internationaler Akteur*, Kehl, Strasbourg, 1982.

Schmuck, Otto, *Vermittler zwischen Nord und Süd: Das Europaische Parlament und die Entwicklungspolitik*, Europa-Union Verlag, Bonn, 1988.

Shaw, Timothy M., 'EEC–ECP interactions and images as redefinitions of Eurafrica: exemplary, exclusive and/or exploitive?', *Journal of Common Market Studies*, Vol. XVIII, No. 2/1979, pp. 135–57.

Wessels, Wolfgang and Otto Schmuck, 'The Community's development policy: the problem of inter- (intra) institutional coordination' in Cosgrove, Carol and Joseph Jamar (eds). op cit., pp. 33–58.

Zartman, I. William, 'Relic of the 1970s or Model for the 1990s?', ibid. pp. 59–74.

4 The Euro–Arab Dialogue: procedurally innovative, substantially weak

Elfriede Regelsberger

Academics and policy-makers alike find it difficult to assess the relationship that has been established between the European Community and its member states and the 22 members of the Arab League in the framework of the Euro-Arab Dialogue (EAD). This group-to-group approach has been described variously as an 'exercise in political good will'[1] and as a 'realité internationale d'un type nouveau'.[2] The intra-European dimension of the Dialogue has been characterized as 'the very new and rather unique relationship between the two European institutional systems'.[3] Official EC documents place the EAD in the section of the Community's external relations while also referring to it in the part on European Political Cooperation (EPC).[4] Those involved in the Dialogue tend to characterize it as an informal political–economic dialogue,[5] conducted at both the Community and the EPC level.

The approach: the gradual reconciliation of divergent interests

The reasons why classifying the Euro-Arab Dialogue is so difficult can be traced back to its early days in the mid-1970s. None of the group-to-group relations dealt with in this volume has witnessed so many ups and downs as the EAD. Several factors have been relevant. Among developments in the Middle East, there has been the peace treaty between Egypt and Israel (Camp David, 1979) and the consequent Egyptian exclusion from the Arab League (which did not end until 1989). There have also been the problems emanating from the size of the two groupings, the degree of coordination both within and between the partners and the cultural differences between Europe and the Arab world. However, the biggest hindrance to allowing the Dialogue to get off the ground has had to do with deep-rooted controversies over the aims and the approach of the new relationship.

For the Arab countries, the motives were clearly political: those among them with large energy supplies had learned how to use them for political purposes in the course of the Yom Kippur war. Given the vulnerability of Western Europe and its dependence on AOPEC supplies, the Arab side intended to exert pressure to force EC countries to change their position on the Arab–Israeli conflict. Other motives, such as establishing links with the European Community in order to foster economic and social development, were of only minor relevance. Similarly, the attractiveness of the EC as a model of integration relevant to the Arab world was limited. The idea of establishing some sort of permanent link with the Europeans therefore arose. If the too massive oil-weapon appeared inappropriate in the longer term, it needed to be replaced by a more moderate and sustainable approach in order to influence Europe's policy towards the Middle East in the 'dialogue'.

When the proposal for a dialogue was tabled by a number of Arab ministers to the heads of state and government of the EC — not all of whom were surprised — at their summit in Copenhagen in 1973, the Europeans found themselves in a dilemma. On the one hand, the Mediterranean and Middle East region was accepted as being of considerable importance in both political–strategic and economic terms. Consequently, the then Nine were keen 'to preserve the historical links with the countries of the Middle East and to cooperate over the establishment and maintenance of peace, stability and progress in the region'.[6] On the other hand, and at the same time, the impression had to be avoided that the cooperation planned with the Arab side could be interpreted merely as giving in to external pressure. The Nine agreed that it would be wrong to reject the Arab offer. They were, however, uncertain about the substance of their response. How were they to react, for example, to the Arab League's demands for the recognition of the PLO as the sole legitimate representative of the Palestinian people? Or the Arab request for the EC to withdraw from its cooperation with Israel?

The prospects for 'speaking with one voice' were not promising. The Nine's first steps in formulating a collective stance on the Arab–Israeli conflict had been only partially successful. The gap between the supporters of a pro-Arab policy, led by France, and the pro-Israeli minority, composed mainly of the Federal Republic, the Netherlands and Denmark, was still wide, even though the latter had already moved towards the majority position.[7] Tension also existed over the definition of a common Western energy policy, both among the countries of the Community and with the United States. And to make transatlantic relations even worse, the Europeans appeared to be going beyond safeguarding their 'regional' interests. Washington followed the development of EPC with great suspicion, particularly in those cases where it threatened to interfere with American interests and viewpoints, which was precisely the case in the Arab–Israeli conflict.

Experiences with this sort of inter-regional cooperation were practically non-existent in the early 1970s. Doubts therefore arose over whether a group-to-group approach could work given the numerous participants on both sides. For the EC/Nine, it was unclear whether homogeneity in procedures and substance could be achieved, especially in view of the division of competences in the field of a 'European foreign policy' and the different institutional structures, each one guarded by its supporters against interference from the other.[8]

The 1970s: the EAD's low-key profile and deadlock

Once the basic decision to cooperate had been taken by the Foreign Ministers and the guidelines had been set,[9] negotiations began at both official and ministerial level. Those among the Nine who were concerned that cooperation with the Arab League would damage relations with the United States and discredit Israel insisted on some compensatory measures. The result was that Washington was granted privileged access to EPC in the form of being informed and consulted about the Nine's foreign policy activities.[10] Israeli authorities were assured of being informed about EAD negotiations and were offered special treatment within the Community's Mediterranean policy.[11]

Existing literature tends to describe the EC/Nine as the active party, tabling proposals on the structure of the Dialogue and the timetable for negotiations. As conceived by the Nine, the EAD was to cover cooperation in a number of areas, ranging from industry, trade and agriculture to science and technology, cultural and social affairs. The question of energy supplies and the 'political' question of the Arab–Israeli conflict were not mentioned at all — largely for the reasons suggested above. According to the Nine, contacts should be established between the EPC Presidency and its counterpart on the Arab side, and a General Commission should be set up as the key institution at official level. Once this preparatory work had been successfully undertaken, a meeting of the Foreign Ministers of both sides could be envisaged to take further decisions.[12]

On the basis of these ideas, negotiations with the Arab League seemed to progress during the second half of 1974. However, they came to a halt when the Arab side insisted on the participation of the PLO as the sole representative of the Palestinian people. While it causes the EC/Twelve no problem today, in 1974 the Nine were divided over whether to accept this request. The first meeting of the General Commission scheduled for November 1974 had to be postponed as intensive diplomatic contacts were undertaken to overcome this deadlock. In February 1975, a formula was found, opening up admission for PLO representation but without explicitly naming them. Each party would consist of only a single delegation, the composition of which was the responsibility of each group.

Based on this formula, discussions continued at expert level in preparation for the first meeting of the General Commission. This preparatory stage lasted until May 1976 due to the persistent divergence on the political dimension of the Dialogue. While the EC/

Nine emphasized areas of cooperation in the non-political fields, the Arab approach was the opposite, referring whenever possible to the political situation in the Middle East. Not surprisingly, the Europeans' initial readiness to establish cooperation at a high political level gradually diminished at the same time as their partners perceived such a step as the culmination of their efforts.[13] In the end, the European quest for a non-political agenda found some acceptance at working-group level but not in the General Commission. There, it had to be reconciled with the Arabs' opposite approach. Its four regular meetings, held between 1976 and 1978, consequently covered both political and other issues. This parallelism was also reflected in the joint communiqués issued after each meeting. The first part was usually devoted to the political situation in the Middle East (such as the fate of the Palestininan people and the role of the PLO, the policy of Israel, or the Lebanon) and to the political dimension of the Euro-Arab Dialogue (the establishment of a political dialogue entrusted to a special commission of regular meetings at Foreign Ministers' level). The second part of the communiqués normally dealt with all the other subjects discussed and the results achieved in the various working groups.

The Camp David peace accords and the later suspension of Egypt's membership in the Arab League led the League into deep crisis. Strong tensions between the radical and the more moderate of its members replaced the earlier homogeneity. As a consequence the EAD's value became obsolete. From a European point of view, this intra-Arab struggle meant a lessening of the political pressure exerted on them. But the exclusion of Egypt was also strongly regretted and was seen as a factor damaging to a continuation of Euro-Arab cooperation. At the same time, however, the EC governments thought it worthwhile to keep the Dialogue alive — and even to develop its political dimension.[14] The reasons behind this change in attitudes were twofold: first, destabilization in the Gulf region, most obviously in the war between Iran and Iraq after 1979, was considered as another threat to Europe's economic well-being and security. Despite its limits, the existing network of contacts with the Arab League was seen as a helpful means of avoiding or at least reducing the possible negative effects for Europe. The second factor militating against cutting ties with the Arab world had more to do with the Nine's greater cohesion in foreign affairs, including the *acquis politique* in the Arab–Israeli conflict, and their willingness to 'shape events' with regard to the peace process in the Middle East.

The 1980s: the emergence of the EAD's political dimension

It took the two sides almost a decade to find enough common ground to revive and upgrade the Euro-Arab Dialogue. Various attempts during the early 1980s failed. The differences in perceptions on the Middle East conflict were still too great in certain fields, not only between the two sides, but also within the two groupings. Nor was there any agreement on the format in which the revitalized EAD should be demonstrated towards the outside world. In the second half of the 1980s, there was a further obstacle in that the British government strongly opposed any moves towards reviving the Dialogue. This was part of London's policy to combat those in the Arab League who practised state-supported terrorism, sometimes almost regardless of whether proof of involvement was available or not. This attitude met with strong reservations on the part of most of the EPC partners, who believed that countries like Syria were too important to be neglected in the Twelve's search for a solution to the Middle East conflict.

As consensus is the ruling principle of EPC, it was only in the second half of 1987, after London had withdrawn its opposition, that the Presidency could take up contacts with Syrian authorities and enter into another phase of negotiations on the political dimension of the Euro-Arab Dialogue. During the first half of 1988, the views of the Dialogue partners seemed to be closer than ever before. The two Foreign Ministers who chaired the two groups at the time — the German and the Saudi ministers — were the driving forces. A ministerial meeting using the Troika formula was held in June 1988 in Bonn, preceded by negotiations at ambassadorial level. In a short statement, the EPC Presidency confirmed the 'strong interest' of both sides in giving new impetus to the Dialogue at all its levels. The meeting was said to have led to a 'friendly and comprehensive exchange of views ... which included all questions of mutual interest'. However, little was said about the details on the agenda and the degree of convergence on the substance of the Dialogue.[15]

Despite the new start, a follow-up did not come about as speedily as had been envisaged by the ministerial meeting. Even though it was announced that the General Commission would meet 'soon', two years have passed and, at the time of writing, it is not yet certain whether the General Commission will be convened as planned during the Irish Presidency of the first half of 1990. In order to keep the new momentum alive, the French Presidency in 1989 felt the need to do something and called for another ministerial meeting. However, the launching of the idea was largely uncoordinated by the French, in part the result of miscalculation stemming from French self-esteem, though the initiative taken in Paris was in line with what the Ten/Twelve had continuously stated.

The meeting held in December 1989 in Paris assembled the Foreign Ministers of all the countries of both sides — in fact the formula the Arab League had long demanded. While they were happy with the approach, it met with reservations on the EPC side. Again the British government raised doubts as to the usefulness and appropriateness of sitting together with representatives of governments involved in terrorist activities especially at such a high level. Others among the

Twelve, and the Commission representatives, were also unhappy with the chosen formula, arguing in favour of restricted participation to safeguard efficiency and reduce the organizational burden. These reservations did not go unheard when decisions had to be taken on the build-up of the political dimension of the EAD. It was agreed that group-to-group conferences at ministerial level should be held only in exceptional cases; the 'normal' Dialogue should be conducted with restricted high-level participation.[16]

The format: a proliferation infrastructure

Compared to the patterns of other dialogues dealt in this volume, the format of the Euro-Arab Dialogue has two distinctive characteristics: the non-existent legal or other framework between the EC/Twelve and the Arab League; and on the European side, the nature of the inter-relationship between EPC and the EC institutions.

The commitment to cooperate in the EAD has been only a political one despite, or perhaps because of, the absence of a legal framework. Around 50 working groups, sub-committees etc. exist below the General Commission. The lack of any treaty basis indicates the specific approach of the EAD, that of offering a framework for the mutual exchange of information and views over a wide range of topics of more or less common interest to all the participants. Cooperation in concrete terms takes place on a bilateral basis which is seen as the most appropriate way of securing individual interests. Most of the members of the Arab League are thus linked on a contractual basis with the European Community, whether through the EC's global Mediterranean policy, the Lomé Convention (as in the case of Mauritania), or the Cooperation Agreement with the Gulf Cooperation Council. Thus the political dimension of the EAD is for some Arab League members in addition to a bilateral relationship (for example, the Maghreb countries) or through a group-to-group approach (such as the Gulf Cooperation countries, and the signatories of the Lomé Convention).

The clearest account of how the EAD should be organized dates back to 1976. Annex 4 to the Joint Communiqué of the first meeting of the General Commission describes the 'organs' of cooperation, their composition, their mandates, the calendar for their meetings and other organizational questions (including chairmanship).[17] Since then, procedural and organizational adaptations seem to have been based on a common political agreement, not necessarily laid down in specific texts. This pragmatic approach applies also in the decision to hold ministerial meetings. It cannot be excluded that some sort of an internal agreement exists in written form, but such a loose arrangement contrasts with the approach of several other group-to-group ministerial meetings where the political will to institutionalize such a dialogue is expressed usually in a joint communiqué or, in the case of the Contadora and the Central American States, in the form of a political, not legally binding, Act.

Since 1988, meetings of the Foreign Ministers have constituted the highest authority of the EAD. According to the decision of the Paris conference of December 1989, meetings are to take place annually, obviously at alternating sites, as is the practice in most of the other group-to-group dialogues. There were differing views over the composition of the Ministerial delegations; the Arabs favoured the full representation of all the 22 members of the Arab League and the European Community, while the Twelve and the EC Commission insisted on the Troika formula. In the end, the latter proposal was applied, even though the Europeans admitted that in cases of emergency and outstanding circumstances, Ministerial sessions with full representation could be held.

With the institutionalization of Ministerial conferences, the need arose for a definition of the relationship with the existing core of the EAD, the General Commission. According to the Paris meeting, the politicians will have the overall responsibility for both the political and economic aspects of Euro-Arab cooperation, while the General Commission's main focus will be on the non-political dimensions of the Dialogue. The surveillance function given to the Ambassadorial level corresponds widely to the tasks entrusted to the Cooperation Committees, which were created in other dialogues described here. Given the highly politicized framework within which the EAD has worked so far, it remains to be seen whether this new sharing of responsibilities will work.

Furthermore, at their December 1989 meeting, the Foreign Ministers agreed to reduce the number of working groups, sub-groups and task forces that seemed to have moved beyond the control of the General Commission. The European proposal, suggesting the elimination of two basic working groups dealing with general economic cooperation and social/cultural affairs, was more radical than that put forward by the Arab League countries. The latter proposed, in addition, to continue the expert meetings on financial/commercial and scientific/technological questions. The final compromise paid tribute to the interests of both sides.

The other particular characteristic of the EAD concerns the intra-European decision-making process. It refers to two different aspects: the first concerns the creation of a coordinating group composed of officials from the national foreign ministries and the EC Commission to prepare the meetings of the General Commission. As its agenda had to cover both EPC and Community-related aspects, it had to report to both the Political Committee and the Committee of Permanent Representatives. This approach constituted a novelty at the time, for emphasis was then put on a clear-cut distinction between EPC machinery and the EC's institutional structure. At the very beginning of the EAD, the EPC working group on the Middle East was exclusively in charge of preparing for cooperation with the Arab countries. As the EC governments at that time did not wish to allow the Commission to participate at the working-group level, a specific forum had to be set up, in order to manage the complex issues that needed to be handled and to respect the competences of the EC (in the field of trade) which had been transferred from the national to the European level. The second aspect of this intra-European dimension of the EAD is that, contrary to the usual principle of rotating Presidencies among the member states, the term of office is a permanent one and delegated to individual EC member states and the Commission. It was chosen because of the manifold issues covered by the EAD and the common desire to safeguard some sort of continuity, at least at the expert level.

The results: atmospheric confidence-building and some convergence in substance

Compared to the other group-to-group relations described in this volume, the EAD has been highly controversial, both over procedural questions and matters of policy substance. It took the two sides more than a decade to complement the initially limited approach and to establish a political dimension. Despite all the misunderstandings and divergencies of view, neither side has considered abolishing the network of cooperation. On the contrary, there was proliferation at the working level and a gradual stabilization of the Dialogue at the political level. To the extent that the EC government's *acquis* on problems related to the Middle and Far East became more solid, the existing gap on the substance of policy could be bridged, at least with the more moderate forces among the Arab League countries.

With the Arab members of the Gulf Cooperation Council, the EC/Twelve are connected through an individual group-to-group dialogue.[18] Even though both sides stress the importance of both fora of cooperation as complementary, competition cannot be excluded. Given the smaller number of participants and their greater homogeneity, both inside and between the two groupings, it is more likely than not that the EC/Twelve–GCC relationship will prosper, even though obstacles persist, particularly in the field of trade. There cannot be the same degree of certainty that the new momentum of the EAD will be maintained in the 1990s.

Notes

1 Robert Rüdiger, 'Euro-arabischer Dialog', Wichard, Woyke (ed.), *Pipers Wörterbuch zur Politik, Vol. III*, Europäische Gemeinschaft, Munich and Zurich, 1984, pp. 43–6.

2 Françoise de la Serre, 'Conflict du Proche-Orient et dialogue euro-arabe: la position de l'Europe des Neuf', Jacques Bourrinet (ed.), *Le Dialogue Euro-Arabe*, Paris, 1979, pp. 79–93.

3 David Allen, 'Political Cooperation and the Euro-Arab Dialogue', in David Allen, Rummel Reinhardt, Wolfgang Wessels (eds), *European Political Cooperation*, London, 1982, pp. 69–82.

4 Commission of the European Communities (ed.), *22nd Annual Report*, 1988, Brussels and Luxembourg, 1989.

5 See the contribution of Simon Nuttall in this volume.

6 Point 13 of the document on the European identity, published by the Foreign Ministers, Copenhagen, 14 December 1973: Press and Information Office of the Federal Government (ed.), *European Political Cooperation (EPC)*, 4th ed, Bonn, 1982, p. 61.

7 For further details see David Allen and Alfred Pijpers (eds), *European Foreign Policy-Making and the Arab Israeli Conflict*, Martinus Nijhoff, The Hague, 1984.

8 For further details on foreign policy-making at the European level see Alfred Pijpers, Elfriede Regelsberger and Wolfgang Wessels (eds), *European Political Cooperation in the 1980s*, Martinus Nijhoff, Dordrecht, Boston and London, 1988; de Philippe Schoutheete, *La Coopération Politique Européenne*, 2nd edn, Brussels, 1986, pp. 4–9; Guy de Bassom pierre, *Changing the Guard in Brussels: An Insider's View of the EC Presidency*, New York, Westport and London, 1988.

9 During their first informal Gymnich-type meeting, the Foreign Ministers of the Nine agreed to an *aide-mémoire*, which contained the aims and the mandate for negotiations from a European perspective. For the text of this document see Bourrinet, 1979, op. cit., p. 295.

10 This procedural arrangement, known as the Gymnich gentlemen's agreement of 1974, marks the beginning of what is known today as the Twelve's dialogue with third countries and regional groupings (Article 30, 8 SEA). Initially it was designed to associate the 'friendly and allied states' with EPC. Today it is open for a wider range of countries all over the world. See Chapter 1 in this volume.

11 Israel was the first out of the 13 countries of the Mediterranean basin to sign a cooperation agreement with the EC, including a financial protocol.

12 See the *aide-mémoire* of June 1974, op. cit.

13 Illustrative in this respect is the joint memorandum formulated by the expert group in 1975. In Bourrinet, 1979, op. cit., p. 296.

14 Declaration of the European Council, 12/13 June 1980, Venice.

15 For the text of the statement of 24 June 1988 see European University Institute and Institut für Europäische Politik (eds), *European Political Cooperation Documentation Bulletin 1988*, Vol. IV, No. 1, Luxembourg, 1989, p. 181.

16 *Agence Europe*, 28 December 1989.

17 Text of the document in Bourrinet, 1979, op. cit, p. 331.

18 See the contribution of Eberhard Rhein in this volume.

5 Cooperation with ASEAN: A success story

Manfred Mols

Introduction

'For years, ASEAN States have constituted a growth region with optimistic perspectives for the future.'[1] Such a judgement is representative of European evaluations of the Association of South East Asian Nations (ASEAN) composed of Indonesia, Malaysia, the Philippines, Singapore, Thailand, and (since January 1984) Brunei, which was founded in 1967 by a relatively vague statement of foreign ministers, the Bangkok Declaration.

ASEAN came into being as a loosely structured intergovernmental organization designed to promote 'cooperation in the fields of economic, social and cultural affairs'.[2] Although it was not a political organization *per definitionem*, 'the establishment in itself was a political act.'[3] During the first decade of its existence (and to a certain extent even now), a satisfactory relationship and workable balance between national and regional interests was never easily achieved. A weak organizational structure[4] reflected a beginning that was more non-committal than a clear statement of a developed philosophy of regional cooperation. Mainly as a result of substantive changes in the international environment in East and South East Asia (such as the end of the Vietnam war and the partial withdrawal of the United States from mainland Asia), ASEAN's political leaders increasingly recognized the need for closer cooperation. Two summits (1976 in Bali and 1977 in Kuala Lumpur) underlined the political will both for improving intra-relationships and establishing a more systematic international stance. The Bali conference closed with two important, future-oriented documents, the Treaty of Amity and Cooperation in South East Asia and the Declaration of ASEAN Concord.[5] The Kuala Lumpur conference should have further strengthened economic cooperation, but was primarily designed to stress the determination of the ASEAN heads of government to enter more vigorously into the fields of foreign policy including regular dialogues with third partners.

It was in this context that EC–ASEAN cooperation was established in 1978 at the level of Foreign Ministers. Relations had begun at an institutional level in 1972 partly as a result of Britain's entry into the European Community and the corresponding need to redefine relations with its former colonies of Malaysia and Singapore. The present state of the relationship is well summed up in the words of the German Foreign Minister, Hans-Dietrich Genscher, when he declared on 2 May 1988:

The founding of ASEAN was a decisive step forward. The European Community and its member states from the outset have considered it an important task to promote this association and to assist the development of the links between the two regions from their modest beginnings to what they are today: an important partnership, which is of benefit to the parties involved and is also on the way to exercise a beneficial influence throughout the world.[6]

This is not to be taken as an expression of tremendous enthusiasm, but rather one of open satisfaction with having started something that makes good sense, and whose continuation is obviously regarded as worthwhile. For the Europe of the Twelve, the relationship with ASEAN and its member states has become a solid and, on the whole, a reliable element in its foreign relations. And for their part, the South East Asian countries also consider the relationship with Europe a successful enterprise which still offers — in the words of the Indonesian Minister for Foreign Affairs, Mochtar Kusumaatmadja — 'room for improvement',[7] but which has been for a long time an indispensable part of the ASEAN community's international engagement. As one of the ASEAN Ambassadors to the EC in Brussels put it, 'There is no other ASEAN relationship to match this in intensity'.[8]

The structure of European-South East Asian Cooperation

From the beginning, the objective of the then five signatory states to the Bangkok Declaration of August 1967 was 'To maintain close and beneficial cooperation with existing international and regional organizations with similar aims and purposes'.[9] It was therefore only natural that the new community should approach the EC, even more so since in South East Asia, as in other parts of the world, Western European efforts at unification were (and still are) seen as an important model. The initiative was taken in 1972 by the Indonesian Minister of Commerce, Sumitro Djodjokadikusomo, and by June of the same year, it had become possible to establish the first ASEAN Committee in a third country, in Brussels.

Two years later, a Joint Study Group of EC and ASEAN officials was set up which held meetings over several years and carried out the preparatory work for the subsequent agreements. In November 1978, the first EC–ASEAN meeting at the ministerial level was held. In 1980, a formal EC–ASEAN Cooperation Agreement, a Joint Statement on Political Issues, and a Joint Declaration on the possibilities of economic and technical cooperation were signed in Kuala Lumpur.[10] That, from the very beginning, the EC was interested in an orderly dialogue with ASEAN can be inferred from the fact that in 1979 an EC liaison office

had been set up in the Far East. Its geographical competence was
certainly not limited to the territory of ASEAN member states, but by
taking its seat in Bangkok, it gave a clear and well-understood signal
about the priorities of EC cooperation in the region.[11] There has been a
constant EC–ASEAN dialogue at a high level ever since.

Politically, the most important instrument are the meetings of
Foreign Ministers. They have so far met seven times, with interludes
between each meeting of about 18 months. Compared to its meetings
with other dialogue partners (United States, Japan, Australia, New
Zealand), the EC has been strongly represented since normally the
Foreign Ministers of the Twelve and the European Commission take
part. In addition, a second type of high-level political EC–ASEAN
exchange takes place in the form of the so-called post-ministerial
dialogue conferences which ASEAN organizes annually with its
international partners in connection with ASEAN Ministerial
Meetings.[12] The ASEAN Committees in Brussels, Bonn, London and
Paris also serve as important links. In the Federal Republic of Germany
and in Belgium, there are semi-annual working dinners between the
Foreign Minister and the respective ASEAN Committee; in other EC
countries, there are at least meetings of ASEAN Ambassadors with
officials at the level of Political Directors. There is a counterpart to all
this in the capitals of ASEAN in that the Foreign Ministers and other
high-ranking officials periodically see the Ambassadors of the EC
countries.[13] Meetings between the European Parliament and the
ASEAN Interparliamentary Organization also form part of the political
dimension to EC–ASEAN activities.[14] They have, however, mainly
symbolic significance: the ASEAN Interparliamentary Organization
remains outside the formal ASEAN structures.

Apart from the fact that the Economic Ministers of the two regions
met first in Bangkok in 1985, the most important regular links in the
economic sphere are those of the Joint Cooperation Committee, which is
made up of senior officials which meets more or less once a year. There
are also the so-called groups of contact responsible for the continuity of
mutual dialogue and coordination between the regular meetings.[15]

There are numerous additional foras which meet either regularly or
on an *ad hoc* basis, such as the ASEAN–EC Business Council, the Joint
ASEAN–EC Investment Committees in each of the ASEAN capitals
and the so-called Partner Research Network which, among other
things, promotes joint ventures. There are also seminars and missions
and other regular meetings of businessmen and others. There are also
institutions like the ASEAN Trade Promotion Centre in Rotterdam, as
well as an ASEAN–EC Energy Management Training and Research
Centre, to be located in Brunei.[16] All this is reinforced by meetings of
other groups such as trade unionists (in November 1985, for example).
Although European knowledge of ASEAN and its member states
remains unsatisfactory and, conversely, there are complaints that
ASEAN familiarity with the EC is declining[17] (partly because there is

no Centre for European Studies in any of the ASEAN countries), economists, sociologists, political scientists etc. from both regions occasionally come together for joint conferences, workshops and symposia.

Beyond these multilateral ASEAN–EC relationships there is, of course, a dense network of bilateral relations between ASEAN and EC member states which both sides have shown interest in promoting. These relationships are in part a product of history, but in part also they derive from ideas about a geographically functional division of labour within the European Community. The British presence in South East Asia, especially in Singapore, Malaysia and Brunei, is complemented by the strong economic commitment of the Federal Republic of Germany, which has made the Germans something like a *de facto* spokesman for the EC.[18] It is no accident that Mr Genscher, especially, supported the Kuala Lumpur Agreement of 1980, and that the foreign policy of the Federal Republic is well regarded in all ASEAN states. But Italy is apparently in the process of expanding its commitment in South East Asia on a multilateral (ASEAN) as well as on a country-by-country basis.[19] As for the Netherlands, whose past relationship with Indonesia was somewhat delicate, its growing commitment in the areas of foreign trade and development aid policies has helped to normalize relations. French relations are in part a product of its long history in Indochina. The whole of South East Asia, beyond only the six ASEAN countries, has thus had a significant place in French foreign policy conceptions,[20] including cultural policy as indicated by the successful activities of the Alliance Française.

There is sufficient reason to believe that the attention Europe gives ASEAN is reinforced by the very existence of the latter as an institutionalized system of cooperation.[21] In the same way, the countries of Western Europe would be less interesting for ASEAN and its member states without the existence of the European Community and its mechanisms of cooperation. Only in exceptional cases therefore can the relationship between the EC and ASEAN, which on the whole functions rather well, be seen separately from the equally satisfactory cooperation between the FRG and Singapore, Italy and Malaysia, Great Britain and Brunei, and so on.

At first glance, one might say that the Kuala Lumpur Agreement of 1980 and its underlying philosophy has proved unique for both sides in the sense that it was not states but regional communities that took steps towards each other. It was possibly due to the negotiation skills of the South East Asians that not only was a commercial agreement signed (which had initially been the idea of the EC), but an entire political and diplomatic network of interrelations was constructed,[22] which includes economic cooperation. There is today a certain imbalance between the two levels of cooperation. Cooperation between the EC and ASEAN, including bilateral relations between the individual member states, is more profound in the political than in the economic sphere. While at the level of Foreign Ministers and senior foreign policy representatives, a significant degree of familiarity exists along with considerable mutual understanding on many global questions, economic cooperation, despite numerous isolated successes, has still not passed the stage of being a programme for which most of the homework remains to be done.

Motives and reciprocal interests in EC–ASEAN cooperation

Cooperation in the foreign policy or foreign trade policy sector, whether between states or between regional groups, is subject to specifiable cost-benefit analyses.[23] The accounts of each side, however, do not necessarily contain similar, much less similarly weighted items. In the case of EC–ASEAN cooperation, the underlying interests and motives of each side are obvious. The ASEAN group which, it should be remembered, had taken the initiative towards the EC, has sought to counter the danger of a paralysing dependence on foreign interests while, at the same time, attempting to strengthen its autonomy and viability by diversifying its external links. 'Coping with dependence' is the significant sub-title of a recent analysis of ASEAN.[24] A second important motive, especially in the years when ASEAN deliberately courted the EC, was the wish to find stronger support in the West against communism which appeared to be gaining ground in the region (in Indochina, partially in Thailand and Malaysia, and, during the time of Sukarno, in Indonesia, a fact his political heirs have always kept in mind). This was considered all the more important as the United States seemed to be withdrawing from the region, at least from the countries on the continent, after their defeat in Indochina.[25] The moment — and this leads us to the European side of the picture — was favourable for initiatives of this kind.

Europe for its part had become more self-confident in the second half of the 1970s, and it sought to appear on the international scene in a more independent way than before. A connection with the ASEAN group had several fascinating aspects. The sub-region was considered more stable politically than most other parts of the Third World. Its growth rates, which were well above average according to universal standards, gave,[26] and continue to give,[27] hope for a future accompanied by a marked growth potential. The opportunity to use the connections with ASEAN to gain access to the Pacific Community, whose contours were beginning to become visible, also played a role; even the European Commission openly talked about the possibility of finding a 'stepping stone into the Pacific' by way of ASEAN.[28] And besides, as Detlef Lorenz has suggested,[29] the European presence in South East Asia offered them the chance to reassert their position, in a geo-strategically relevant area, within the competitive relationship of the so-called trilaterals (United States, Europe, Japan).

This clearly indicates the convergence of interests between the Europe of the EC and the ASEAN group.[30] For the South East Asians, the interest from the very beginning was the possibility of co-determining the geo-political and geo-strategic balance of power within the region. This was regarded as especially important in view of the overlapping spheres of interests of the two superpowers and those powers claiming regional leadership, including China, Vietnam, as well as Japan and, to a certain degree, Australia. The ultimate goal was to keep the communist powers out, but without allowing any of the Western powers to gain a position of monopolistic hegemony. This argument was initially directed rather more against the United States, but for the last 15 years or so it has referred particularly to Japan whose economic penetration of the region has never encountered pure enthusiasm, however much it has been needed as an economic partner, a source of development aid, or a counterweight to the two regional communist states.

As for the European relationship with ASEAN, it has not given rise to the change of intruding into the 'backyard' of a third power (unlike the case in Latin America). Nor have intra-European sensitivities of the kind experienced with respect to some of the ACP states been apparent in connection with ASEAN. But the primary European argument is that ASEAN and its member states are partners with a predictable position in the international system, who rely in their foreign policy on regional zones with a calculable international balance,[31] and, in their economic policies, on similar philosophies of the market economy, free enterprise and international trade as an engine for economic growth.[32] Given this background, the two groups have been able to use each other as mediators in those fora where they themselves have no direct access. The EC (especially, again, the FRG) has gained a role akin to that of a mediator in favour of ASEAN at the World Economic Summits; ASEAN's role as a conciliatory bridgehead in the North–South dialogue has been held in high esteem by the Europeans.[33] The argument can be extended to suggest that the interest of Western Europeans in other international bodies has been stimulated by the link with ASEAN: the role, for example, of Malaysia, Indonesia and Singapore in the Non-Aligned Movement; the membership of Indonesia and Malaysia in the Organization of Islamic Countries; Malaysia's and Singapore's activities in the British Commonwealth of Nations and in the regional Asia–Pacific Commonwealth; and Indonesia's membership in the OPEC.[34] Hence perhaps the statement of Guilio Andreotti, the sometime Italian Foreign Minister and Prime Minister, that EC–ASEAN cooperation is a model for North–South cooperation.[35]

The political and strategical dimensions

The relatively close economic dialogue between the EC and ASEAN has at no time been able to obscure the fact that the political–strategic dimension has been of incomparably greater relevance, including its basic philosophy of regionalism as a structural principle of international relations.[36] Detlef Lorenz has suggested: 'The first motive is that of an elementary interest in political cooperation, which is also understood by the majority as the primary motive.'[37] A number of reasons can be given for this primacy of the political dimension which are complementary although they belong to different levels. No matter how pluri-dimensional the numerous ASEAN–EC conversations may be, the solid nucleus of the dialogue is reduced to the regular meetings of the Foreign Ministers and the officials preparing for them. There is, in addition, the quality of ASEAN itself; it has always been primarily a venture in political cooperation (even before the explicit expression in the Manila Declaration of December 1987),[38] or at least it is a regional alliance in which political performance and political benefits have been more obvious than the economic aspect. The Joint Declaration on Political Issues of 7 March 1980[39] laid the foundations of a dialogue that was forward-looking and concerned with securing international peace, a concern which has not been abandoned. This can be seen in the EC/Twelve's support for ASEAN's ZOPFAN project (Zone of Peace, Freedom and Neutrality), as well as the attempt on the part of both sides to stabilize situations of particular importance to the other — as, for example, in the Twelve's support for ASEAN's position on Kampuchea, in the UN, or the pro-European position of the ASEAN group on Afghanistan or, especially, the Middle East. It is tempting to argue that in foreign policy, in contrast at least to foreign trade, investment or technology policy, what has evolved is what Hans-Dietrich Genscher has described as 'new forms of diplomacy':

Increasingly, bilateral negotiations are replaced by an almost parliamentarian system of multilateral diplomacy, where the objective is no longer to get as many concessions from the other side as possible, but rather to develop autonomous positions of whose beneficial nature a majority of states can be convinced.[40]

This new diplomacy differs from classical diplomacy, which in game-theoretic terms might be characterized as a zero-sum game, by being more oriented towards longer-term perspective to the benefit of all. This remains valid even when concerns are neither immediate nor equally felt by all, on the assumption that 'mixed motives' complement each other, or at least are not seen as too interfering.[41] The comprehensive agenda of the Seventh ASEAN–EC Ministerial Meeting held on 2–3 May 1988, in Dusseldorf, confirmed the tendency which had been discernible in earlier years in high-level EC–ASEAN talks. The final Joint Declaration,[42] under the heading 'International Political Issues', contains the following topics: East–West Relations, Disarmament and Arms Control, Kampuchea, Indochinese Refugees, Afghanistan, Middle East, Southern Africa, International Terrorism,

Narcotics, International Economic Situation, Uruguay Round, Commodities, EC–ASEAN Economic Cooperation, Trade, Investment and Industrial Cooperation and Development Cooperation.

The list clearly includes issues of varying importance to each side; the question remains therefore as to whether the negotiations have been so encompassing and successful because a degree of interdependence has been reached in the relationship that is procedurally more solid than its substance.[43] This observation is not intended to underestimate the possibility that, at the political level the limits may have been reached of what is possible between regional schemes living neither in a geo-political, geo-strategic nor even security–political proximity and which belong to different worlds of development, different cultures and incongruent political systems. Thus, when the German Foreign Minister somewhat dramatically suggested that in the ministerial talks in Dusseldorf 'an outsider could not distinguish whether a Foreign Minister from an ASEAN or an EC country was talking',[44] it was intended primarily as a reminder of the degree of familiarity reached in EC–ASEAN relations and not the extent of agreement on priorities. However, would the German Foreign Minister (or any other of the 18 Foreign Ministers present!) have been able to make the same statement if concerns vital to his own government had been affected? Foreign policy is certainly not limited to non-committal symbolism (to take up a point made in the internal considerations of the reform of ASEAN preceding the Third Summit in Manila,[45] under the slogan 'Politics may thrive on symbolism, but economics cannot'), but it is much easier to set up and develop a conference diplomacy which ultimately produces 'only' resolutions rather than distributive or even redistributive measures,[46] or policies which touch on the essentials of political order. That the political dialogue between the EC and ASEAN has limits can be demonstrated by the fact that a general discussion on human rights, which has been a strong factor in other EC–Third World discussions, but which would focus attention on a weak point in practically all ASEAN countries, has been neglected. Is this only due to prudence on the part of the EC/Twelve *vis-à-vis* ASEAN or does it indicate limits to mutual understanding of man in society?

The economic dimension reconsidered

It was reported that during the Fifth ASEAN–EC Ministerial Meeting in January 1985 in Dublin, the Malaysian Foreign Minister, Ahmad Rithauddeen, voiced concern[47] about decreasing investments from the EC and went on, somewhat angrily, 'Sometimes we ask ourselves whether you are still interested in cooperating with us.' Similarly, on the European side, there has been talk about a 'discrepancy between the level of expectations and the cooperation that has been realized'.[48] For Europe, 'a re-appraisal of economic relations, taking into account the

political and economic progress as well as the future perspectives of the
ASEAN region and deriving from it constructive conclusions and
measures, is still in its initial state'.[49] Only at first sight does this seem
surprising. In principle, the European Community, its member states
and European private business has rarely overlooked the fact that the
ASEAN region not only enjoyed magnificent economic growth rates,[50]
but that it has also been considered a promising economic partner for
the foreseeable future. That Thailand or Singapore[51] enjoy especially
good economic results, while other ASEAN countries show a tendency to
fall back on economic 'normality' does not substantially impair a
generally positive impression.

Nevertheless, the honeymoon period has apparently come to an end.
There seem to be economic and political limits to inter-regional
cooperation; the EC and ASEAN will remain for some time to come
unequal economic partners. The EC has refused — largely because of its
obligations in the Mediterranean and towards the ACP countries — to
concede privileges to the ASEAN states which go beyond the most-
favoured-nation clause of the GATT. The essential articles of the Kuala
Lumpur Cooperation Agreement (Articles 2, 3 and 4) refer to the
expansion and diversification of trade relations at 'the highest possible
level', the 'promotion of closer economic links through mutually
beneficial investment', and a carefully directed development
cooperation.[52] This was not intended to lead to any formally agreed
preferential treatment but, rather, to the encouragement of free
enterprise, the conditions for which were to be created by the two
communities and their respective national governments through
organisational measures and supporting legislation.

Today, it is less an issue of whether or not cooperation in trade,
investment or development between the EC and ASEAN is functioning,
but rather that so much remains to be done. The standard complaint
from the ASEAN region[53] is of growing protectionism on the part of the
industrialized countries, which in the case of the EC has serious
consequences especially for agriculture in third countries because of the
subsidies given. It is also believed that the ASEAN region is not
receiving priority in investments to the extent that might have been
expected given the declarations of mutual friendship which have so
frequently been made at Ministerial Meetings. The objections from the
European side are no less unequivocal,[54] that ASEAN is not sufficiently
consolidated as an economic community to qualify as a homogeneous
market. European products often do not find large enough markets.
Foreign investors in ASEAN can face substantial impediments,
ranging from low labour productivity (in spite of low wages), lack of
infrastructure to paralysing bureaucracy and 'high special tributes'.[55]
On this last point, at a meeting of the ASEAN/EC Business Council in
Kuala Lumpur some years ago, Hans Singer succinctly remarked 'that
investments will be made in the country with the least red tape'.[56]

There are, of course, differences among the member states of ASEAN which have inhibited the development of the economic side of ASEAN–EC relations to match the density of the political relationship. Improvements could be made by both sides, not least a more systematic European investment policy, which is a prerequisite to holding ground in the region against tough Japanese and North American competition. But, on the whole, one will probably have to agree with Rüdiger Machetzki, that 'With respect to the future, it must be assumed that even for the Asia–Pacific region, the time of constantly growing demand–push from the OECD countries is over'.[57]

This is not to negate the relationship and the possibilities of further economic cooperation. The EC long ago for example began to practise a less 'colonial-type trade' of raw materials for finished products with ASEAN, and instead bought more and more finished products. Secondly, ASEAN has an annual surplus in its trade with the EC of 1 billion dollars. Thirdly, EC development aid, currently amounting to more than 600 million dollars annually, is given on softer conditions than Japanese aid.[58] And finally, both sides have maintained and encouraged multiple forms of economic cooperation through training and information measures, etc. Nevertheless, for the time being it remains true that the ASEAN group is not the top priority area for the EC.

Evaluation and perspectives of EC–ASEAN relations

Cooperation has been advantageous for both groups and is likely to remain so. For none of the participating countries have there been disadvantages or excessive costs. For the EC, ASEAN has been a predictable, reliable dialogue partner in a region which, from the point of view of vitality, is likely to do well in the future: it has allowed the EC to profit through access to ASEAN commodity and investment markets. The relationship has, at least indirectly, also provided a presence in the talks over the future of the greater Pacific region. There are perhaps two other advantages: Europe, through the 'model' of EC–ASEAN cooperation, can show that it is willing and capable of entering into a regular dialogue at a high political level with other groups in the Third World; and may also convince others that, by pursuing individual measures,[59] it is not always practising a policy of divide and conquer, but can be encouraging regional unity.

The advantages for the South East Asian side are as evident. They include the fact that Europe contributes, whether through political dialogue, trade, investments or development aid to a diversification away from dependency relationships. In this way, Europe becomes an alternative to Japan, and to a lesser extent to the United States. Europe is a part of the defensive line-up against communism, whose manifest and latent presence is felt in the region, despite the opening of China, a more conciliatory Soviet Union, at least since Mr Gorbachev's speech in Vladivostok in July 1987,[60] and the progress that has been made on the question of Kampuchea.[61] Through its systematic dialogue with the United States, Canada, Australia, New Zealand, Japan and, last but not least, with Europe, ASEAN has acquired an internationally recognized position that none of the member countries by itself could even come close to — and this is as true for the 'tiger' Singapore[62] as it is for Indonesia with its huge population.[63] Nevertheless, there are limits to the mutual relationship, and there are even difficulties and strains.

No matter how advantageous the current levels of cooperation are for both sides, and how explicitly it has been stressed, not least by senior European officials, that the South East Asian potential for development differs substantially from that of other parts of the Third World,[64] it cannot be ignored that for neither region is the other a really vital political or economic priority. Europe defines its international role primarily with reference to the two global powers, to its geo-political environment, perhaps to some leading powers of the Third World (China, India, Brazil), and economically and especially technologically to Japan. The relationship with the ASEAN group has a complementary function; it is important, but not indispensable for the future of the Community of the Twelve. Conversely, in South East Asian evaluations of their own priorities in the international system,[65] Europe's role too is limited to being a complementary partner — without whom, however, it would be impossible to live without substantial losses.

Secondly, both partners have difficulties in dealing with each other in most areas outside the 'official' EC–ASEAN network. This begins with European businessmen who need to adapt better especially their behaviour to conditions in South East Asia.[66] It carries over to the delicate question of the distribution of competences in the mutual relationship. The EC suffers from an almost paralysing over-bureaucratization in practical working relationships with third countries, though ASEAN does not always help itself either internally or externally with its principle of rotating competences and the absolute underdevelopment of its community institutions.[67] But there are also difficulties which derive from the limited influence that Brussels and European governments normally have over the behaviour of private entrepreneurs.[68] At best, they can create incentives — for example, for investments abroad or joint ventures — but in each case decisions are based on whether or not private business feels attracted by these measures.

In contrast, economic and political sectors are incomparably more closely interlinked in the ASEAN countries, as elsewhere in the Third World. The fact that for Europeans ministerial resolutions on economic policy often have only the character of recommendations is not well understood outside Europe (with the exception of the northern industrialized countries). Tensions can result from misguided expectations, and so strain cooperation. Closer attention needs to be paid to looking beyond negotiated texts to understand the specific preferences of individual partner countries and the cooperation policies of each community[69] especially in terms of potentially binding economic policy.

The EC–ASEAN relationship also carries the burden of asymmetries and dichotomies of a 'senior–junior relationship',[70] although the guardians of diplomatic protocol spare no effort to enforce the principle of equality. This is not only due to psychological reasons (a marked sensitivity in questions of status can be observed in all countries where the political élites have experienced colonial rule and where the process of nation-building is still far from complete), but has structural causes. Although the ASEAN countries and the Europe of the Twelve are comparable with respect to the size of their populations (in the mid-1980s, the ASEAN group counted approximately 310 million inhabitants, the Europe of the EC 322 million),[71] the accumulated gross domestic products show a wide gap (approximately 200 billion US dollars against some 3,000 billion). Another important indicator for the imbalance between EC and ASEAN is the volume of their mutual trade:[72] the EC in 1984 had a share of 10.9 per cent of the foreign trade of the ASEAN region (Japan: 23.2 per cent, United States: 17 per cent); conversely, ASEAN's share of the foreign trade of the EC amounted to approximately 2.5 per cent on, as with investments, a slightly decreasing trend. Thus, ASEAN is incomparably more vulnerable to EC measures than vice versa. The ASEAN group has so far always reacted to this situation with the demand for increased privileges and EC concessions. However, this means giving up the principle of equality in matters of substance.

Concluding remarks

In conclusion, it is necessary to ask whether enough substance is left to go on calling EC–ASEAN relations a success story, and whether to advocate further expansion of this cooperative relationship. I think the answer is positive — the limitations and difficulties notwithstanding. To point out difficulties and elements of strain does not negate benefits. Neither the ASEAN group nor the European Community has reason for regretting the Kuala Lumpur Agreement or the high-level dialogue as such and the expansion to which all this has given rise. But both sides should be careful not to allow frustration to increase because of exaggerated expectations. From the perspective of 1989, no fundamentally new 'grand design' for an EC–ASEAN Agreement will need to be developed in the foreseeable future. Instead, it will be much more important to cultivate and consolidate, step by step (and with patience on both sides), a venture which on the whole has proved satisfactory. Many of the proposals already presented — on improving of European perceptions of ASEAN and its member states, for example,[73] or the proposals of the EC/ASEAN High Level Working Party on Investment presented some years ago[74] — could be taken up with few problems. The parameters are three basic structural factors: the development of ASEAN itself which, according to a wise phrase by Lee Kuan Yew at the Manila summit of 1987,[75] will be turned over to the responsibility of a new generation of leaders who will be installed in all ASEAN countries in the near future; the changing quality of the EC after 1992; and the possible consequences of the intensification of relations in the Asia–Pacific region, including those for the ASEAN group.

Notes

1 Werner Gocht and Hubertus Seifert in Gabriele Schrittmacher, *Kooperationsstrategien westeuropäischer und japanischer Banken in den ASEAN-Staaten* (Baden-Baden: Nomos-Verlagsgesellschaft, 1984), p. 5.

2 C.P.F. Luhulima, 'ASEAN institutions and modus operandi: Looking back and looking forward', in Noordin Sopiee, Chew Lay See and Lim Siang Jin (eds), *ASEAN at the Crossroads. Obstacles, Options and Opportunities in Economic Cooperation* (Kuala Lumpur: Institute of Strategic and International Studies (ISIS) Malaysia, not dated (1987), p. 32.

3 ibid.

4 cf. Manfred Mols, 'ASEAN Leugo de la tercera reunion cumbre', *Estudios Internacionales*, Vol. XXI, No. 81 (1988), pp. 45–60.

5 See text in e.g. Purificacion Valera-Quisumbing and Elizabeth Aguilling-Pengalagon (eds), *Vital ASEAN Documents* (Quezon City: Academy of ASEAN Law and Jurisprudence, 1985).

6 *Bulletin des Presse- und Informationsamtes der Bundesregierung* No. 57 from 10 May 1983, p. 553 (quoted from *Südostasien aktuell*, July 1988, p. 336). Mr Genscher as President of the Council was acting as host to the Seventh EC–ASEAN Conference.

7 Quoted in *Europe and South East Asia* (Bangkok), No 6 (June 1986), p 3.

8 Chiang Hai Ding, 'ASEAN-EC Relations: An ASEAN View', in Bernhard Dahm and Wolfgang Harbrecht (eds), *ASEAN und die Europäische Gemeinschaft: Partner, Probleme, Perspektiven* (Hamburg: Deutsches Übersee-Institut, 1988), pp. 110–19, here 110. (This book, including contributions by Mark B. M. Suh, Kai M. Schellhorn, Hans Christoph Rieger, Andreas Lukas, Wolfgang Harbrecht, Detlef Lorenz and others is so far the best publication available on the subject.)

9 cf. note 5.

10 For a chronology, see Stuart Harris and Brian Bridges, *European Interests in ASEAN* (London *et al*: Routledge & Kegan Paul, 1984); Will Reckman, *EC–ASEAN Almanac* (Bangkok: Press and Information Service of the Delegation of the Commission of the European Communities, not dated (1985)).

11 cf. Narciso G. Reyes, 'Building Bridges and Opening Doors', in Narongchai Akrasanee and Hans Christoph Rieger (eds), *ASEAN–EEC Economic Relations* (Singapore: Institute of South East Asian Studies, 1982), pp. 1–7.

12 Andreas Lukas, 'EC-ASEAN, Modell für interregionale Zusammenarbeit', in Dahm and Harbrecht, op. cit.
13 For details see Chiang Hai Ding, op. cit.
14 On the structure of parliamentarian cooperation within ASEAN see Eberhard Knappe,'Die AIPO–ASEAN Inter-Parliamentarische Organization', in Holger Hanel et al, Bericht über das Projekt ASEAN — Ziele, Formen, Probleme und Konsequenzen regionaler Zusammenarbeit in Südostasien, mimeo, Free University Berlin, presented to the Stiftung Volkswagenwerk (1987), pp. 118–55. In this context, it must be noted that in South East Asia, including the member countries of ASEAN, parliaments in general do not nearly have the political relevance they enjoy in the representative democracies of Western Europe, and increasingly also within the Western European integration process.
15 cf. Narongchai Akrasanee and Hans Christoph Rieger, op. cit, pp. 2f.
16 cf. ASEAN Newsletter No. 27 (May–June 1988), p. 13.
17 Chiang Hai Ding, op. cit, p. 119.
18 cf. Stuart Harris and Brian Bridges, op. cit, p. 51; cf. also note 21 of Hiemenz and Langhammer, op. cit., on the question of European economic presence in South East Asia in general. Of interest in this context Martin Gross, The Extent, Structure and Change of German, Japanese and US American Direct Investment in ASEAN Countries, Kiel Working Paper No. 239 (August 1985). For data about trade cf. EUROSTAT, EC–ASEAN Trade: A Statistical Analysis 1970–1984 (Brussels/Luxembourg: Office des publications officielles des Communautés européennes, 1987).
19 cf. Thailand Foreign Affairs Newsletter No. 2 (1987), pp. 9–10.
20 Typical of this more strategic perspective on the part of the French, for example, Georges Ordonnaud, 'L'ANSEA a l'âge adulte' in François Joyaux and Patrick Wajsman (eds), La nouvelle Asie (Paris: Livres de Poche, 1984), pp. 311–31.
21 Manfred Mols, 'ASEAN am Vorabend der Dritten Gipfelkonferenz', Europa-Archiv (1987), Vol. 42, 655–64.
22 Eric Theo, 'ASEAN–EEC Diplomatic Consultations on the Eve of an Extended Kuala Lumpur Agreement', Contemporary South East Asia (1985), Vol. 7, 116–26, esp. 117.
23 cf. Robert O. Keohane, After Hegemony: Cooperation and Discord in the World Political Economy (Princeton: Princeton University Press, 1984), particularly Part II.
24 Donald K. Crone, The ASEAN States: Coping with Dependence (New York: Praeger, 1983).
25 cf. on this and the following Eric Theo, op. cit.
26 For details see Ulrich Hiemenz, Rolf Langhammer et al., The Competitive Strength of European, Japanese and US Suppliers on ASEAN Markets (Tubingen: J. C. B. Mohr (Paul Siebeck), 1987), especially table A1.
27 cf. ASIA Yearbook, volumes for 1987 and 1988, especially the Regional Performance Figures reproduced in the first part (Hong Kong: Far Eastern Economic Review, 1987 and 1988).
28 Thus Robert Hull of the Commission in Brussels, according to Eric Theo, op. cit, p. 124. cf. on this topic Staffan Burenstam Linder, The Pacific Century: Economic and Political Consequences of Asian–Pacific Dynamism (Stanford: Stanford University Press, 1986); Kurt Furgler et al., Das Dreieck Europa–Amerika–Asien (Zürich: Verlag Rüegger, 1986); Ulrich Hiemenz, Verpaßt

Europa den Anschluss in Fernost? (Kiel: Institut für Weltwirtschaft, Kieler Diskussionbeiträge No. 101, September 1984).
29 cf. Detlef Lorenz, 'International Division of Labour or Closer Cooperation? A look at ASEAN-EC economic relations', *ASEAN Economic Bulletin*. (1986), Vol. 2, No. 3.
30 From an economic perspective, Detlef Lorenz has called these two converging batches of motives the 'motive of affiliation' ('Anschlußmotiv') and the 'motive and diversification' ('Diversifizierungsmotiv'). cf. by the same author, 'Motive und Mòglichkeiten einer engeren wirtschaftlichen Kooperation EG–ASEAN in der Zukunft', *Konjunkturpolitik* (1987), Vol. 33, No. 5, 285–302. From a political science and partially geopolitical perspective, Reuben Mondejar, *An Asian Challenge to Europe* (Barcelona: Universidad de Navarre, 1986).
31 cf. 'Italian Foreign Minister Calls for More Ties between EC and ASEAN', in *Thailand Foreign Affairs Newsletter* No. 11 (1987), p. 10.
32 Hans Christoph Rieger, *ASEAN–EC Economic Cooperation*, mimeo (Singapore, December 1984).
33 cf. Jürgen Koch, 'EG–ASEAN: Zwei Gemeinschaften schliessen einen Pakt', *EG Magazin* (1980), pp. 9–11.
34 cf. Chiang Hai Ding, 'Europe and South East Asia', *Contemporary South East Asia* (1981), Vol. 2, No. 4, p. 330.
35 Quoted from Thailand Foreign Affairs Newsletter, op. cit.
36 cf. Hans H. Indorf, 'Political Dimensions of Interregional Cooperation: The Case of ASEAN and the EEC', *The Round Table* (1983), Vol. 286, 119–36.
37 Detlef Lorenz, 'Möglichkeiten und Grenzen ...', op. cit, p. 5.
38 What is new, for the context just mentioned, in the Manila Declaration approved on the occasion of the Third ASEAN Summit is the sequence of the goals of cooperation. 'Political Cooperation' is mentioned before all other forms of cooperation. This may seem sensational, in view of the constitutive Bangkok Declaration from 1967, and of the important documents from 1976 (Declaration of ASEAN Concord, Treaty of Amity and Cooperation in South East Asia), but it does in fact only acknowledge the effective priorities for cooperation within ASEAN.
39 Eric Theo has called it a 'unique document' in international terms, 'ASEAN–EEC Diplomatic Consultations ....', op. cit., p. 119.
40 Hans Dietrich Genscher (ed.), *Nach vorn gedacht: Perspektiven deutscher Aussenpolitik* (Stuttgart: Bonn Aktuell, 1987), p. 23.
41 Such considerations play an important role in the more recent discussion about 'political regimes'. cf. e.g. Stephen D. Krasner (ed.), *International Regimes* (Ithaca and London: Cornell University Press, 1983); Michael Zürn, *Gerechte internationale Regime: Bedingungen und Restriktionen der Entstehung nicht-hegemonialer internationaler Regime untersucht am Beispiel der Weltkommunikationsordnung* (Frankfurt-on-Main: Haag & Herchen, 1987). I have been able to show the actual importance such 'mixed motives' can acquire in specific cases, for the example of the Latin American Economic System SELA; cf. Manfred Mols, 'Das Lateinamerikanische Wirtschaftssystem SELA', in Mols (ed.), *Integration und Kooperation in Lateinamerika* (Paderborn *et al.*: Ferdinand Schöningh, 1981), pp. 249–309.
42 Reproduced in *Südostasien aktuell* (July 1988), pp. 338ff.
43 cf. the distinction between 'procedural interdependence' and 'substantive interdependence' in Jock A. Finlayson and Mark W. Zacher, 'The GATT and

the regulation of trade barriers: regime dynamics and functions', in Krasner, op. cit, pp. 273–314, especially p. 309.

44 Quoted in *Bonn ASEAN Committee Newsletter* No. 26 (May–June 1988), p. 11.

45 cf. Luhulima, op. cit.

46 On this important distinction, cf. Adrienne Windhoff-Héritier, *Policy-Analyse: Eine Einführung* (Frankfurt/New York: Campus-Verlag, 1987), especially Chapter II.

47 Quoted from *Südostasien aktuell*, Heft 1 (January 1985), p. 5 (Fifth ASEAN–EC Meeting of Foreign Ministers in Dublin).

48 Hans-Christoph Reichel, 'Die Europäische Gemeinschaft und die ASEAN', *Aussenpolitik* (1985), 36, 189–96, especially p. 194.

49 ibid.

50 cf. among others, Marjorie L. Suriyamongkol, *Politics of ASEAN Economic Cooperation: The Case of ASEAN Industrial Projects* (Singapore et al.: Oxford University Press, 1988).

51 cf. among others, Toh Kin Woon, 'The Market Economies of South East Asia in 1987: Let Down by Agriculture', *South East Asian Affairs 1988* (Singapore: Institute of South East Asian Studies, 1988), pp. 22–31.

52 cf. Andreas Lukas, *Regionale Wirtschaftsgemeinschaften im internationalen System: Eine Analyse ausgewählter Wirtschaftsgemeinschaften und ihrer Interaktionen, insbesondere zwischen der EG und der ASEAN* (Frankfurt-on-Main et al.: Peter Lang, 1985), pp. 216ff, as well as the Kuala Lumpur Agreement, reproduced on pp. 304–17.

53 cf. Narongchai Akrasanee and Hans Christoph Rieger, *ASEAN–EEC Economic Relations*, op. cit., and Chee Peng Lim, 'ASEAN–EEC External Relations: Cooperation, Trade and Investment', in The Economic Society of Singapore (ed.), *ASEAN External Economic Relations* (Singapore: Chopmen Publishers, 1982), pp. 242–56.

54 cf. the cited works by Reichel and Lorenz, as well as Werner Draguhn (ed.), *Die wirtschaftliche Position der Bundesrepublik Deutschland in ausgewählten asiatisch–pazifischen Ländern: Gegenwärtiger Stand, Konkurrenz und Perspektiven* (Hamburg: Verbund Stiftung Deutsches Überseeinstitut, 1987).

55 cf. Karl Fasbender, 'Indonesien', and Klaus-A. Pretzell, 'Thailand/Malaysia' both in Draguhn, op. cit., pp. 77–94 and 95–128. The observations made there can be generalized, even though not every single judgement applies to every single country of the Association.

56 Quoted in Staff Writer, 'Less Red Tape: More Investment', *Europe and South East Asia*, No. 4 (December 1985), p. 7.

57 Rüdiger Machetzki, 'Möglichkeiten und Wege einer Verbesserung der Position der deutschen Wirtschaft im asiatisch-pazifischen Raum', in Draguhn, op. cit., pp. 249–56, especially p. 255.

58 On conditionaly, cf. Hans-Christoph Reichel, op. cit., p. 198. On the data, cf. Opening Statement by Hans Dietrich Genscher at the 7th ASEAN–EC Ministerial Meeting on 2 May 1988, in Düsseldorf, reproduced in *Südostasien aktuell*, op. cit., p. 337.

59 There was special concern about an improved creation of industrial joint ventures. cf. especially point 17 of the communiqué of the Seventh Meeting of Foreign Ministers cited in note 43.

60 On the state of Soviet foreign policy, cf. Joachim Glaubitz and Dieter Heinzig (eds), *Die Sowjetunion und Asien in den 80er Jahren: Ziele und Grenzen sowjetischer Politik zwischen Indischem Ozean und Pazifik* (Baden-Baden: Nomos-Verlagsgesellschaft, 1988). cf. also Leszek Buszynski, *Soviet Foreign Policy and South East Asia* (London and Sidney: Croom Helm, 1986); Joseph M. Ha, 'Gorbachev's Bold Asian Initiatives: Wladiwostok and Beyond', *Asian Perspective* (Seoul), Vol. 12, No. 1 (1988).

61 cf. e.g. Mohamed Noordin Sopiee, *Kampuchea: One Way Forward* (Kuala Lumpur: Institute of Strategic and International Studies (ISIS Research Note), 1988); Muthiah Alagappa (ed.), *In Search for Peace: Confidence building and conflict reduction in the Pacific* (Kuala Lumpur: Institute of Strategic and International Studies, 1987).

62 Singapore, together with South Korea, Taiwan and Hong Kong, is considered one of the most successful New Industrializing Countries (NICs) in the world. This group of countries is often called the 'Tigers' in South East Asia.

63 cf. the four articles on Indonesia in the two yearbooks *South East Asian Affairs* 1987 and 1988, op. cit. (note 47).

64 Very clearly, e.g. Claude Cheysson in an interview given to Jane Morris, reproduced in *Europe and South East Asia*, No. 3 (1985), pp. 3–5.

65 cf. e.g. Likhit Dhiravegin, *ASEAN and the Major Powers: Today and Tomorrow* (Bangkok, 1984 (Research Centre, Faculty of Political Science, Thammasat University: Monograph Series No 7); cf. also M. Rajendran, *ASEAN's Foreign Relations: The Shift to Collective Action* (Kuala Lumpur: arenabuku sdn. bhd, 1985).

66 Bernhard Coe, President of the British Chamber of Commerce in Thailand, once put it in the following way: 'The fire-eating, assertive, dynamic executive is not a success in South East Asia.'

67 cf. again, C.P.F. Luhulima, *ASEAN Institutions and modus operandi*, op. cit., *The Far Eastern Economic Review* comes to an equally hard judgement in its *ASIA 1988 Yearbook*, op. cit. p. 74: 'Relations with the industralized dialogue partners remained steady, but had more form than substance ... Part of the problem centred on ASEAN's structure, with a plethora of committees but little in the way of a single corporate authority through which to channel aid and technology.'

68 This point is stressed very intensely by Coe, 'Europe ought to be at an advantage', op. cit.

69 cf. e.g. Indorf, *Political Dimensions of Interregional Cooperation*, op. cit., p. 131.

70 ibid.

71 These data are taken from resp. calculated after: *ASIA 1988 Yearbook*, op. cit., pp. 8 and 9 (Regional Performance Figures) and from the collection of statistics 'Europa in Zahlen', 1988 edition (ed. Office for Official Publications of the European Communities, Luxembourg and Brussels). The data for the gross national products can only indicate proportions, since due to substantial fluctuations in the exchange rates of the dollar and the ECU absolute values are meaningless.

72 cf. Office des publications officielles des Communautés européennes, EC–ASEAN, *Trade: A Statistical Analysis 1970–1984* (Brussels and Luxembourg, CECA–CEE–CEEA, 1987), esp. section 2.

73 cf. the interview with Bernhard Coe, cit. (note 62).

74 cf. summary in *Europe and South East Asia*, No. 7 (1986), pp. 10 and 11.
75 cf. Opening Statement by Prime Minister Lee Kuan Yew of the Republic of Singapore at third ASEAN Summit, 14 December 1987 (mimeo).

6 Relations with Central and Southern America: a question of over-reach?

*Wolf Grabendorff**

Introduction

The relationship of the European Community (EC) with Latin America is characterized by an asymmetry between the importance attached to its political aspects and the low profile allowed to economic links. The gap between political relations on the one hand and economic ones on the other actually widened during the 1980s, as the EC took an active part in Latin American political affairs while economic relations steadily declined.

Europe's traditional cultural ties with Latin America, which have always contributed to a general affinity between the regions, were enriched by the region-wide process of (re)democratization during the 1980s. The contacts established between European and Latin American political parties and other groups representing civil society during the years of authoritarianism transformed Europe into Latin America's favourite broker once new democratic regimes had taken office. Furthermore, Latin America's interest in diversifying its foreign policy focus, particularly away from the United States, coincided with Europe's eagerness to demonstrate its presence on the continent.

Europe's stated responsibility for the stabilization and the promotion of democracy in Latin American through economic cooperation contrasts with the poor economic relationship between the regions. Commercially, Latin America's share in EC imports has averaged 6 per cent over recent years. Although the EC plays a more important role in Latin America's imports (around 20 per cent for the same period of time), the EC's share still falls far behind imports from the United States (around 41 per cent). These figures do not reflect mutual indifference. On the contrary, the EC has explicitly recognized the vast potential of the Latin American economies in terms of their endowment of both natural and human resources. The Latin American countries have repeatedly stressed the significance of broadening their economic

* The author wishes to thank Kea Wollrad for her excellent research and editorial assistance in preparing this chapter.

relations with the EC in order to counterbalance their heavy orientation towards the US market. However, these figures do reflect Latin America's preoccupation with Europe's agricultural policy and its position in the EC's trading hierarchy for it ranks last after the countries of the Mediterranean, the ACP, the Gulf states and ASEAN.

The asymmetry between the political and economic dimensions of the relationship is reflected in the group-to-group dialogue between the EC and Latin America. Although the EC has always had a vested interest in securing Latin American intermediaries appropriate to an inter-regional dialogue, a consistent framework has only been developed on the basis of the *political* interest shown by the Community in the Central American conflict. Attempts in the 1970s to set up a dialogue between the EC and Latin America as a whole, as in the case of the Latin American ambassadors to the EC (GRULA or the Grupo de Latinoamérica) and the SELA (Sistema Económico de Latinoamérica), were denied a solid basis because they lacked either a clear mandate or an institutional infrastructure. The first dialogue at a sub-regional level, the conclusion of a cooperation agreement with the Andean Pact in 1983, has shown more promise, although it has been limited so far to a more technical level within the framework of the treaty.

With the possible de-escalation of the Central American crisis, the EC/Twelve's dialogue with the region — a regular item on the EPC agenda for many years — is likely to lose much of its importance. Hence, the continuity of the European dialogue with Latin America will very much depend on a new regional counterpart and the development of an agenda able to provide the foundation for a sustainable relationship. Since the mid-1980s, the transition from authoritarian to democratic regimes and the difficult economic situation in some countries of South America have again shifted international attention towards the south of the continent. The EC took careful note of this evolution by recognizing the increasingly important role of the Group of Eight (G-8) in Latin America. However, it remains to be seen whether the G-8 will be able to strengthen, or even maintain, Europe's political and economic commitment to Latin America.

The EC dialogue with Central America

Motives and interests

EC relations with Central America follow the pattern of Europe's links with Latin America in general. The driving force behind the dialogue remained rooted in the political dimension of cooperation — as emphasized by the EC — while its economic aspect — of greater interest to the Central Americans — clearly came only second.

The *political* interest of the EC/Twelve in a dialogue with Central America arises, firstly, from the change of political regimes which the Europeans have watched very closely. The Nicaraguan Revolution, and the transition from authoritarian to democratic rule in El Salvador, renewed and gave impetus to the existing network of contacts between governments and non-governmental institutions of the two regions. In particular, the party internationals supported and promoted the emergence of their respective affiliates in Central America.

The second motive for a European presence in Central America developed in tandem with the deterioration of the political and economic situation in the Isthmus, and the efforts made among the parties involved to settle the regional conflict. European support, first for the Contadora initiative and later for the Esquipulas process, highlights the strategy of advocating genuine regional solutions which steer clear of superpower rivalry. Or, to put it differently, the Central American conflict — like many others in the Third World — has been seen as neither rooted, nor resolvable, in terms of military security; political stability in countries traditionally marked by an extremely uneven distribution of national income and influence can only be achieved by economic development and profound social reforms.

The third motive rests more with Europe than in the structure of the dialogue. The deepening of the regional conflict coincided with a difficult period in transatlantic relations and growing European self-confidence *vis-à-vis* Washington. It is for this reason that the EC did not hesitate to offer its services in a region which had previously been considered an exclusively US sphere of influence. Although Europe's cooperation with Central America was neither meant to undermine Washington nor to mediate between the countries of the Isthmus and the United States, the EC/Twelves's approach of 'patient diplomacy' explicitly condemned the policy of 'providing aid to non-regular forces and insurrectional movements'.[1] Although confrontation with the United States throughout the cooperation process varied according to the political hue of European governments, and the state of East–West relations in general, Central America became the litmus test for European self-assertion *vis-à-vis* the United States.[2]

The dominant role of the United States in the region likewise played an important part in encouraging Central America to reactivate its contacts with the EC. The European initiative in support of regional solutions was welcomed precisely because the EC was perceived as an honourable broker with motives free from any self-interest in Central America's strategic position. Furthermore, unlike the United States and in spite of the variety of positions within the EC, the Community's attitude has always been one of welcoming any initiative capable of accelerating the peace and integration process in Central America.

However, the importance of the group-to-group dialogue with the EC was, for the Central Americans, clearly focused on its *economic* dimension. In view of the sharp economic crisis in Central America, which paralysed all efforts to revive the integration process and reactivate intra-regional trade, the countries of the Isthmus saw the Community — with its particular interest in integration processes — as the ideal counterpart in the reconstruction of the region. Furthermore, by strengthening their trade relations with the EC, the Central Americans sought to redress their dependence on the United States, not just politically but also economically.

From the Central American's perspective, the declared *political* interest of the Community in the affairs of the Isthmus has never been accompanied by a commensurate level of *economic* commitment. Throughout the group-to-group contact, Central America has seen itself as the 'demandeur' on the economic side, thus giving the EC considerable leeway in setting the rules of the game, i.e. in defining the relationship between political dialogue on the one hand and economic cooperation on the other.

Format and agenda

On 28 and 29 September 1984, the first EC–Central American conference was held with the participation of the Ministers of Foreign Affairs of the EC member states and those of the Contadora Group. This meeting was to be the beginning of a dialogue that was institutionalized in 1985, taking the form of a yearly conference on a ministerial level. The so-called San José process is characterized by its formal division into political and economic parts, the latter also including Panama.

According to the provisions of the Cooperation Agreement, signed on 12 November 1985 on the occasion of the second ministerial conference, a Mixed Commission was set up which would be responsible for the preparation and implementation of projects within the framework of the agreement. To date, the Mixed Commission has held three meetings. Furthermore, three sub-commissions have been established to deal with projects, primary products and trade, and with scientific and technical cooperation.

The *overall agenda* of the group-to-group dialogue has varied very little.[3] Its main feature is the special link established between progress in the intra-regional dialogue on the one hand and the EC's economic commitment to Central America on the other. While the EC has fully recognized the importance given by the countries of the Isthmus to economic aid as a precondition of any solution of the conflict and long-term political stability, the Central Americans have had to accept that such economic aid would be tied to the fulfilment of expectations of democratization and intra-regional cooperation. The EC has always stressed the importance of fostering the regional integation process through its economic cooperation with support, for example, for projects designed to revive regional integration institutions. With regard to the latter, it is notable that on the occasion of the conference in San Pedro

Sula (San José V) in 1989, economic integration was given top priority. The approved budget is around 100 million ECUs per annum, from which 40 million ECUs are to be assigned to integration projects over each of the next three years.

On the *political side*, the evolution of the San José conference series exhibits an interesting feature. While the 1984 meeting was widely regarded as a success, by the following year the dialogue had already lost momentum. With the Contadora peace initiative slowly withering, an important limitation to Europe's involvement in Central America was pointed out: dependence on initiatives taken by other parties to the conflict. However, it was precisely the emergence of a new, genuinely Central American peace effort that gave new impetus to the European interest in the region. The Esquipulas peace plan, signed on 7 August 1987, which prompted a step-by-step approach towards a simultaneous process of national democratization and of regional conflict settlement, was received with enthusiasm by the EC. The San José meeting in Hamburg on 29 February–1 March 1988 reflected the disposition of the EC/Twelve to support further steps towards the implementation of the Esquipulas agreement. On that occasion particular importance was given to the Central American Parliament — towards whose creation the Community agreed to contribute a total of 20 million ECUs.

On the *economic side*, the results of the San José conferences have always fallen short of Central American expectations. The Cooperation Agreement defined the scope and the limitations of European economic cooperation. The Central Americans expected a sort of 'Marshall Plan' with, among other things, preferential access to the European market beyond the GSP scheme, and Central American eligibility for credits granted by the European Investment Bank (EIB). However, neither points were seriously considered by the Council of Ministers since they threatened to undermine the special relationship which the Community has traditionally maintained with other regions or groups of states such as the Mediterranean countries and the ACP. In general terms, the treaty with Central America did not go beyond the framework of non-preferential cooperation agreements signed with other regions (including the Andean Pact and ASEAN). In its commercial section, it did not go beyond the preferences already conceded. Only in the area of development cooperation, which provided for a substantial increase in financial aid, did the Community make a concession that began to meet the demands of the Central Americans.[4]

Over the following years, the EC did indeed increase its financial aid to Central America. From an average of 40 million ECU per annum between 1979 and 1985, the EC approved an increase in aid to 71.8 million ECU in 1987 and 106.4 million ECU in 1988. However, financial cooperation is supposed to have peaked in 1988 and to have stabilized at around 100 million ECUs on a medium-term basis. On the other hand, these figures express only the budget approved and not the amount of aid granted. Recent experience has shown that the Central

Americans have not always been able to design feasible projects and secure their implementation, which has reduced the absorptive capacity of the money approved.

The actors

From the *European side*, the dialogue with Central America initially relied on the very general consensus of supporting and promoting the regional peace process already under way. However, this consensus was not strong enough to allow for the active role in Central America that some members wished to assign to the Community. The fact that every move made by the Community in the region would automatically be commented on in Washington limited the possibilities of a concerted European position from the outset. Each member state's relations with the United States have thus been the determining factor in setting its position on Central America.

Given this, it is not surprising that those members with a special interest in a more independent European role in world affairs were the most enthusiastic advocates of engagement in Central America, namely, the Federal Republic of Germany, France and Spain. On the opposite side, Great Britain, for the very reason of its special relationship with the United States, has always been an outspoken opponent of the EC 'meddling' in Washington's backyard.

The EC consensus on its Central American policy has been crumbling since 1985. The rise of more conservative foreign policy positions and a growing impatience in Europe with the record of the Sandinista regime, coincided with a sharp increase in tension between the United States and Nicaragua. President Reagan's decision on 1 May 1985 to impose a trade embargo against Nicaragua eventually split the Europeans over Nicaragua and, consequently, over how to continue the dialogue with the region. Although the Esquipulas peace accord undoubtedly revived European interest in Central American affairs, the San José process has never been able to restore the EC's commitment as expressed during both the preparatory phase and the first ministerial meeting. The decline in interest on the part of the EC/Twelve is reflected in its level of representation at the annual San José meetings. While in 1984 the EC was represented by all the Ministers of Foreign Affairs, only three Ministers attended the conference of San Pedro Sula in 1989.

The *European Commission*, as an observer to the San José meetings, has played a prominent role throughout the dialogue not only with regard to its economic dimension, but also as a participant with a clear cut political standpoint. On the Cooperation Agreement, the Commission seized the opportunity and worked out a proposal, thus defining the framework of discussion within the Council. However, given the requirement of unanimity in the Council's decisions on development cooperation issues and cooperation agreements with non-associated countries, Commission's draft — which came close to Central American expectations — had to be modified substantially to fit the objections of some member states.

The *European Parliament* has also been an important actor on the European side. Continuous efforts to increase its influence on the Council's decisions usually facilitate consensus among the deputies. This observation applies equally to the Central American case. Thus, it was on the insistence of the Parliament that early initiatives by the Commission to increase financial aid for Central America were taken up again by the Council. Furthermore, the Parliament threw its full support behind the Esquipulas II Accord, its resolutions being frequently far more explicit than the moderate San José communiqués in condemning, for example, external military interference in the region and the violation of human rights. In this respect, the Parliament assumed its traditional role of providing EC policy with a 'moral' dimension. The creation of a Central American Parliament created particular interest among the European parliamentarians who not only endorsed the establishment of a similar institution in Central America, but who also actively promoted an exchange of opinion and experience with Central American representatives involved in the creation of the regional Parliament.

The 1988 ministerial conference in Hamburg (San José IV) and the approval, on 12 May 1988, of the UN Special Plan of Economic Cooperation for Central America (PEC) drew worldwide attention to the need for measures aimed at the economic recovery of the region. In *Central America*, these prompted immediate efforts to reactivate regional decision-making fora and create new consultation mechanisms for responding to the offer of international support. Contacts have been intensified particularly at the level of vice-ministers, Ministers of Foreign and Economic Affairs, regional institutions and GRULA — the Central American diplomatic representation to the EC — the United Nations and the Organization of American States in order to harmonize positions *vis-à-vis* the international community.

At San José IV, the EC stated its willingness to study the means of participating in the process of economic recovery in Central America. The PEC was dealt with in detail at the meetings of the Mixed Commission and the sub-commissions throughout 1988 and 1989. The importance of the PEC for the reconstruction of the regional economies was decisive in allowing Central America to speak with one voice, particularly *vis-à-vis* the Community. However, the outcome of regional consultations underwent an evolution over time which, at any given moment, mirrored the state of play of the regional peace process.

During a first stage, consultations were facilitated by the positive atmosphere stemming from the Esquipulas agreement. However, the moment an increase in intra-regional tensions overshadowed the accord, the disposition to come to terms on extra-regional aid declined. Traditional differences over the scope of the integration process began to re-emerge once projects had to be drafted in detail. Moreover, the delay in financial aid for the most urgent problems prompted enormous disappointment in the PEC and a general indifference towards regional policy coordination.

As a third party involved in the dialogue of the Twelve with Central America, the *Contadora Group* has taken part in the San José process ever since it started in 1984. The participation of the Contadora countries (Colombia, Mexico, Panama and Venezuela) was, at first, aimed at highlighting the Community's endorsement of the peace proposal presented by the Group. Later, however, when the Contadora plan was no longer on the agenda, the involvement of the four countries served to place the European initiative in Central America in a broader Latin American context and to intensify a general political dialogue which, ultimately, paved the way for the establishment of relations with the Group of Eight.

Assessment

Between 1983, when the idea of a bi-regional meeting was born, and 1989, Central America has been high on the EPC agenda. Although from the beginning interest among the Europeans varied considerably and differences of principle on the Central American issue led eventually to a lower European profile in the region, the group-to-group dialogue with Central America contributed considerably to the shaping of a 'European foreign policy'. A number of factors were involved, including:

— the fact that Europe has no overriding interests in Central America facilitated a common standpoint and helped to underscore the picture of the Community as a 'single actor' in world affairs;
— European involvement and, therefore, intra-European consultations on the issue were particularly intense over a relatively short period of time;
— the dominant role of the United States in the region transformed the dialogue into a test case for the development of a genuinely European position, thus adding — at least for some countries — an additional incentive to speak with one voice.

However, the genuine link between Europe's involvement in Central America and the evolution of the regional crisis implies that the dialogue is bound to be reduced when the conflict is settled. Since the victory of the Union Nacional Oposiora (ONU) in the Nicaraguan elections of 25 February 1990, a definitive agreement between the opposing parties seems closer than ever before. The Community will still be asked to assist the process as a contributor to the economic recovery of the region and some of its members may be involved as participants in an international verification commission to supervise the future security and confidence-building measures of the peace process. But the Central American issue as a conflict that formed part of the East–West power struggle is about to disappear. So will one of the primary motives for Europe's involvement in Central American affairs.

EC relations with the Group of Eight: a shift towards the south of the continent?

In 1987, the EC initiated consultations with the Group of Eight (G-8) or Rio Group. The G-8 embodies the countries of the Contadora Group and its Support Group (Argentina, Brazil, Peru and Uruguay). Since February 1988, the G-8 has consisted only of seven members due to Panama's temporary exclusion from the group in the wake of the internal institutional crisis that led to the downfall of President Delvalle the same month.

The G-8 was formally established at a meeting of Foreign Ministers in Rio de Janeiro on 18 and 19 December 1986. On that occasion the 'Permanent Mechanism of Consultation and Political Coordination' was set up to provide for informal meetings at ministerial level three times a year. In addition, three meetings have been held between the heads of state of the G-8.[5]

The interest of the *Community* in the G-8 can be put down to, first, the contacts held, and common experience shared, with the Contadora Group on the Central American issue. Although the Support Group, which had been set up in July 1985 to give fresh impetus to the Central American peace process, did not participate directly in the EC–Central American dialogue, the common interest in the issue was to become an important link between the Twelve and the Support Group. Secondly, the G-8 pools together the largest and most influential states of Latin America (Argentina, Brazil, Mexico) with smaller — but at the international level undoubtedly prestigious — countries (such as Uruguay). It therefore provides a forum with considerable diplomatic resources. More significant, however, is the fact that the G-8 represents over 80 per cent of the population and of the gross national product of the region, and that it includes the most developed countries in terms of industrial, scientific, technological and export capacity. The EC recognized the importance of the group in the 'Conclusions of the Council and representatives of the member states of the EC on relations between the Community and Latin America', adopted on 22 June 1987. The document, which aimed at political and economic reconciliation between two regions, identified the G-8 as the principal actor for the Twelve as far as the EPC was concerned.

The *Group of Eight*, on the other hand, has an interest *sui generis* in a group-to-group dialogue with the EC. Apart from the Central American conflict which featured strongly among the topics of consultation in the initial period, the G-8 has been dealing with subjects that touch on the most pressing problems of Latin America's economic relations with the Community. At the top of the agenda has been the debt problem, followed by issues such as trade and the related problems of protectionism, drug-trafficking and Latin American integration.

Moreover, it is no accident that the consultation mechanism of the G-8 has been inspired by, and modelled on, European Political Cooperation, i.e. it is based on on the principle of inter-governmental cooperation and the unanimity rule; the idea has evolved gradually and progressively; and consultations are selective in nature, in the sense that they do not necessarily cover all facets of member states' foreign policies nor do they attempt to solve any disputes arising between member states.

The talks between the Foreign Ministers of the EC and of the G-8 began on 23 September 1987 in New York, during a session of the UN General Assembly. Further meetings were held on the occasion of the IV EC–Central America conference in Hamburg on 1 March 1988, and in New York on 28 September, which coincided with a new session of the General Assembly. At their meeting in Punta del Este on 25 October 1989, the Foreign Ministers of the Group of Eight invited Commissioner Cheysson for an exchange of views on foreign debt. Moreover, they met with European participants who attended the summit in Toronto of the seven most industrialized nations (G-7) in March 1988. The first specially convened meeting between the Foreign Ministers of the EC/Twelve took place in Granada on 15–16 April 1989. A further meeting was held on 28 September 1989 during the session of the UN General Assembly, while the last meeting was scheduled, again in the context of the San José process, to coincide with the ministerial conference on 10 April 1990 in Dublin.

The different fora in which the dialogue has been taking place shows the informality of the consultative procedure. The exception to this rule is the Granada meeting, the only one set up exclusively for group-to-group consultations. In terms of content, the most serious problems affecting Latin America — the debt problem, the Central American crisis, the threat to democracy, drug-trafficking — as well as questions of a more general nature such as East–West relations, have been broached. The Granada meeting was undoubtedly a milestone in the EC/G-8 relationship as, for the first time, the EC openly admitted that the debt problem constituted a serious obstacle to political stability and economic development. However, the meeting only yielded vague and general support for the Brady Plan. Because of the lack of consensus, the Twelve carefully avoided an open discussion on the question of debt relief and resorted to the usual formula that the EC as such has no mandate to negotiate financial issues with third parties.

Assessment

The G-8, as the new interlocutor for the Twelve in Latin America, embodies a set of characteristics which undoubtedly favour continuity in the dialogue. First it includes the most important and economically most powerful countries of Latin America. Thus the topics addressed within the dialogue provide a representative picture. Secondly, the agenda of the dialogue is, in principle, open. This provides, on the one hand, for flexibility in the setting of priorities and, on the other, it allows for the possibility of encompassing topics beyond those of direct concern to both regions. Thirdly, dialogue has been very informal, thereby opening channels of communication that are not bound (as in the Central American case) to the formal structure of conferences. This has contributed to the enhanced weight of the G-8 as a voice of Latin America in international affairs.

However, each of these arguments can be turned against the successful deepening of relations between the EC and the G-8.

— The very heterogenity of the G-8 may impede successful coordination in the field of foreign policy. Different orientations in external relations and, particularly, in foreign economic relations became obvious during the last presidential meeting of the G-8 in Ica (Peru) on 11–12 October 1989. The strong interest of countries like Mexico and Venezuela in entering into the US market prevailed even over the imperative of Latin American integration. This may give rise to scepticism over the genuine interest in a dialogue with the EC, not to speak of the development of a common policy on specific issues.

— An open agenda in the relationship is only useful if the parties coincide on the setting of priorities. The most pressing topic for the Latin American countries has so far been the debt question, followed by industrial cooperation, trade relations and direct investment. The Europeans, however, have kept quite a low profile on all economic questions — the debt problem in particular. Their agenda, which is headed by topics like drug-trafficking and environment, reflects specific European interests in the dialogue. It remains to be seen whether, and to what extent, the EC and the G-8 can come to terms on the content of their relations.

— The informality of structures can be an obstacle to cooperation if one or other party involved loses interest in the dialogue. In the Central American case, the institutionalization of the San José process has contributed to carrying relations through difficult phases. Furthermore, Central America could count on intra-regional mechanisms of consultation which go far beyond the structure which has been built up within the G-8. In this sense, the ongoing discussion of who will be included in the G-8 — Chile, Bolivia and Ecuador are candidates — weakens the group as a representative Latin American actor.

Although contacts between the EC and G-8 are still very new, initial European expectations of a dialogue on a region-wide level with Latin America have already been scaled down. The Twelve are still interested in the G-8 and the dialogue is likely to continue. However, a forum for political cooperation like the G-8 does not constitute an alternative to economic integration, which is unlikely to prosper within the group as a whole. The establishment of a framework for integration would be a pre-condition for assuring Europe's (economic) interest in the G-8 in the long run. Hence, the Group may not play a key role in the Community's renewed interest in the south of the continent. On the other hand, the development of a Southern Cone integration scheme which integrates Chile and Paraguay into the existing agreements between Argentina, Brazil and Uruguay seems to be promising from an EC perspective.

Conclusions and perspectives for EC: Latin American relations

The European involvement in Central America and its role as an interlocutor in the process of democratization indicate the high degree of 'politicization' of bi-regional relations. The political dimension contrasts sharply with the expectations that the Latin Americans have been projecting on to their economic links with the EC, and that are seen as still to be fulfilled.

The likelihood of redressing the balance between the political and economic aspects of the relationship is today less than ever before. The deep economic crisis throughout Latin America which, *a priori*, reduces the attractiveness of the continent in terms of foreign economic initiatives, coincides with the implementation of the Internal Market in Europe and, more recently, with the attention paid by EC to the changes in Eastern Europe. Although the Commission had made it clear that the level of financial aid for Latin America will be maintained, it is obvious that Europe's official as well as private economic commitment to Latin America will, at best, stagnate in the medium term. Concerns expressed by politicians like the Mexican President Salinas de Gortari that Europe might focus exclusively on its own problems and might forget the world beyond its borders[6] are clearly justified by the magnitude — in political as well as economic terms — of the envisaged EC commitment to Eastern Europe.

However, the very sharpening of the economic crisis in Latin America, which had already had negative repercussions on the political stability of some countries (such as Venezuela and Argentina) has demonstrated the importance of fostering economic integration on a sub-regional level. Initiatives here could pave the way for new group-to-group relations between the EC and Latin America. The bilateral integration project between Argentina and Brazil formally agreed upon in July 1986, and which gave rise to high expectations at an early stage, has been partly slowed down because of the difficult political and economic situation in both countries.

Yet the possibility of the newly installed Chilean democracy joining the scheme would give fresh impetus to the process of integration in the Southern Cone. The Community's interest in the industrial development potential of the region suggests that a new cooperation structure for the economic as well as the political field could be created. Such a development would accord with the Community's sub-regional approach to Latin America to which Mexico constitutes the only exception. Within this policy approach, Central America, the Andean Pact and the Southern Cone all mirror not only the different development levels of the countries involved but also their varying cooperation agendas with the EC.

Given the ever decreasing interest of the United States in South America, such a shift in the EC attitude would also contribute to avoiding conflict with third partners in a redesigned group-to-group dialogue with the Andean Pact and a newly constructed one with the Southern Cone.

Notes

1   'Joint Political Declaration of the Hamburg Ministerial Conference on Political Dialogue and Economic Cooperation between the European Community and its Member States, and the Countries of Central America and of the Contadora Group, held on 29 February and 1 March 1988' (mimeo): 7 (par. 13).
2   For a more detailed discussion see my article 'Central America: A Dilemma for European–US relations?', *Harvard International Review*, Cambridge (MA) (1986) 9:1 37–9.
3   For the evolution of San José process compare Klaus Bodemer, *Europa Occidental–America Latina: Experiencias y desafiós*, Barcelona/Caracas: Alfa (1987): 65–131.
4   Guido AShoff, 'La cooperación para el desarrollo entre la Comunidad Europea y America Latin: Experiencias y perspectivas', *Documento de Trabajo* 16, Madrid: IRELA (1989): 23–35.
5   Institute for European-Latin American Relations (IRELA), *The Group of Eight: A new regional actor for Latin America?*, Dossier 17, Madrid: IRELA (March 1989).
6   Frankfurter Allgemeine Zeitung, Frankfurt, 30 January 1990.

7 EC–EFTA relations: neighbours in search of a new partnership[1]

Thomas Pedersen

EC–EFTA relations as a case of group-to-group relations

Seen from a comparative perspective, EFTA is undoubtedly the regional grouping with which the EC has developed the closest of ties. This is not surprising. In at least three respects, EC–EFTA relations stand out as unique compared with other cases of group-to-group relations. First of all, there is a close cultural–political affinity between the 18 member countries of the EC and EFTA and even closer linguistic and cultural bonds which cut across the EC/EFTA divide — notably between Denmark and the other Nordic countries and between the FRG and Austria and Switzerland. Secondly, membership of the EC is an option for at least some of members of EFTA, which obviously gives EC–EFTA relations a certain saliency seen from Brussels. Thirdly, the degree of economic interconnectedness between the two groupings is very high. Equally important, however, there are important structural similarities between the major EC economics and the major EFTA economies. EFTA exports are often close substitutes to EC exports. While the internal market will probably lead to some demand expansion with beneficial effects for EFTA, it should not be overlooked that it will also lead to some trade diversion, the brunt of which will probably be borne by EFTA.

To say that EC–EFTA relations are exceptional is not necessarily the same as saying that they are good or, indeed, that they are given high priority. While the cultural familiarity and the high degree of economic inter-connectedness are forces favouring a closer cooperation, the constraints on EC–EFTA cooperation are also considerable. Whereas most EC countries are to varying degrees a part of NATO and the Atlantic Alliance, four of the six EFTA countries are neutrals. This represents a barrier to wide-ranging EC–EFTA cooperation in two respects. First, were the neutral EFTA countries to move closer to the EC, this might be interpreted by the outside world as reflecting a political *rapprochement* with the NATO bloc. Secondly, as national sovereignty is generally considered to be a prerequisite for conducting a neutral foreign policy, participation in a more binding West European integration process is likely to have a negative impact on the credibility of some EFTA countries' neutrality. Moreover, there is no strong security interest involved in EC–EFTA relations unlike the case of, for example, EC–Middle East relations. Nor is EC–EFTA cooperation inspired by normative goals such as support for democracy or the fight against poverty, which might give relations with EFTA a symbolic value and serve to sharpen the Community's international profile. To understand the constraints on EC–EFTA cooperation one also has to take into account the historical rivalry between the different concepts of integration symbolized by the two organizations.

The historical background

It is worth recalling that after the Second World War, attempts were made at the Congress of Europe in the Hague in 1948 to create a grand integrated Europe. When these attempts failed,[2] a smaller grouping of West European states succeeded in creating the ECSC, the EEC and Euratom, a unique series of international organisations based on the principle of transfer of national sovereignty to supranational institutions. In 1956, fearful of being isolated, the United Kingdom proposed the creation of a wider free trade area, but the ensuing negotiations within the OEEC eventually broke down, essentially because of Franco-British disagreements.

Seven of the remaining OEEC countries, including the United Kingdom, formed EFTA in 1960 as a reaction to the EC. It is important to note that EFTA is in a very real sense an offspring of the EC, and that for most EFTA countries EFTA has always been a second best, the preferred trade arrangement being a wider European free trade system. Individual EFTA countries like the United Kingdom, Ireland, Denmark and Norway soon defected from EFTA, recognizing the greater dynamism of the EC, though they were not admitted to the EC until 1972. The Norwegian decision to join the EC was thwarted when the government lost a referendum on membership in 1972.

The 1970s were a period of pragmatic bilateralism. At the insistence of the United Kingdom and Denmark, the EC concluded free trade agreements with all the remaining EFTA countries in 1973 so as to avoid the erection of new trade barriers between the United Kingdom and Denmark on the one hand and EFTA on the other. Though some progress was made on the nitty-gritty of trade management, relations at the political level relations remained remote and strictly bilateral throughout the 1970s. The 1980s, however, have seen a reintroduction of elements of multilateralism in the EC–EFTA dialogue. In 1984, EFTA proposed a multilateral dialogue with the EC on a number of economic and trade issues. This initiative led to the so-called Luxembourg Declaration of April 1984, in which the EC and EFTA countries committed themselves to wide-ranging economic cooperation. By the end of the 1980s discussions had begun on how to proceed to establish some sort of group-to-group structure. In a sense, therefore,

Western Europe has come full circle and is currently reactivating the debate of the late 1940s and 1950s on a grand integrated Europe.

The new EC–EFTA dialogue: what has changed?

The pattern of EC–EFTA interaction has changed significantly since the 1970s. For EFTA, the main factor behind its new EC policy is that it is facing a stronger EC in a tougher world economy. The EC has become a stronger organization, not simply because of the internal market nor even the progress made towards political union, crucial though these factors are. In addition, there is the fact that the United Kingdom has come to terms with Community membership, and that France has more or less accepted a European role for Britain. For years EC–EFTA relations were to a very large extent the continuation of Franco-British rivalry by other means.[3] It is unlikely that France would have accepted a wider West European cooperation in the 1970s. Today, the United Kingdom is no longer the only driving force in promoting EC–EFTA integration so that its support for wider European cooperation is no longer regarded as an attempt to dissolve the EC as a piece of sugar in a cup of tea, as it was once aptly put.

Secondly, the EFTA subsystem has to operate within a tougher international economy. It is worth noting that EFTA's new interest in a dialogue with the EC preceded the adoption of the Commission's White Paper on the internal market. Quite apart from the EC discussions on constitutional reform and economic modernization, by 1984 the challenge from the new growth centres of East Asia had created an incentive for the whole of Europe to close ranks. Thus major EFTA countries like Sweden seem to have been enthused by the EC's new technological impetus, which began with the first technological framework programme of 1983.

During the 1980s, the international economy also showed clear signs of protectionism in a new guise. In 1984, the EC adopted the so-called 'new trade policy instrument' in response to what it regarded as unfair trade practices by other countries.[4] This neo-protectionist trend has continued, and the new academic debate on strategic trade policy shows that the mood is changing.[5] The world economy is increasingly becoming tripolar and the free trade system is being succeeded by a mixed system characterized by what Robert Gilpin has called 'mercantilistic competition, economic regionalism and sectoral protectionism'.[6] Since the early 1980s there has been some concern in EFTA lest the complexity and magnitude of trilateral problems preoccupy Brussels to the extent of losing sight of economic collaboration within a wider European framework.

On the Community side, during the early 1970s the EC simply rejected EFTA countries' proposals for more binding links between the two organizations. It has taken a new interest in EFTA in part, undoubtedly, because of changing trade patterns. In relative terms, EFTA has gained considerably in importance as a trading partner for the EC.[7] It is also obvious that in the context of more politicized international trade and monetary talks, it becomes important for the EC to bolster its negotiating position. The need for closer EC–EFTA cooperation on international economic issues was indeed stressed in the Luxembourg Declaration.[8] However, there are also specific national interests involved, as well as the shifts in the internal balance of power within the EC, particularly the growing international political role of the FRG.

EC–EFTA relations and EC coalition politics

The evolution of EC–EFTA relations is to a significant degree affected by specific national interests and by the coalition politics of the FRG, France and the United Kingdom. The asymmetries of the relationship also have to be taken into account. EFTA is clearly in the position of the demandeur. From the perspective of power politics, the fate of wider West European cooperation is very much dependent on the interests and coalition politics of the big powers in the EC. EFTA policy fits into a wider internal EC discussion on the future of the Community, where EC–EFTA integration is not always seen as an end in itself, but sometimes also as an instrument meant to further other objectives.[9]

The endeavour to create a political partnership between the EC and EFTA might be interpreted as an attempt by the Central–Northern coalition in the EC led by the FRG and the United Kingdom to counterbalance the new powerful Central–Southern coalition within the EC. There is both a general political and a financial aspect to this. The accession of Spain has strengthened the position of France in a variety of issue areas, creating a rough balance between the UK-German position and the Franco-Italian–Spanish–(Greek) position on trade policy matters, where Northern Europe used to have the upper hand.

From a British and German perspective, closer EC–EFTA relations are a way of strengthening the hand of the 'free-traders' in the EC against the demands for a tougher trade policy emerging from Paris, Rome and Madrid. The problem is that to win over the rather strong Central–Southern grouping, the Northern coalition, to which Denmark and the Netherlands also belong, will have to make significant political side-payments. A likely demand from the southerners is a tougher external trade stance towards Japan and the United States as compensation for an opening of the internal market to the competitive EFTA economies. Thus the effect on Europe's external trade stance of an even considerably closer EC–EFTA cooperation is likely to be limited, though not insignificant.

The United Kingdom has historically had close ties with the Nordic countries, especially Norway, and might hope to bolster its position in EC-coalition politics by reviving the spirit of UNISCAN. The United Kingdom, or at least the more open-minded sections of the British public, is uncomfortably aware that on issues like monetary union, the United Kingdom is becoming isolated within the EC, with Denmark as its only and rather questionable ally. Though Norway is not a big power, Norwegian accession would be seen from London to be a welcome contribution to the reconstruction of a British-led European coalition.

The United Kingdom also seems to favour closer EC–EFTA cooperation as a means of building closer ties with Bonn, playing on the contradictions between France and West Germany. There are, however, limits to British support for EC–EFTA cooperation. The United Kingdom is not as keen on far-reaching EC–EFTA cooperation as is the FRG (and Denmark) and the present British government is sceptical about Austrian accession. London recognizes that the FRG has more to gain from far-reaching EC–EFTA integration than any one else. Besides, the accession of neutral Austria would in the British view block progress towards security cooperation within the EC and thus in a sense give the Russians a *de facto* veto power over the future evolution of the Community.

The FRG and Denmark — not the United Kingdom — are probably the countries most wholeheartedly sympathetic towards the new EC–EFTA *rapprochement*. At the informal EC–EFTA meeting of Foreign Ministers in March 1989, for example, Bonn proposed that EFTA ministers sit in on certain EC Council meetings. EFTA trade is much more important for Bonn and Copenhagen than for the other EC countries. But there also very important foreign policy interests at stake. In the present climate of European *détente*, Bonn regards the neutral EFTA countries — and Austria in particular — as useful stepping-stones on the way towards Eastern Europe. As a member of the EC, Austria would be able to play a valuable role as a bridge-builder between Western and Eastern Europe and as the EC's window towards the East.

However, support for the twin goals of European union and all-European cooperation place Bonn in a dilemma. On the one hand, there is a natural wish in Bonn to support the Austrians in their ambitious EC policy. On the other hand, elements within the CDU/CSU emphasize that a neutral Austria may block further progress towards a foreign policy and security cooperation.

The French government has rather more mixed feelings about EC–EFTA cooperation. France has welcomed pragmatic sectoral cooperation as witnessed by the EUREKA proposal. But unlike West Germany, it wants the EC to adopt a firm negotiating stance towards EFTA. And France is far from thrilled by the idea of yet another enlargement at a time when it is working to achieve economic and monetary union. Generally, the French seem to regard cooperation with

EFTA more as a means than as a valuable end in itself. France wants the internal market to be matched by parallel measures towards the outside world to safeguard the interests of European business; it may have moved away from its former strongly protectionist stance, but it still favours some sort of strategic trade policy.

The problem, as stressed by Wolfgang Hager, is that because of the FRG's close links with most of EFTA, a 'European option' has to be defined to include these countries in order to be acceptable to Bonn.[10] France regards cooperation with EFTA as more a political necessity than an economic opportunity. French diplomats argue that unless the EC as a whole shows a minimum of openness towards EFTA, the FRG will 'go it alone' and forge stronger bilateral ties with the EFTA countries. This might be a too negative — and outdated — description of the French position for there are signs that under the second Mitterrand Presidency Paris is cautiously revising its policy towards Eastern Europe, and this is likely to have spill-over effects on the policy towards the neutral EFTA countries.

The points worth emphasizing are, first, that since the early 1970s the FRG has further strengthened its position as Europe's biggest power along with the Soviet Union. This has enabled Bonn to pull the Community in the direction of a more active role in a wider European cooperation. Second, the Franco-German *rapprochement* has calmed some of the traditional anxieties of France as regards Germany, giving Bonn a greater leeway in pressing for wider European cooperation. Third, the Franco-German understanding has forced the United Kingdom into a new process of coalition-building, in which the Nordic region plays an important role.

The new EC–EFTA dialogue: what has been achieved?

The new phase in EC–EFTA relations started with the adoption of the Luxembourg Declaration in April 1984 at the first joint ministerial meeting of the two regional groupings. The Declaration spoke of the need for greater cooperation in a number of areas, especially: research and development; industrial cooperation through measures such as a truly free internal market; common action in international economic fora; and cooperation with regard to the Third World.[11] The official aim of the new multilateral dialogue was to be the creation of a European economic space (EES), encompassing the 18 member countries. However, with the endorsement of the Commission's White Paper in 1985 attention immediately focused on the trade problems related to the internal market.

Institutionally, a new multilateral cooperation structure was established. The EC Commission, represented by the Commissioner for External Relations, now attends one of the two yearly EFTA ministerial meetings. Several multilateral working groups were set up, the number of which has increased with almost dizzying speed, reaching 35 by the end of 1989, according to Commission officials. In terms of concrete results, the two most important decisions are probably the agreement in May 1987 on two conventions: the first establishes that the Single Administrative Document (SAD), introduced in the EC to simplify trade, shall also apply to EFTA countries; the second lays down common rules for transit. At joint ministerial meetings in 1988, the two groupings discussed practical improvements in a variety of other fields such as intellectual property, transparency of state subsidies, and public procurement.

Thus, whereas before the Luxembourg meeting EC—EFTA relations were almost exclusively trade-related, cooperation between the two groupings has now moved beyond this. Gradually, all four economic freedoms have entered into the multilateral discussions. Since 1987, there have also been preliminary multilateral talks on educational and environmental problems, and the social dimension is now also being touched upon. At the bilateral level, cooperation has expanded as well. Progress has been particularly marked in the field of research and development, where, in 1986, the EC concluded framework agreements with all EFTA countries except Iceland. EFTA countries have also taken part in the EUREKA programme from the beginning, and several EC programmes, not only in the technology field, have been opened to EFTA countries.

However, at the insistence of the neutral EFTA countries, EPC matters are deliberately kept off the agenda of the EC—EFTA negotiations. But it should not be overlooked that bilateral arrangements for informal exchanges on foreign policy issues are now in place, at least for Norway, while regular exchanges take place within the framework of the Council of Europe.

Norway has developed extensive bilateral ties with the EC/Twelve in the foreign policy area. At the beginning of the 1980s, Norway and the EC set up a consultation procedure, which allowed for regular half-yearly meetings between the Norwegian Foreign Minister and the incoming EC Presidency. The arrangement was improved in 1988 during the German Presidency with the decision to extend consultations to the level of Political Directors. Austria has also tried to obtain some sort of bilateral arrangement, but so far (the end of 1989), it seems, with little success.

The EC entered into negotiations with EFTA in a pragmatic spirit, stressing that the Luxembourg commitment was, in principle, open-ended, but that cooperation with EFTA could neither place obstacles in the way of the EC's own integration programme nor unhinge the sensitive balance achieved in the Single European Act. At the EFTA ministerial meeting in Interlaken in May 1987, the Commission spelt out the EC's position in terms of three main principles: (i) priority; (ii) autonomy; and (iii) cohesion.

The priority principle is short-hand for the view that the completion of the internal market must have first priority, and that relationships with third countries must not be allowed to delay the 1992 process. In large measure, this is an administrative problem in that the Commission would find it difficult to cope with any new tasks on top of the burdens of the 1992 programme. The principle of autonomy refers to the EC's insistence on the need for the Community to retain full decision-making autonomy. Essentially, it is a question of protecting the *acquis de l'integration* and avoiding actions that might stimulate tendencies towards the formation of a two- or three-speed Europe. However, some EFTA countries, especially Switzerland, have already embarked upon a very wide-ranging process of national adaptation to the internal market, matching adaptation to proposals for bilateral bridging-agreements with the EC that aim to confer a *de facto* right of co-decision on the particular EFTA country in the event of any changes in relevant EC legislation.

The principle of cohesion is justified by the need to preserve an overall balance between the costs and benefits of the participants in the internal market. The main problem is that the advanced EFTA economies are gradually gaining free access to the internal market, including the new member states of Spain and Portugal, without having to pay the 'social compensation' demanded of the northern EC members, through, for example, funding the structural funds. Thus the EC Commission has, on the insistence of the southern member states, especially Spain, asked the EFTA countries to participate in some sort of burden-sharing arrangement. To this end, EFTA countries have been asked to make direct contributions to the economic modernization of the Iberian peninsular, and it has been proposed that EFTA countries ease the access of Spanish agricultural and fishery products to the EFTA market. Spain has argued that such a concession is only fair, as the Community's Free Trade Agreements with EFTA do not cover agricultural exports, which are of particular importance to Spain.

By the end of the 1980s, however, negotiations with EFTA ran into increasing difficulties. Austria placed greater emphasis on bilateralism and submitted an application for membership in July 1989. Norway seemed to be considering the possibility of following suit. The trend has caused concern in Brussels. At an informal Commission meeting in April 1988, it was decided that the time was not right for further enlargement. The Commission's preference was to shift the focus back to the multilateral framework or, perhaps, the establishment of a new collaborative structure.

The motives are both practical and political. There is a fear in the Commission that bilateralism in general and enlargement negotiations in particular would create an administrative overload in the Community system. The Commission has argued that, in practical terms, enlargement prior to 1992 is simply not feasible. Accession negotiations have always been extremely time-consuming. It would probably take a year for the Commission to express an opinion. It would take at least another year for the Council of Ministers to reach a common position. On top of that, the Single European Act has given the European Parliament a new role in the decision-making agreements with third countries. But quite apart from the problems of capacity and time, there are political doubts about the wisdom of admitting neutral Austria. Might it not 'dilute' EC integration and block the progress towards monetary and political union?

Group-to-group relations as an option

It is against this background that one should interpret the speech by Jacques Delors, the President of the Commission in February 1989.[12] In presenting the new Commission's programme to the European Parliament, M. Delors called for an extension of wider European cooperation, indicating, *inter alia*, that provided the EFTA countries were able and willing to strengthen the organization and political cohesion of EFTA, it might be possible to create common structures of decision-making and implementation, encompassing both the EC and EFTA. In concrete terms this might mean setting up a West European Customs Union. M. Delors also proposed an expansion of the EC–EFTA agenda to include areas like culture, social affairs and financial questions.

It is not quite clear to what extent M. Delors spoke in a personal capacity. What is certain is that his speech gave rise to intense speculation in EFTA capitals. The idea of a new institutional structure for EC–EFTA cooperation was naturally given maximum attention at the EFTA summit in Oslo in March 1989. The final communiqué from the meeting expressed EFTA's willingness to participate in the liberalization of all the four areas suggested by the EC and stated its willingness to examine ways of achieving a more structured cooperation. However, despite intense campaigning from the Norwegian Presidency, it proved impossible for the EFTA countries to agree on a proposal for a Customs Union. The Swiss were loath to accept any hint of supranationality, and the Austrians stuck to their bilateral strategy notwithstanding considerable pressure from their partners. At the insistence of Austria, the communiqué explicitly left the bilateral backdoor open.

The Oslo summit was followed by a joint ministerial meeting in Brussels at the end of March. EFTA ministers arrived in a state of euphoria, but the EC ministers were not particularly forthcoming. The conclusions reached were purely procedural; it was decided to set up an informal high-level group. The group was asked to examine two sets of issues: (a) the whole range of technical problems to do with the four freedoms; (b) institutional and legal reforms. A new joint ministerial meeting was scheduled for the end of 1989. According to sources in the

Commission, the high-level group tended to concentrate on the practical issue of harmonization, postponing the institutional dimension.

Has there been a systemic change in wider European cooperation? It is probably fairer to say that EC–EFTA relations have entered a transitional phase. One should not overestimate the changes in the relationship. It is still characterized by a mixture of multilateralism, bilateralism and national adaptation. A new inter-regional structure is being discussed, but we are still in a phase of brain-storming rather than decision-making, as a Commission official put it. One should be aware that Delors's speech was itself partly motivated by tactical considerations. To that extent it was an exercise in diversionary tactics as regards the issue of Austrian membership. But in part only for there is clearly a new recognition in parts of the Commission that wider European solutions have to be seriously considered. One sign of this is the Commission's proposal for a European environmental agency that would be open to both EFTA countries and Eastern European countries.

Space does not allow an in-depth discussion of the various concrete forms a structured group-to-group approach might take in the EC–EFTA case. Interesting suggestions have been made by Helen Wallace and Wolfgang Wessels; among the options they sketch is one which they call a privileged partnership between the EC and EFTA.[13] This would mean an upgrading of EC–EFTA relations to a status beyond association, establishing a 'close interconnection and interpenetration of decision-making processes of both organizations with areas of common interests jointly defined and pursued'.

The new legal arrangement implied in this model would be particularly binding in the field of trade and could conceivably stretch as far as to a West European Customs Union. EFTA would be linked to most or all levels of EC decision-making, though EFTA could not expect to be given equality, but only an important 'droit de regard'. In practice this could involve arrangements such as meetings of the Presidencies of the EFTA and EC Councils prior to each session of the European Council, an arrangement for the Commission to consult EFTA experts, a timetable for a common EFTA position to be transmitted to the Council and possibly the setting up of an enlarged COREPER, comprising ambassadors from both the EC and EFTA, and an enlarged Council of Ministers in certain issue areas.

For EFTA, the advantage of such a structure is obvious: it would give EFTA countries a certain amount of influence over internal market legislation without forcing EFTA countries to become members of the Community. The status quo is clearly unacceptable to them; adapting to legislation, over which they have no say, sooner or later creates problems of legitimacy for national governments. For the EC, the main advantages would be more effective and binding outcomes in negotiations with EFTA countries and in general a more rational management of EC–EFTA relations that would represent an attractive alternative to enlargement.

The question is, of course, whether this is a realistic option. Obviously the EC could only accept EFTA as a privileged partner, if it could be sure that the new arrangement would not seriously delay the Community's own plans. EFTA would be expected to reform its organizational structure and its members would have to develop new habits of binding international cooperation, which would represent a radical new departure for them. Do they have the capacity and political will to do so? But could EFTA countries be given a right of co-decision in policy areas, where EC member states themselves have not got much of a say — in, for example, competition policy and parts of agricultural policy?

The notion of a West European Customs Union is problematic in more ways than one. Would EFTA countries be willing to accept the inclusion of agricultural products? Would neutrals like Sweden, Finland and Austria be able to accept the use of economic sanctions for foreign policy purposes?

As Harto Hakovirta has stressed, most EFTA countries have historically been seeking a comprehensive settlement in Western Europe. The free trade agreements of the early 1970s were the maximum acceptable solution only to Finland; judging from their statements in 1962 and 1970, the neutrals Sweden, Austria and Switzerland had been willing to go much further — probably as far as to some sort of Customs and partial economic union.[14] EFTA is obviously interested in widening the scope of West European integration. But are they prepared to engage in a deepening of wider European integration?

An EC–EFTA partnership is supposed to rest on two pillars. The further integration of EFTA is a prerequisite for structured group-to-group relations in Western Europe. However, lack of geographical continguity, differences in economic structure and differences in foreign policy traditions all work against a deepening of EFTA integration. In other words, a loose multilateral forum with a wide though not exhaustive agenda is a more realistic outcome of the current negotiations than a fully fledged partnership.

The present phase of EC–EFTA interaction is characterized by a new momentum within the Community, which weakens the cohesion of EFTA. The new external challenges not only make EFTA countries realize the extent to which they have common problems, they also expose the differences in the range of options open to to them individually or in groups. Moreover, the pressing need for adaptation to the internal market puts a premium on efficiency and rapid decision-making. This inevitably focuses attention on, for example, the existence of a quite cohesive Nordic subgroup within EFTA, which despite all its problems has developed habits of smooth and flexible harmonization and consultation in the social and economic field. If Austria goes ahead with its membership application, the Northern EFTA members will feel tempted to give priority to the Nordic grouping as the main framework for negotiations with the EC, the more so since Switzerland has already become somewhat isolated in the discussions on the new EC proposals.

The Nordic Council of Ministers has published several interesting reports, which call for more concerted Nordic action to confront the challenge of 1992.[15] Concrete initiatives have also been taken. In Autumn 1988, the Nordic Council of Ministers launched the so-called NORDPLUS programme, a Nordic parallel to ERASMUS. Given the high degree of Nordic consensus on issues like environmental protection and safety standards for workers, there is scope for Nordic pre-emption of the EC in these areas. On the other hand, Sweden would probably question the bargaining value of a 'dwarfed' EFTA without Switzerland. Thus an Austrian application could just as well lead to a 'bilateral chain reaction' within EFTA.

The institutionalized group-to-group model is facing some difficulties on the EC side as well. There is the risk that, in trying to avoid the administrative burden of enlargement negotiations, the EC will end up creating a new administrative overload. The negotiations on new binding collaborative structures will be time-consuming and exceedingly complex. Existing inter-regional arrangements offer little guidance, as EFTA countries would be asking for more than just consultations and some element of supranationalism might have to be contemplated.

On the other hand, the FRG in particular regards the group-to-group approach as useful in the EC–EFTA context. The West German government takes the view that a structured group-to-group arrangement between the EC and EFTA might serve as a model for the EC's cooperation with the Eastern European countries, and has suggested that, in part for domestic political reasons, it would be wise to give greater visibility to wider European cooperation.

Officially, the EC is still bound by Interlaken principles of priority to EC integration, decision-making autonomy and cohesion. The Commission has formed an opinion on the advantages of some sort of inter-regionalism, but the Community as such has not officially changed its position. Nor is there universal agreement within the Commission on the virtues of group-to-group relations or inter-regionalism in the EFTA case.

An alternative option: enlargement

This raises the question of the extent to which enlargement of the Community is an attractive and realistic option. Clearly, in the short term, enlargement is not an option, though it may be for several EFTA states in the medium and longer term. Austria is already waiting. Whether the EC's Council of Ministers is ready to accept Austria even after 1992 is not yet clear. But given the acceleration of European détente, it may be that time is working in favour of Austrian membership. Norway is also inching closer to the Community.

For none of the applicants would membership be an easy option. EFTA countries joining the Community in the first half of the 1990s would face severe problems of adaptation. Not only would they have to adapt to the legal obligations of membership. They would also have to prepare for the challenges of the internal market. The most important benefit would be the possibility of influencing decision-making on internal market legislation, to which they would anyway have to adapt.

From the Community's perspective, there is a conflict between widening and deepening of integration. Realistically, a new round of major enlargement would therefore require political side-payments to integrationists in the Parliament and Council of Ministers. It is hardly a coincidence that the first enlargement of the EC was accompanied by attempts at a deepening of integration. There is also a problem of maintaining a rough balance between North and South in the Community.

A further problem arises arises from the so-called hierarchy of third-country relations. It is difficult for the EC Commission to give its opinion on an Austrian accession without reference to its opinion on Turkish accession, which, for a number of reasons, it found difficult to contemplate. For political as well as administrative reasons the Community would probably prefer parallel accession negotiations with Austria and Norway (and perhaps Turkey). These considerations point to the conclusion that enlargement is a possibility in the medium and long term, but that it will probably have to take place as part of a major package deal involving some deepening of integration.

All European perspectives

The conflict between deepening and widening of integration is of course a real one. Would it be possible to admit two or more new members without mortally wounding the process of European unification? On the other hand, there is a risk that in blind pursuance of its successful economic rearmament programme, the EC will fail to exploit unique political opportunities for stirring the foundations of the post-war division of Europe. Nobody knows who will rule the Kremlin in 1992. The present trend, characterized by cumulative *détente*, clearly also changes the external context of European neutrality; in a relaxed East–West climate, there is less of a need for neutral go-betweens for the support of the non-committed is of less value to the two blocs. Moreover, despite their overlapping memberships, the differences between NATO and the Community have become even clearer, thus reducing the latter's bloc character at least in the traditional sense. It should be added, though, that the EC has through the reintroduction of majority voting acquired a more marked supranational character, and that it has made some headway in foreign policy and security cooperation — with negative implications for wider European integration. The tension between the dynamics of European Union and all-European cooperation creates acute dilemmas, which in the short term can probably only be solved by additional doses of two- or three-speed integration and variable geometry.

The current developments in Eastern Europe offer possibilities for creating more solid functional ties between the two parts of the continent. The Soviet leadership has signalled a profound change in its attitude to the EC which has deeply significant implications for pan-European cooperation.[16] Hungary's political leadership has signalled an interest in membership of EFTA and, possibly at some stage, even the EC. Can one speculate whether for some Eastern European countries EFTA may come to represent an alternative to the CMEA or, perhaps more realistically, a transit area within the European family? By flagging the notion of a broader political partnership between the EC and the other European countries, the EC might in any case hope to stimulate the loosening of ties between some Eastern European countries and the CMEA. It is in the EC's interest to formulate an open-minded and forward-looking EFTA policy that does not slam the door in the face of neighbouring countries, who are in the process of reinterpreting their international role.

Notes

1 The research for this chapter is partly based on a series of interviews in March 1988 with officials in the Commission and the national representations who understandably want to remain anonymous and who bear no responsibility for this text.

2 The reader is referred to the interesting discussion in Pierre du Bois and B. Hurni (eds), *EFTA from Yesterday to Tomorrow*, Geneva, 1987, which contains testimonies by officials who took part in the negotiations of the 1950s.

3 ibid.

4 R. C. Hine, *The Political Economy of European Trade*, Wheatsheaf Books, Brighton, 1985, p. 93.

5 See the articles on this subject in the 1989 volumes of *International Organization*.

6 See Robert Gilpin, *The Political Economy of International Relations*, Princeton University Press, Princeton, 1987.

7 See Herman de Lange, 'Taking Stock of the EC–EFTA dialogue' in H. Wallace and J. Jamar (eds), *EEC–EFTA: More than just good friends?* College of Europe, 1988, pp. 310ff.

8 See The Luxembourg Declaration of 9 April 1984.

9 An elaboration of these arguments can be found in Thomas Pedersen, *The Wider Western Europe: EC Policy Towards the EFTA Countries*, RIIA Discussion Papers 10, Chatham House, 1988.

10 See Wolfgang Hager, 'Little Europe, Wider Europe and Western Economic Cooperation' in L. Tsoukalis (ed.), *The European Community: Past, Present and Future*, Basil Blackwell Oxford, 1983, pp. 171ff.

11 See The Luxembourg Agreement of 9 April 1984.
12 Jacques Delors, *Die Orientierungen der Kommission*, EG-Nachrichten, nr. 3 v 7 February 1989.
13 See Helen Wallace and Wolfgang Wessels, *Towards a New Partnership: The EC and EFTA in the Wider Western Europe*, EFTA Occasional Paper No. 28, March 1989.
14 See Harto Hakovirta, *East–West Conflict and European Neutrality*. Clarendon Press, Oxford, 1988, p. 130f.
15 See internationella samarbétsfrågar i Nordiska rådet, 1988: 4 Betänkanda avgivet av Nordiska rådets internationella samarbetskommitè, Nordisk Råd, Stockholm, 1989, and Arbejdsprogram 'Norden i Europa 1989–1992'. Nord, 1989: 50, Nordisk Ministerråd, Copenhagen, 1989.
16 The influential IMEMO Institute in 1988 published 14 theses on Western Europe, which contain a positive theoretical evaluation of the EC.

8 Agreement with the Gulf Cooperation Council: a promising if difficult beginning

Eberhard Rhein

A late start of a structured relationship

Among all the regions in the world the Arab Peninsula is of the greatest strategical importance for the EC. It is here that roughly 50 per cent of the non-communist world's proven oil reserves lie in the ground. It is from here that the Community gets about a quarter of its total oil imports. It is this region that will outlast all other oil producers in the world, its reserves lasting well into the middle of the next century (at present production rates). The Community therefore has a vital interest in close friendly relations with this region, at least as long as its economic well-being continues to be so closely hinged upon a regular, unimpeded supply of oil.

It is more surprising that it took the Community more than 20 years before it started taking a closer look at the region [1] and another 10 years before it found a contractual partner in the Gulf Cooperation Council (GCC). [2] Even the process of establishing diplomatic relations with the individual countries of the region was very slow and hesitant, in particular when compared with Iran. [3]

The turning point in EC–Gulf relations was undoubtedly the setting up in 1981 of a regional structure comprising six of the eight countries situated between the Red Sea and the Gulf. [4] The creation of the Gulf Cooperation Council was the reaction to regional instability and the threats emanating from the Iran–Iraq war and the Soviet occupation of Afghanistan. In that sense, a certain analogy can be established with the origins of the EC in the early 1950s or that of ASEAN in 1969. But there was surprise that the GCC envisaged, from the start, a much broader, but also less economic model of regional cooperation than the European precedent with its heavy bias on economics. [5]

The initiative for a group-to-group relationship was taken by the Federal Republic of Germany. It was Hans-Dietrich Genscher who, in late 1979, even before the GCC had been established, took the matter up with colleagues in the Council of Ministers, suggesting that the Community approach the Gulf states including Iraq and North Yemen and declare its readiness to negotiate a non-preferential trade and cooperation agreement of the type the Community had recently concluded with the five ASEAN countries. This initiative did not get very far. The GCC side had much more pressing needs at home. It had to get its own act together, establish a functioning secretariat, and define the strategies for closer regional cooperation among its own member countries. Negotiating an agreement with the Community or any third countries was evidently not their first priority.

Still, the messages sent from the EC in 1980 gave rise to the first tentative contacts between the EC Commission and the newly established GCC Secretariat in Riyadh. M. Bishara, the GCC Secretary-General, paid his first visit to Brussels in 1982 and a Community delegation visited the GCC headquarters in 1984 for informal exploratory talks on a possible cooperation agreement.

The making of the Cooperation Agreement

From 1985 onwards relations between the Community and the GCC entered into a new, more active phase. The substance of relations underwent significant changes. In the first place, since 1985 it has been the GCC which has become the dynamic, more pressing partner. The Community found itself on the defensive. Secondly, the GCC had defined its long-term strategy for the relationship with the EC as one of obtaining long-term free access to the enormous and nearby Community market for the refining and petrochemical industries, which have been coming on stream since the 1980s. The Community offer of a most-favoured-nation (MFN) agreement on the lines of the ASEAN agreement was rejected as not good enough. The EC–Israel free trade agreement was considered as the model for EC–GCC relations.

Thirdly, there were the beginnings of an informal political dialogue, especially after 1986 when the pressure of the Iran–Iraq war rose, prompting the GCC to look out for 'allies'. Finally, contacts became progressively closer. The EC and GCC Presidents, plus the Commission and the GCC Secretariat met for the first time on 14 October 1985. This was followed by a Troika meeting in Brussels two years later (23 June 1987). The Cooperation Agreement of 15 June 1988 finally provided for a Joint Council for GCC–Community cooperation, which was to meet regularly in order to 'define the general guidelines of cooperation' (Article 10). What had changed since 1980 when the Council first envisaged entering into a contractual relationship?

The oil price had dropped to a level that nobody had thought possible in 1975–81; the seller's market had turned into an oil glut. The Europeans were no longer scared about the security of their energy supply. Moreover, the Gulf countries had ceased to generate a vast foreign exchange surplus that needed 'financial recycling'. The oil boom was over, the Gulf market had lost a good deal of its previous attractiveness. EC exports to the GCC fell by one-third within two years (from 1985 to 1987), after having risen twenty times between 1973, the year of the first oil shock, and 1982. And, in addition, the Gulf countries had built up refining, petrochemical, aluminium and other energy intensive industries, all of them vitally dependent on exports. At the same time, in Europe, such industries were undergoing a painful adjustment and restructuring process, trying hard to reduce excessive capacities so as to fit with the lower demand and new competitive conditions. Thus, within a short period of time the respective interests of the two parties had undergone profound change, which in turn led to a reassessment of how relations between EC and GCC should be shaped.

The Cooperation Agreement of 15 June 1988 fully reflects the ambivalence of the respective interests. Both sides wanted an agreement, essentially for political reasons: the Community because it wanted to demonstrate the importance it attributes to the Gulf region and in particular to the GCC; the GCC because they considered an agreement with the Community as an expression of special relations and as a first step to their ultimate goal of a free trade zone.

For the GCC, the agreement constituted a 'première' on the international arena. Never before had they negotiated *en bloc* or signed an international agreement; the signature itself meant an upgrading of the international status of the GCC, even though only its member states (and not the GCC as such) are parties to the agreement. It is not surprising, therefore, that since June 1988 other countries have discreetly expressed their willingness to negotiate similar agreements.

Moreover, the signing took place at a decisive moment of the Iran–Iraq war. Parallel to it, the parties issued a joint declaration, in which 'they reiterated their full interest for the early implementation of Security Council Resolution 598' and 'explicitly emphasized that freedom of navigation is a cardinal principle in internal relations'. For the Community, the signing of the agreement was a much more routine act of external relations. It finally filled a vacuum in the Community's 'foreign policy' by formalizing the relationship with one of its major economic partners, comparable to the ACP or the Latin American Group, but considerably more *important* than ASEAN.

But beyond the basic political consensus on an agreement, each side wanted to see a text of quite different contents. The Gulf side wanted a fully fledged free trade agreement; the European side preferred a framework agreement expressing the readiness of the two parties to cooperate more closely in industrial, scientific, energy, agricultural matters, etc. The text finally agreed on fully reflected the two sides' different approaches.

In its substance it resembles other cooperation agreements concluded by the Community, for example, with ASEAN, India, Mexico or Brazil. Unlike those agreements, however, it went a step further in the direction of what the GCC wanted to see embedded in such an agreement. Indeed, the Community specifically agreed to examine the possibility of negotiating a trade expansion and liberalization agreement, provided it would be in full conformity with the provisions of the GATT and not undermine the Community's efforts to maintain a production capacity in the oil refining and petrochemical industries (Joint Declaration concerning Article 11(2) of the Agreement).

For all these reasons, the Cooperation Agreement could be finalized in record time, the signature occurring less than nine months after the Commission had asked the Council for a negotiating directive. Both the Commission and the Presidency, held by the FRG, were instrumental in pushing matters forward.

Assessment and perspectives

It is too early to conclude that the GCC and the Community have established a meaningful group-to-group dialogue or even cooperation. There is no doubt that the establishment of a regional organization in the Gulf in 1981 caused relations to intensify. As in other cases of regional groupings (such as ASEAN, Central America, Caricom and the Andean Group), the Community has been prompted to seek closer cooperation with the GCC, too.

However, there have been no tangible results so far. Of course, there have been occasional group-to-group meetings, and ministers have got together for luncheons on the occasion of the UN Assemblies in New York. But the political dialogue has not gone beyond strictly regional questions, with the Gulf pressing its case on Iran and the Palestinian issue. In the economic field, discussions have so far been focused almost entirely on the issue of free trade and, related to this, on the access of petrochemical products to the Community market.

No energy dialogue at a political level has so far taken place. This has been partly because there was not much need for it, the ball being entirely in the producers' court and partly because the European side may still have felt inhibited by the thwarted attempts of the consumer–producer dialogue in the 1970s. Admittedly, all this has not so far been terribly exciting for Community ministers. But it should also be borne in mind that the Cooperation Agreement has not yet been ratified and therefore no institutional dialogue has been set up.

So far the group-to-group dialogue has fallen short of expectations. This is especially so for the GCC side. Indeed, the GCC will settle for no less than a free trade area which, they hope, will assure them long-term access to the Community market for their processed oil products. As long as the Community finds itself unable, for whatever reasons, to respond favourably to fundamental GCC requests, both the economical and the political dialogue are likely to remain low-key, and the Cooperation Agreement may well remain one of the many paper documents that furnish the history of modern diplomacy without shaping it.

It is therefore useful to reflect on what is at stake for the Community when considering the free-trade option with the GCC. In an nutshell, the issue is twofold: does the Community want to extend the scope of its 'preferential' economic and commercial relations beyond Western Europe and the Mediterranean? And is the Community prepared to accept a more important transfer of its refining and basic petrochemical industries to more advantageous locations near the oil and gas sources in the Gulf? Since the end of 1988 the Community has been able to agree on a position on these two fundamental questions. The Community is prepared to enter into a free-trade agreement to be progressively implemented towards the beginning of the twenty-first century with long-term strategic considerations. The key arguments in favour of free trade between the Community and the GCC are easily set out. Whatever happens over the next three to four decades, the Gulf region will hold a major key for mankind's economic survival. It is therefore of critical importance for the Community to be linked as closely as possible to the region, politically and economically. A free-trade area, coupled with political stability, might be expected to produce close links and that interdependence in turn will finally create common interests (EC–EFTA relations being the classic example of such a linkage of interests).

There is no way of preventing the Gulf countries from upgrading their oil and gas production and developing their refining and petrochemical industries, for which they clearly possess comparative advantages. The European petrochemical industry would be well advised to enter into joint ventures with the Gulf and thereby to dispose of a cheap feed-stock base for the more sophisticated research intensive productions to be concentrated in Europe. The progressive abolition of duties by the Community would by no means endanger the existence of a thriving European petrochemical industry, but would only accelerate necessary and overdue adjustments and allow for an optimum division of labour between the Community and the Gulf.

Those who oppose such a marriage of interests between the EC and the GCC advance two basic arguments. First, the Community must not indulge in a further proliferation of regional free-trade areas.[6] As the world's major trading group, it has a vital interest in the maintainence of free world trade governed by universal adherence to the MFN clause. It should not offer any arguments to the United States or Japan to pursue regional trading blocks in their respective regions. Secondly, the petrochemical industry is too important and too sensitive to be put into any predicament. This is particularly so as the trade advantages likely to accrue to the Community from free trade are anything but certain because of the one-sidedness of the economical structure of the GCC, which hinges essentially on the energy sector.[7]

Whatever the outcome of the discussions on the pros and cons of EC–GCC free trade, it is abundantly clear that fruitful group-to-group relations can only thrive where there is also a dense network of economic, financial, trade, industrial, technological, cultural and even social relations between the partners concerned. Political dialogue does not take place in a vacuum. It needs a healthy sub-stratum of common interests and, if possible, a common outlook on fundamental political issues. Despite the fact that the GCC as a group is among the Community's major trading partners (behind EFTA, United States, Japan and well ahead of ASEAN), the intimacy of relations and dialogue still leaves much to be desired. This can be attributed essentially to four factors: a fundamental though subconscious feeling of suspicion and a lack of trust on the part of many Europeans, stemming above all from inadequate knowledge of the Arabs; the existence of cultural differences, and of differences in the legal, social and political structures of the respective societies; the predominance of the energy sector which makes a broad-based dialogue more difficult; and finally the fact that the GCC has only recently emerged as a major power factor in the international scene.

These inhibiting factors are bound to disappear only slowly. The establishment of a free-trade area between the Community and the GCC would most likely encourage closer industrial, financial and trade cooperation. But even so it would be wise not to expect any revolutionary changes, at least in the short term, towards a very intimate group-to-group dialogue.

Notes

1 The Arab Peninsula covers an area of 3.5 million sq.km. (including both North and South Yemen) compared to 2.2 million sq.km. for the Community. But its population is only about 20 million people, most of the area being desert. Kuwait, Bahrain, Qatar, the United Emirates and South Yemen (Aden) became independent states only in the 1960s. Thanks to the oil boom of the 1970s, the area has undergone profound economic and social changes. The average per capita income is comparable to that of the Community with the exception of North and South Yemen, which are still very poor and do not belong to the Gulf Cooperation Council.

2 A Cooperation Agreement was signed in Luxembourg on 15 June 1988.

3 Iran in 1963, Saudi Arabia in 1967, Qatar in 1976, Oman in 1975, UAE in 1982, Kuwait in 1986, Bahrain has not yet established diplomatic relations with the Community.

4 Saudi Arabia, Kuwait, Bahrain, Qatar, United Arab Emirates and Oman.

5 cf. Charter of the Cooperation Council for the Arab States of the Gulf in Ursula Braun, *Der Kooperationsrat arabischer Staaten am Golf: eine neue Kraft?*, Baden-Baden, 1984.

6 In this context the Community cannot, of course, dismiss the question of how to respond if Iraq and Iran, both of which are closely following the development of Community–GCC relations, one day knocked at the Community's door and also requested to enter into free trade with the Community.

7 For the GCC import duties fulfill essentially a revenue function, and not one of protection. Under a free-trade arrangement the GCC could theoretically

abolish all duties and replace these by internal taxes applicable *ergo omnes*. The Community would thus not benefit from any preferential treatment on the GCC markets, while offering such preferential treatment to the Gulf on processed oil/gas products.

9 EC–CMEA relations: normalisation and beyond

Barbara Lippert

The significance of the Council for Mutual Economic Assistance (CMEA) as a dialogue partner

Over the last few decades, distance and ignorance rather than dialogue and cooperation have characterised relations between the EC and its analogous group in Eastern Europe, the CMEA. The CMEA was regarded as dominated by the Soviet Union and was therefore treated as part of the global East–West conflict. The EC was cautious not to support a 'powerful and efficient group' of integrated countries behind the Iron Curtain. This outlook has given particular significance to the group-to-group dialogue with the CMEA, marking it as a special case.

Prospects have become brighter as the Soviet and therefore the CMEA's policy towards the West has been redefined in line with the 'new political thinking' in international affairs. This redefinition led to a reassessment of the nature of the EC as a unique and dynamic system of integration; the Moscow Institute of World Economy and International Affairs put it thus:

The integration process in Western Europe reflects a progressive tendency towards the strengthening of intercommunication between states ... In this sense, Western European integration has great potential, a capacity to demonstrate a positive influence on international relations in Europe, to assist in the reduction of the level of military tension and to help in the development of equal and mutually advantageous cooperation agreements.[1]

Watersheds in post-war history

The rapid erosion and breakdown of Soviet-type regimes in Eastern Europe in the late 1980s marked what President Gorbachev did not hesitate to call a second revolution.[2] These changes also affect the intra-bloc relationships among the European members of the CMEA. Mechanisms of power and control that were shaped in the 1950s by Stalinist policies and the rules of cold war diplomacy are undergoing fundamental changes which allow its allies broader and more independent decision-making capacities.[3] These centrifugal tendencies have ended the monolithic nature of the Eastern bloc, provoking the question of whether, and to what extent, Eastern Europe is an appropriate partner for dialogue and cooperation with Western Europe and especially with the EC.

From an Eastern European perspective, the EC, with its comparatively sophisticated and efficient decision-making authority, has a new and exciting attractiveness; it is even viewed as a model worth striving for. While the Community is heading for integration on the basis of the Single European Act (SEA), the creation of a single market in the 1990s and a European Union, disintegration is at present the dominant feature in Eastern Europe, especially within the CMEA. If these dynamics of East and West were originally hardly connected, their new inter-connectedness marks a watershed in post-war history.

The movement towards a new closeness between the EC and the CMEA has to be understood within the wider framework of a changing post-war international system. There is, for example, the new understanding and summit diplomacy between the two super powers, the United States and the Soviet Union. At the same time, a more pluralist and multipolar international order has emerged, which no longer follows a mere antagonistic bloc pattern. The most prominent catchword from the East for this process is 'interdependence'. It may have seemed an ironic turn of history when Gorbachev implicitly revised the Leninist tenet of 'imperialism as the highest stage of capitalism' when he told the Assembly of the Council of Europe that today the 'interdependence of countries' can be perceived 'as a higher stage of the process of internationalization'.[4] This internationalization forces the so-called socialist world system to adapt; global and universal challenges have replaced 'the traditional balance of forces with a balance of interests'.[5] This has required Eastern European élites to adopt a sense of *realpolitik* with some urgency, which has contributed to a general de-ideologization[6] of Soviet and socialist foreign policy. This has given the Community an opportunity to break new ground in pursuit of an overall European framework.

The 'dialogue of the deaf'

In reviewing the efforts to formalise relations between the EC and the CMEA since Brezhnev's first 'invitation to talks' in 1972, the close connection between Soviet thinking and the initiatives of the CMEA is clear. Traditionally, the Soviet Union opposed all efforts towards Western European integration. The Community was considered an instrument of monopoly capitalism acting like a cartel.[7]

In 1972 Brezhnev partly overcame this hostility when he called the EC a 'reality in international politics' which had to be taken into account.[8] Consequently, the CMEA decided at its Twenty-seventh Session in 1973 to begin talks with the EC. Contacts opened in August 1973 at the level of a 'private visit' of General Secretary Fadeev of the

CMEA Executive Committee to the Danish Foreign Minister Norgard, who was then President of the Council of Ministers.[9] The newly enlarged Community (from six to nine) had just developed the first mechanisms of Political Cooperation (EPC). It is very likely that the CMEA's, and more notably the Soviet's, initiative in a 'European direction'[10] were a reaction to these new dynamics in the Western integration process and to the effects of Community policies.

However, the systemic incompatibilities of market- and state-directed economies, as well as the different legal natures and competencies of the EC and the CMEA, set limits to any cooperation.[11] The fact that the CMEA is not a supranational organisation but one based on the sovereignty of its member countries was not the main reason for the EC's reluctance — such asymmetries have not stopped the EC from shaping a special regime for cooperation in other cases of group-to-group relations. The sovereignty of CMEA member countries was limited to a degree determined by the Soviet Union, which assumed the role of an overall hegemony. The sometimes oppressive Soviet dominance resulted not only from geopolitical, demographic, military and other material factors but also from its power to interpret *ex cathedra* the lines of Marxist/Leninist orthodoxy. The EC was very much aware of this power constellation within the CMEA and, therefore, took the strategic decision not to encourage — as it had deliberately done so in other parts of the world — deeper intra-CMEA integration and bloc coherence. Instead it preferred to foster bilateral contacts with individual Eastern European countries. Yet the formalisation of EC–CMEA contacts was not totally rejected, hence the Community's 'parallel approach'.

The CMEA's Executive Committee submitted a draft outline of an agreement to the Council of Ministers in February 1976, after a revision of the CMEA's statute in 1974 had confirmed its treaty-making power and after a meeting between officials of the Commission and the CMEA Secretariat had been held in Moscow in February 1975.[12] The draft was based on the Helsinki Final Act and limited EC relations with individual CMEA members to technical matters. But in addition to establishing official relations with the EC, the draft contained a full-scale programme for trade cooperation. The EC Commission's counter-draft in November 1976 neither offered the CMEA official recognition (only 'working relations') nor did it allow for cooperation in areas that concerned trade, finance and other aspects of economic cooperation. These areas, the Commission held, should be dealt with exclusively on a bilateral basis with CMEA member countries. Moreover, the EC would not accept the CMEA's efforts to establish bilateral and multilateral cross-relations with the EC and its member states on the grounds that this undermined the Community's authority to act collectively on behalf of its members in fields provided for in the Treaties.

Formal talks were opened in May 1978. However, there was no substantial progress. Expert meetings in Brussels and in Moscow in

November 1978 only stressed the incompatibility of each side's views. The main disagreements were over the assessment of the authority and competencies of each body and the treatment of West Berlin, whose interests the EC claimed fully to represent on the legal basis of the Joint Declaration concerning Berlin which was an integral part of the EEC treaties of 1957.

The CMEA's demands for the creation of a joint committee to examine and control the bilateral agreements of its members towards the EC, as well as the claim for fixing the most-favoured-nation clause went well beyond the EC's willingness to find a compromise. Although the CMEA finally gave in and accepted the Commission as the only negotiating partner, talks with the EC in Geneva in July 1980 ended in deadlock and were suspended in October 1980.[13] Mr Haferkamp's letter to the CMEA's Secretary in March 1981 — offering a declaration on mutual recognition — remained unanswered. As J. Maslen pointed out, it was these circumstances, and not the invasion of Afghanistan and the deterioration of global East–West relations, that put an end to negotiations.[14]

Interim and issue-centred solutions

The Community's attempt to minimise the role of the CMEA in its relations with Eastern Europe was a strategy opposed by the CMEA and orthodox party élites in the East. It was, though, seen as compatible with the national interests of the smaller CMEA countries who intensified their Western policies during the period of *détente*. By 1974, the exclusive competence for external trade had been transferred to the Community (under Article 113 of the EC Treaty), thereby restricting the powers of the member states to negotiate on trade issues.[15] It was the Community, therefore, that launched an initiative to conclude bilateral trade agreements, which offered most-favoured-nation status to each of the CMEA countries. It forwarded the appropriate drafts in November 1974. They were, however, ignored or sent back to Brussels.

To overcome the deadlock and in order to find an interim solution, the EC set up the so-called 'autonomous import arrangements' in 1975. These largely comprised the prescriptions of EC member states and made up an EC list of quotas for imports from the CMEA that were continuously updated.[16] Although they had been introduced unilaterally, individual CMEA countries explored ways of communicating their interests to the Commission. Thus contacts between the EC and CMEA countries on single issues never completely broke down. Political élites in Eastern Europe, however, sought to limit trade agreements with the EC to sectoral bilateral agreements on textiles, steel and other sensitive products.[17] The agreements on textiles were based on the Multi-Fibre Agreement (MFA) within the GATT and were signed by Romania, Hungary, Poland and Czechoslovakia and by the non-GATT member, Bulgaria, between 1976 and 1981. In addition, there were separate agreements with the same five countries covering steel, as well as sensitive products in the agricultural sector such as cheese, wine, eggs, sheep and goat meat imports. An agreement on sheep and goat meat was also signed by the GDR in 1987. These arrangements followed GATT rules and recognised the position of individual CMEA countries, which was largely defined by special protocols.[18]

The onset of normalisation between unequal groups

A new phase in East–West relations which prepared the ground for a further effort to negotiate began in 1984–5. In June 1984 at the summit of CMEA party leaders in Moscow, proposals were put forward once more for the conclusion of an 'appropriate agreement between the CMEA and the EC' as well as contributions to 'the development of trade and economic relations that exist between the member countries of these organizations'.[19] However, the CMEA's proposals were treated by the Commission as a belated answer to its 1981 letter.

It was not therefore before the redefinition of global Soviet foreign policy that a really new impetus was given to the EC–CMEA contacts. With the advent to the leadership by Mr Gorbachev in April 1985, signals were sent out encouraging an intensification of East–West relations. A month later, Mr Gorbachev told Mr Bettino Craxi, the then President of the Council of Ministers who was visiting Moscow, that the Soviet Union was ready to 'organize mutually advantageous relations between the CMEA and the EC in economic matters. To the extent that the countries of the Community function as a political entity', the Soviet Union was willing to 'explore with them, in a common language, specific international problems'.[20] This proposal indirectly invited a political dialogue and hinted at the Soviet's high evaluation of EPC. CMEA Secretary Sychev then took the initiative and, on 14 June 1985, wrote to President Delors proposing a Joint Declaration on mutual recognition to precede any bilateral relations between the EC and the CMEA member countries. The CMEA had dropped its ambitions for a substantial trade agreement with the EC. The formal proposal followed in September 1985. The Joint Declaration was to provide for the establishment of official relations between the CMEA and the EC that would 'take into account the powers of the two organisations'.[21] The proposal formed the basis of exploratory talks which began in Geneva in September 1986 and which continued in March 1987.[22]

In all, it took until 25 June 1988 to conclude the Joint Declaration which in about 250 words provided only for mutual recognition and placed on a legal footing what had been practised for some time. The EC concluded the Joint Declaration on the basis of Article 235 of the EC Treaty, the EP adopting the Commission's proposal according to the procedure laid down in Article 228. The Joint Declaration did not provide for any institutions but referred only to 'means of contacts and discussions' between representatives of both parties.[23] The level at which meetings might take place as well as their frequency were left open. The Joint Declaration advised both parties to 'develop cooperation in areas which fall within their respective spheres of competence and where there is common interest'. But the cooperation element remained vague and ambivalent, saying that 'The parties will, if necessary, examine the possibility of determining areas, forms and methods of cooperation'.

What made the negotiations on the Joint Declaration so cumbersome was the safeguarding of the EC's policy of giving priority to bilateral contacts with the members of the CMEA and the territorial dispute over West Berlin. Initially, there was little agreement within the Community on how to achieve parallelism,[24] a policy which, in effect, was designed to downplay the authority and competence of the CMEA. In keeping with the policy, the EC in January/February 1986 offered to negotiate an overall trade agreement with each CMEA country, thus repeating its invitation of 1974. At the same time, the Commission explored their general attitude towards the proposed Joint Declaration between Brussels and the CMEA.[25] This 'parallel approach' by the Community, which was repeatedly declared a *sine qua non*, was answered positively in the following months by the CMEA and each of its members[26] even if with different positions and priorities. The GDR, the Soviet Union and Bulgaria emphasised that the Joint Declaration had to precede the bilateral agreements. The GDR declared, furthermore, that it would only discuss problems of mutual interest.[27] On the other hand, as early as 1983, Hungary and Czechoslovakia had asked the Community to broaden existing relations substantially and not merely to update the sectoral agreements.

The issue over Berlin was not settled until May 1988. The Declaration was based on the so-called 'Hungarian formula', which stressed that the 'Quadripartite Agreement and in particular the agreement of 3 September 1971' was in no way affected.[28] The Joint Declaration and the bilateral agreements include a territorial clause that refers 'to the territories in which the Treaty establishing the European Economic Community is applied'.

It is unlikely that either the Joint Declaration's limited institutional arrangements or its substance will be improved in the future. Meetings at senior official or even ministerial level are not to be expected. The evolutive capacity of the Declaration, too, is highly restrictive and is unlikely to contribute to a widening of competencies, unless there is a significant change in the EC's general development. The EC accepted the Joint Declaration with the CMEA as the entrance ticket to bilateral agreements with individual countries, not as a framework agreement that fixed an agenda for further bilateral cooperation. In contrast to its dialogues with other groups of states, the Community has denied a bloc to bloc approach towards the CMEA and, even though it is time-consuming, has continued to establish bilateral contacts with CMEA members. The same is true for the envisaged political dialogue at EPC level. The countries of Eastern Europe have, in turn, favoured this treatment and have not sought mechanisms by which to harmonise their foreign policies. It remains an open question whether 'politicisation' and further bloc cohesion is intended in the Warsaw Pact framework. So far, the Soviet Union has continued to denounce a bloc to bloc attitude, whether its allies are communist-led or not. The essence of the EC's dialogue with the CMEA can best be called normalisation, which has been defined by J. Maslen as 'arriving at a situation where each party is willing to have dealings with the other, to communicate with it orally or in writing, to discuss problems of mutual interest and, where appropriate, to conclude agreements on such questions'.[29]

Conditions for cooperation in the 1990s

In analysing East–West relations in Europe, one must recognise the different motives, instruments and capacities of each side. For the EC and its member states, trade with Eastern Europe only amounts to six to seven per cent of its total world trade and has even decreased over recent years.[30] The EC's main motives for cooperation lie therefore in the political field. This is equally true for the FRG which among EC member states traditionally holds the greatest share of, and interest in, trade with the East.[31] The focus on political motives has encouraged, first of all, the normalisation of relations through the establishment of diplomatic relations with the CMEA member states. With the exception of Romania, once a precursor of closer relations, all European CMEA countries presented their credentials to the Community immediately after the adoption of the Joint Declaration in June 1988. Secondly, the conclusion of bilateral trade agreements may help prevent an ever deeper economic and social division in Europe and should improve the working conditions for Western firms and businessmen in Eastern Europe. Thirdly, the development of an institutional framework brings with it procedures by which to discuss and solve problems of cooperation without 'autistic intervals' and contributes to the idea of 'positive interdependence'.[32] Finally, Western Europe is fundamentally interested in the process of democratisation and pluralisation as well as the development of more open, market-based economies in Eastern Europe. This position aims basically at observing the spirit and letter of the Helsinki Final Act, a document regularly referred to in both the Joint Declaration and the bilateral agreements. In the economic field the Community has encouraged the restructuring of the financial and price systems as well as an improvement in the supply of information on import plans and economic forecasting, while discouraging compensated or counter-trade.

From an Eastern European perspective, the primary determinants of policy towards the EC have been economic. The increasingly disastrous economic situation in some parts of Eastern Europe has created an imperative for clear-cut reforms. The problem now is less one of ideological chains that hamper reform measures than of time and competence.[33] Western Europe is looked to to compensate for production deficits, which may even increase during the transition period of restructuring. The division of Europe cut off traditional central European flows and concentrated it within the CMEA and especially with the Soviet Union. But there is now a much greater interest in, and dependence on, an intensification of trade with Western markets: one third of Soviet exports, primarily raw materials, goes to the EC market. The smaller countries of the CMEA hold an export share of 29 per cent. They import from the EC market up to 38 per cent in the case of Hungary or at least 15 per cent in the case of Bulgaria.[34] All lack a diversified export structure, and continue to depend on exports of agricultural, low-technology, and semi-finished products. Their imports are mostly designed to substitute for more refined consumer goods and finished products of higher technological standards.[35] An increase in trade, greater access to Western markets, technology transfers (with the abolition of 'domestic COCOM'[36] as well), credits and foreign investments designed for special projects and currency convertibility are thus the chief interests of Eastern Europe.

Better access to Western markets is dependent on compatible trade structures. The trend towards *de facto* internationalisation illustrates — though with a considerable time lag — the adjustment to the principles on which international organisations such as GATT, the IMF or the World Bank are based. The initial experiences of state-trading countries that gained access to these organisations under special provisions proved the absence of any alternative to a restructuring of their state-run economies and foreign trade systems. The ability and readiness to undertake what are in essence market-type reforms vary from country to country, as is partly reflected in their bilateral agreements with the EC.

The network of bilateral agreements

As for the predominant role of the Soviet Union, its change in attitude towards the EC provided the starting signal for a deliberate attempt of the smaller countries to get in touch with Western European organisations.[37] Poland and Hungary especially have always been more sympathetic to increased cooperation with the EC, and now feel free to follow their orientation towards the West.

Of the obstacles to greater involvement in the world trading system, the 'twin problems'[38] of indebtedness and uncompetitive export structure are the most important. The current bilateral agreements (and those in preparation) are not expected to have a significant impact. The Community shares the opinion that solving these problems depends on economic change within the countries themselves.

So far, three bilateral agreements have entered into force — the agreement with Hungary on 1 December 1988, the one with Czechoslovakia on 1 April 1989, and with Poland on 1 December 1989.[39] The agreement with the Soviet Union enters into force on 1 April 1990. It will be followed by the EC–GDR agreement, which was initialled in March 1990 after only two rounds of negotiations.[40] The transformation of the restricted trade agreement with Czechoslovakia into a global trade and cooperation agreement, which would cover technology transfers, is in preparation.[41] In the case of Bulgaria, appropriate negotiations are likely to be concluded in spring 1990.[42] Negotiations with Romania will reopen on the basis of revised directives, the existing 1980 agreement having been frozen.[43]

The Community's original approach to negotiations with these countries was guided by the principle of 'specificity', i.e. finding the regime and scope of cooperation most appropriate to each country. Nevertheless, we can identify at least four constituent elements of a 'basic trade and cooperation agreement' that has been adapted to individual needs:

(a) *Tariff and trade provisions* which *de jure* grant each CMEA country most-favoured-nation status but no preferential conditions. To varying degrees, the EC will improve Eastern European access to its market by progressively phasing out quantitative restrictions. Anti-dumping regulations are provided to protect the EC's interests in sensitive sectors.

(b) *Commercial cooperation* which merely concerns the improvement of business facilities and exchange of basic economic data.

(c) *Economic cooperation* in a wide range of listed areas.

(d) *The establishment of a Joint Committee* that meets at least annually to manage, discuss and develop all questions touched on by the agreement.

In contrast to the Joint Declaration, the bilateral agreements provide the opportunity for deeper substantive and more elaborate institutional as well as political ties. In the case of Hungary and Poland, for example, the preamble explicitly looks to an extension of relations between both parties. The trade and cooperation agreements are concluded on the legal basis of Articles 113 and 235 on behalf of the Community. Only the agreement with Czechoslovakia, signed on 19 December 1988 for an initial period of four years, lacked any cooperative elements and was concluded on the basis of only Article 113. Moreover, it dealt exclusively with industrial products; its origins lay very much in the tradition of the first generation of sectoral agreements. A 'Consultative Body' to manage the agreement had been set up, which was similar to the Joint

Committees within the trade and cooperation agreements. On the Community's side, the Committees are led by the Commission and supported by its member states.

The trade and cooperation agreement with Hungary, concluded on 26 September 1988, was for some time the most far-reaching of the agreements. It was concluded for an initial period of ten years, compared to the four years of the Polish agreement. However, the later agreements with the Soviet Union and GDR also follow the main provisions of the Hungarian example.

With the democratic breakthroughs throughout Eastern Europe, the Community had to adjust its instruments and guidelines. If the Community had developed a flexible approach towards each of the CMEA countries and had shown itself prepared for broader trade and cooperation agreements, using trade concessions to oblige the countries of Eastern Europe to adjust to world trade and market standards, as well as to confirm its interest in the possibility of long-term partnership,[44] the speed of change in Eastern Europe meant that existing agreements were outdated. Talks opened with Hungary and Poland, for example, on the elimination of specific and non-quantitative import restrictions into the Community from January 1990. The Generalized System of Preferences was also extended, valid for all industrial products covered by the Community scheme and even farm and textile products.[45] But the problems of indebtedness have been particularly acute and the EC decided on the involvement of the EIB, thus opening a new window for the Eastern countries to gain credits. The Community has been wary, though, of creating precedents which might encourage other groups of states to claim special treatment. Nonetheless, on 6 December, the Commission came up with a one billion ECU loan proposal for Hungary and Poland.[46] The Commission has thus followed a cumulative strategy of support measures, though without having a grand design for the CMEA region.

In the case of the Soviet Union, the EC's process of adjustment has been lengthy. After a long period of explanatory and exploratory talks which started in early 1988, the Council of Ministers in July 1989 finally agreed on a mandate for the Community to negotiate an extensive trade and cooperation agreement on behalf of both the EEC and also EURATOM.[47] However, on 15 July 1989, following the partial revision of the EC's overall approach towards Eastern Europe, the Commission was directed to offer a wider agreement which included economic cooperation and touched on nearly all areas of Community competence. K. Schneider has noted that this decision had a favourable impact not only on negotiations with the Soviet Union, but also on the exploratory talks with Bulgaria and Poland, for it 'enabled the Commission to broaden its discussions with these two countries, and which finally led to the Council directives for negotiating an agreement with them on trade *and* cooperation of February 1989'.[48] So far, the Soviet agreement is the only one that in its preamble recalls the Joint

Declaration and the establishment of official relations between the CMEA and EEC. It was signed on 18 December 1989 in Brussels.[49]

In the case of the GDR, both parties stressed the fact that 'inter-German trade', a formula cautiously referred to as 'the special system of trade between the FRG and the GDR', should not be affected. West Germany did not therefore take part in the trade-related provisions of the agreement. With the early finalisation of the agreement, the Community established autonomous links with the GDR; it will not as a result rely solely on the inter-German talks which are preparing the way for the merger of the two countries and which, inevitably, foreshadow a gradual transition to EC standards. The Commission is drawing up two documents for the Special European Council in April 1990 evaluating the impact of the future integration of the GDR into the Community: one considers the repercussions on the institutional structure of the EC and its policies as well as the effects of the German monetary union on EMU; the second reviews the EC's global approach vis-à-vis CMEA countries.[50]

From goodwill declarations to concerted implementation

Since late summer 1989, hardly a day has gone by when EC member governments have not responded to the shattered economic and revolutionary political situation in Eastern Europe. Whether they have been addressing the European Parliament, their own Parliaments, their domestic publics or international meetings, they unfold encyclopaedias of goodwill towards the reforming countries.[51] This does not, however, constitute a consistent Ostpolitik on the part of the Community.

One way of analysing the EC's commitment to an active policy towards Eastern Europe is through European Council meetings. The European Council in Hanover (June 1988) welcomed the conclusion of the Joint Declaration. The German Presidency during the first half of 1988 had intensified consideration of East–West relations, Mr Genscher being eager to conclude the Joint Declaration during his six months in office. The Rhodes European Council (December 1988) received a discussion paper drawn up by the Commission, which elaborated the 'parallel approach' and took notice of the diversity of the region and therefore the need to be guided by the criteria of 'specificity' in bilateral agreements.[52] In Madrid, the European Council reaffirmed the validity and necessity of a comprehensive approach covering political, economic and cooperative aspects, an approach to be adopted by the Community as well as by the member states. The European Council also reiterated the demand for consistency and coherence provided for in the SEA (Article 30.5) between the EC's external relations and the foreign policy as shaped in the EPC framework. A dialogue at the EPC level was initiated with the Soviet Union, when ambassadors of the Twelve met

Foreign Minister Shevardnadze in February 1989 in Moscow. In April, this was followed by a troika meeting of the Political Directors and 'crowned' by the meeting of the twelve Foreign ministers with Mr Shevardnadze on the fringe of the UN General Assembly in September 1989. There, too, the Hungarian and Polish Foreign Ministers G. Horn and K. Skubiszewski briefly met with the Twelve.[53]

The seven Western leaders at the Paris Summit of July 1989[54] called on the EC Commission to work out, coordinate and implement an action and emergency aid programme for Poland and Hungary (PHARE) that was later extended to other Central and Eastern European countries. The Seven recommended that the programme should balance political and economic reforms in such a way that Eastern European leaders could not use the danger of economic ruin as an excuse for undermining political reforms and re-establishing obsolete structures. The food aid for Poland enacted by the Commission in the summer of 1989 amounted to 228 million DM. But the extent of the disorganisation of the Polish economy was such[55] that in November experts, acting on behalf of the Commission and strongly backed by the EP, outlined a second emergency plan to help Poland over the winter.[56] At the same time, President Delors and the President of the Council, the French Foreign Minister, Roland Dumas, talked to the Warsaw and Budapest governments, emphasising that both governments had to accept the IMF's recovery programmes and obligations.

On 13 December, the Group of 24 (G24) discussed, for the first time at ministerial level, further economic measures with Hungarian and Polish participation, and extended the PHARE programme to other Central and Eastern European countries.[57] Their declaration reflected EC guidelines on 'specificity', stressing the 'readiness to coordinate assistance to the German Democratic Republic, Czechoslovakia, Bulgaria Yugoslavia and Romania, adapted to each country's own situation and on the basis of commitments from the countries concerned to political and economic reforms'.[58] All those to whom the programme had been addressed replied within two months. Commission officials then began fact-finding missions to see for themselves the state of the economies in Eastern Europe and to supplement the information provided by governments. The Soviet Union has been treated as a special case and remains outside PHARE's provisions. The Commission is primarily responsible for the management of the programme and has therefore to balance PHARE-related instruments and provisions with the Community's own established network of contacts with CMEA countries. The second ministerial meeting will be held in Brussels in June 1990.

The summit initiatives emphasise first of all that political criteria serve as a yardstick for the EC's willingness to intensify relations and broaden its assistance. The regular consideration of Eastern European affairs at the meetings of the Council of Foreign Ministers has given new impetus to the Community's search for a 'more real and apparent presence'. The EC budget provides for the creation of delegations in Moscow and Budapest in 1990 and subsequently in Warsaw in 1991. It is evident that within both the EPC and the Council frameworks there is a process of constant updating and reassessment of developments.

Despite these preoccupations with coordinating PHARE for Poland and Hungary and being busy with its bilateral contacts with CMEA countries, the Commission was forced to reconsider its global policy towards the East after the 'November revolution' in the GDR.[59] President Mitterrand, who held the EC Presidency, invited the heads government to the Elysée to respond immediately to the new developments in the heart of Europe. In part, too, though, the meeting was an effort to pre-empt the Soviet–American summit in Malta, where talks on the future of Europe could not be avoided. The French took the initiative to demonstrate that the EC made up the 'gravitational centre' of Europe and was mature enough to speak with one voice.[60] Because the Twelve's dinner proceeded so harmoniously, some observers deduced that perhaps questions such as the unification of Germany, its compatibility with progress towards European Union, and the openness towards Eastern Europe had not been debated. The Twelve again welcomed reform in Eastern Europe, especially with the breach of the Berlin Wall.

The Elysée meeting inevitably left open some issues and could not anticipate others. There were, for example, some divisions over the interpretations of the IMF's role, seemingly contradicting President Mitterrand who had emphasised the urgency of the need to assist the East irrespective of the fulfilment of the IMF's obligations.[61] On Poland, Mr Mitterrand proposed a stabilisation fund within the framework of the G24 but managed by the IMF with three prominent American, Japanese and French shares, but with no direct EC involvement.[62] Hungary would be granted a bridging loan of 1 billion ECU to shore up its currency, but only under the condition that Hungary concluded an agreement with the IMF.[63] No decision was taken then on Mr Mitterrand's idea of a special Bank for Eastern Europe modelled on existing regional development banks.[64] This proposal was approved in principle later at the Strasbourg European Council in December 1989 and, in March 1990, the finance officials of 40 countries and institutions (including the EIB, IMF and the World Bank) outlined a draft statute for the European Bank for Reconstruction and Development (EBRD). There was no agreement on whether the Soviet Union was to be a beneficiary or on where to locate the bank.[65]

Member states' perspectives on the EC's position

Whatever the operational problems of implementing concerted action, statements made by the member states hint at characteristic differences in the approach towards the EC/Twelve's Ostpolitik. West

Germany, with its long-standing preoccupation with Eastern Europe, pressed early and hard to bring about a concerted policy on the part of the Twelve. Mr Genscher was one of the first Western statesmen to suggest that Soviet proposals for normalisation and its 'new thinking' should be taken seriously. This appeal (sometimes termed 'Genscherism') was echoed by the President of the Commission who was alarmed by the approaches by the member states to Moscow and other Eastern European capitals to re-establish political and economic relations without proper coordination within the EC framework.[66] Since the autumn of 1989 Mr Genscher has pushed ahead, calling for a 'European plan of solidarity' with Eastern Europe on the scale of a Marshall Plan.[67] To quieten suspicion in the West, he also reaffirmed West Germany's adherence to NATO, quoting the Harmel Report of 1967 and the political goal of European Union as the predominant principles of West German foreign policy. However, his plea for 'open structures' within the EC was at first misunderstood as an indication of possible disassociation from closer integration.[68] Divergent interpretations of his remarks were clear at the Foreign Minister's meeting on 6 November, especially over the procedure and the timetable for bilateral EC–GDR contacts.[69] Despite unanimous Western approval of the changes in East Germany, there was also some irritation. A common language was none the less found in Paris, where the right of self-determination for both Germanies was confirmed, though within the framework of the CSCE process and the process of integration within the EC.[70]

In the United Kingdom, while reforms were welcomed, enthusiasm over their possible implications has been restrained. The British Government has tended to explore primarily national diplomatic channels, particularly with Hungary, Poland and the Soviet Union. The Prime Minister, Mrs Thatcher, somewhat flattered perhaps by Mr Gorbachev's special treatment of Soviet–British relations, had declared in 1984 that Mr Gorbachev was a man to do business with. In June 1989, she promised General Jaruzelski 'to lead a movement of Western countries to help Poland overcome its current situation and relaunch its economy'.[71] With the shift in the political constellation on the continent and with the EC as the major focus of foreign and security policy, Great Britain finds itself increasingly on the periphery in the West. The claims by the Prime Minister that Britain plays a leadership role are therefore difficult to comprehend.[72] Moreover, her attempts to hamper closer integration within the EC may weaken the British position in defining guidelines for a Western European Ostpolitik, including proposals for association agreements for the GDR, Poland and Hungary.[73]

France has shown some eagerness to join the FRG in a comprehensive and distinctive Community approach towards Eastern Europe. This was in part in recognition of the fact that France had somewhat neglected the region after the deterioration of East–West relations during the first half of the 1980s. Traditionally, Ostpolitik in France has meant predominantly Deutschlandpolitik. Mr Mitterrand's Paris summit initiative and the early announcement of his readiness to visit the Modrow Government in East Berlin illustrates the eagerness of the French to make a substantial contribution. Mr Mitterrand's plea for a European Training Foundation in favour of Poland and Hungary was agreed in principle at the Paris special summit and was included in the Strasbourg conclusions of the European Council.[74] His working meeting with Gorbachev in Kiev after the Malta US–Soviet summit focused attention on the 'German Question', the outcome of which was agreement that the question could only be settled in an overall European context. The Bonn–Paris axis, crucial for a Western European security policy and Ostpolitik, showed signs of fragility.[75]

Italy, aware of the needs of its Balkan neighbours, has supported the West German plea for an effective EC programme for Eastern Europe.[76] Spain has felt a considerable sense of identity with the reforming states, like Hungary, where transition from dictatorship to democracy has parallels with Spain in the post-Franco period. However, the smaller EC member states, like Portugal and Greece, may perceive the Eastern European countries as potential rivals on the European market.[77] The commitment towards Eastern Europe within the EC/Twelve reflects a 'division of labour' that flows from traditional foreign policy orientations and specific geopolitical interests. On the other hand, each member state is in the process of assessing the repercussions of the Eastern European revolution on the future of the Community.

Beyond the status quo: association and accession

In July 1989, President Bush reassured his Polish audience that 'in ... what you are doing, we have the unique opportunity to build a Europe ... which will be open, united and free'.[78] Today, architects, and especially bridge-builders, whether academics or political élites, are at work reshaping the map of Europe. Eastern Europe has imposed itself high on the agenda of Western European foreign policy. The deep involvement of the EC/Twelve in the international diplomatic framework gives it a strong position from which to define the range of options and measures in the new East–West relations. The Commission, in particular, finds itself in a new role as the operative hinge as well as the focus for concerted Western support and long-term policy towards Eastern Europe. When the Paris Summit of the Seven announced its declaration on East–West relations, the Commission made it known that it would have preferred a stronger emphasis on the European Community's special responsibility for Eastern Europe.[79]

To transform its 'special responsibility' for Eastern European affairs into a 'coherent and efficient' policy,[80] the Twelve were forced to react to the rapid succession of events. Conditions left little time or capacity to go ahead to 'shape events' as intended. The enhanced status of the EC as an international actor was created more by current challenges and less by its own decisions. It is also due to a gradual disengagement of the United States in European affairs that might lead to a new division of labour in the West with special areas and fields of responsibility.

In the light of the process of normalisation between the EC and the CMEA, it is very unlikely that this restricted group-to-group approach will be the driving force behind East–West relations (especially as the Commission tends to practise delaying tactics in this respect). The significance of the Joint Declaration lies, as J. Maslen has stressed, less in its content than in its existence.[81] However uncertain the CMEA's future, a new balance of external economic and political relations is emerging which favours an intensification of Western contacts. It is difficult to assess the extent to which political and economic ties will force the members of the CMEA to contribute to its restructuring within the framework of an 'integrated market'.[82] It cannot be taken for granted that the countries involved in the CMEA will act as a group in the future.

However, with the exception of the GDR, the Community tends to treat the countries of Eastern Europe as a group of states with converging structural problems and political options. The Twelve's confirmation in Dublin, in January 1990, that it would support a new type of association agreement under Article 238, as suggested by the Commission, was designed as an overall approach towards a disintegrating CMEA region.[83] The new agreements would not imply future membership of the EC but envisaged in 'the institutional aspects of these agreements a true body for dialogue and political and economic cooperation'[84].

If the options open to the countries of Eastern Europe are limited, one of the most attractive put forward is that of a free trade area which would give EFTA-type status to countries that succeed in their reform efforts, thereby ensuring their progressive reintegration into a future European Economic space.[85] The idea first gained momentum from the dynamism of the Single market project which forces even the Eastern Europe to adjust to the standards within the Community. Hungary's wish to join EFTA early leaves no doubt that it sees that organisation as a half-way house to its accession to the EC. However, the use of EFTA as a springboard for EC membership may be misconceived; such a strategy could lead to a dead-end or tempt the EC into passivity. On the other hand, such proposals are not so far-fetched; discussions on the possible accession of CMEA countries to the EC are no longer treated as a joke. Significantly, the Soviet Union, above all, gives the impression of considering a wider range of options. In contrast to his allies, Mr Gorbachev promoted the idea of developing ties between the CMEA and EFTA and using that channel, too, in the construction of new Europe.[86]

The proposal in the Report to the Trilateral Commission to offer a special association status on the basis of Article 238 covering only the economic dimension was quite ambitious at the time.[87] Such specifically shaped association status, with a mixture of institutionalised political dialogue, financial protocols and substantial cooperation provisions (on similar lines, perhaps, to elements of the EC's Mediterranean agreements — Mrs Thatcher even suggested the idea of association on the Turkish model)[88] may work well. President Delors explicitly spoke of association status with the possibility that this could lead to institutionalised access to the Single market and include political dialogue.[89]

Mr Delors also spoke of the need for a special treatment of the GDR which, besides the option of association, may join the EC as an ordinary member, or as part of a unified Germany. The question of the special nature of the East German case in the global approach towards CMEA countries remains a critical one for it stirs up emotions within governments and among people both in the East and West. A solution to the German question has always been regarded as the likely final step in overcoming the partition of Europe. However, the unpredicted acceleration of history and deepening relations between the two Germanies have upset this assumption. Despite agreement that both German states might exercise the right of self-determination, the partition of Germany has sometimes been perceived as a blessing in disguise. Chancellor Kohl's ten-point plan[90] foreseeing a confederal structures for a united Germany, as well as the so-called Genscher plan for negotiations with the Four Powers on the basis of the Ottawa formula of 'two plus four',[91] while constantly informing the Twelve of the process of unification, tried to pre-empt the more alarmist scenarios being discussed in some of its neighbours. The West nevertheless is exploring ways of anchoring Germany in the Western World.

All these scenarios indicate that traditional bloc and group patterns will be outdated by the end of the millennium. Because the map of Europe is being redrawn and the EC serves as the centre of gravity in all the envisioned designs, the Community must reflect on the political finality of these 'affiliation processes' which interfere and coincide with the leap to European Union. The question of the widening or deepening of the EC is also set against this background. These considerations highlight the unique quality and the challenge of the EC's dialogue with the CMEA and its members. The pan-European process touches on military and security aspects as well as the question of German unity. The coincidence of these processes may lead to a transformation of traditional actors, including the EC/Twelve, NATO, WEU, the Council of Europe, and the CSCE. The repercussions might even affect the institutional and material set up of the Community. The Delors strategy to combine the dynamism of change in Eastern Europe with a process of integration towards European Union backs this outlook. This constellation gives the EC's regional approach towards Eastern Europe its tremendous importance and specificity.

Eastern Europe has overcome its hermetic character and is looking for harmonisation and convergence with Western standards in political, social and economic terms. The Community has closed a gap in its external relations with the onset of the normalisation and even association process. It is in the heart of the process of designing policies for cooperation, confidence-building and even peaceful change in a post-Yalta Europe.

Notes

1 Unofficial English translation. The 14 theses on the European Community of the Institute of World Economy and International Affairs are published in *Mirovaja ekonomika i mezdunarodnoe otnosenijja* 12 (1988), pp. 5–18. A German version was printed in *Sowjetwissenschaft-Gesellschaftswissenschaftliche Beitrage* 3 (1989), pp. 268–81.

2 cf. M. S. Gorbachev, *Perestrojka i novoe myslenie dlja nasej strany i dlja vsego mira* (Moscow: Politizdat, 1987, pp. 46–52. Recently Timothy Garton Ash called these processes 'refolution': half-reform, half-revolution, see 'Revolution in Hungary and Poland', *The New York Review*, 17 August 1989, pp. 9–15.

3 The communiqué of the meeting of the Warsaw Pact members in July 1989 can be read as a revision of the doctrine (cf. Sovescanie politiceskogo konsul'tativnogo komiteta gosudarstv-ucastnikov varsavskogo dogovora, Bucharest, 7–8 July 1989, Moscow: *izdatel'stvopoliticeskoj literatury 1989*), and was confirmed at the Malta summit, cf. Europe, No. 5145, 5 December 1989, whereas e.g. the Trilateral Commission doubted the reliability of this course, see V. Giscard d'Estaing *et al.*, *Ost–West-Beziehungen. Ein Bericht an die trilaterale Kommission* (Bonn: Europa Union Verlag 1989), p. 14.

4 *Europe*/Documents, No. 1565, 12 July 1989.

5 ibid., p. 3. On new implications in the Soviet theory of international relations K.v. Beyme, 'Das "neue Denken" in Gorbatschows Außenpolitik', in M.Mommsen and H.-H. Schröder (eds), *Gorbatschows Revolution von oben* (Berlin: Ullstein, 1987), pp. 124–38; also Resolutions of the Congress of People's Deputies of the USSR, On Major Directions of the USSR's Domestic and Foreign Policy, in *Documents and Materials: Congress of People's Deputies of the USSR*, Moscow, Kremlin, May 25–9 June 1989 (Moscow: Novosti Press Agency Publishing House), 1989, pp. 96–112, esp. pp. 110–12.

6 See Report by M. Gorbachev, 'On the Major Directions of the USSR's Domestic and Foreign Policy', Moscow, 30 May 1989, in ibid., p. 34

7 cf. E. Schneider, *Moskau und die europäische Integration* (Munich, Vienna: R. Oldenbourg Verlag, 1977), pp. 75ff with special reference to the 17 theses of 1957 and the 34 theses of 1962.

8 cf. on the history of contacts most of all J. Maslen, 'The European Community's Relations with the State-Trading Countries of Europe 1984–1986', in F.G. Jacobs (ed.), *Yearbook of European Law 1986* (Oxford: Clarendon Press, 1987), p. 335–56; B. Repetzki, 'Der schwierige Weg zwischen der EWG und den europäischen RGW-Ländern', *Osteuropa-Wirtschaft*, No. 3 (1988), pp. 219–36, and S. Verny, *The EEC and the CMEA:*

The Problem of Mutual Recognition, Biblio-Flash, No. 24 (1989), pp. 25–37; B. May, 'Normalisierung der Beziehungen zwischen der EG und dem RGW', *Aus Politik und Zeitgeschichte*, No. 3 (1989), pp. 44–54, and A.Kolinski, 'EEC–Comecon: Difficulties in Reaching an Agreement', Vortrag im Europa Institut der Universität Saarbrücken, 8 February 1989, Saarbrücken, 1989.

9 The Commission told the CMEA Secretary several times that these enquiries should be addressed to the Commission, cf. J. Maslen (1987), op. cit., p. 336.

10 Gorbachev produced this formula before the French Parliament in October 1985; see also A. Bovin, 'Evropejskoe napravlenie', *Izvestija*, 25 September 1985.

11 Finland remained the only Western country to conclude a trade agreement with the CMEA (in 1973) despite Soviet efforts for an extension of the CMEA's authority on this field. cf. O.T. Bogomolov (red.), *Sovremennyj mir: internacionalizacija i otnosenija gosudartsv dvuch sistem* (Moscow: Mezdunarodnye otnosenija, 1988), p. 169.

12 With the submission of a draft declaration the CMEA pre-empted a second preparatory meeting proposed by the EC–Commission, cf. J. Maslen (1987), op. cit., p. 336.

13 ibid., p. 337.

14 J. Maslen, 'A Turning Point: Past and Future of the European Community's Relations with Eastern Europe', *Rivista di studi politici internazionale*, No. 4 (1988), p. 559. Nevertheless, most observers emphasise the impact of global political constellations on EC–CMEA relations.

15 Although a series of bilateral framework agreements on cooperation in selected areas were concluded bilaterally between CMEA members and EC member states during the 1970s.

16 See J. Maslen (1988), op. cit., p. 559, and more elaborate K. Schneider, *The Role of the European Community in East–West Economic relations: A Pan-European Economic Space?* (forthcoming London and Basingstoke: Macmillan Press, 1990). See also the detailed analysis of A. Inotai, 'Probleme der Wirtschaftsbeziehungen der europäischen RGW-Länder mit dem Westen', Stiftung Wissenschaft und Politik (Ebenhausen) Working Paper AZ 2515, April 1987, pp. 51ff.

17 A separate document was therefore needed for the creation of the joint committee to oversee the 1980 agreement with Romania. cf. *Official Journal*, L 352.

18 On anti-dumping measures against CMEA countries cf. from the Hungarian perspective A. Inotai, op.cit., p. 53.

19 S. Verny, op. cit., p. 29.

20 ibid., p. 30, and J. Maslen (1988), op. cit., p. 560.

21 S.Verny, op. cit., p. 30.

22 cf. for the history of these contacts from the CMEA's perspective, CMEA (ed.), *SEV-EES: V nacale puti (dokumenty i materialy)* (Moscow: 1988), pp. 6–8.

23 Joint Declaration annexed to the essay of J. Maslen (1988), op. cit., p. 577.

24 cf. J.Maslen (1987), op. cit., p. 340.

25 ibid., p. 340.

26 On the procedure, cf. ibid., p. 341.

27 See *Bulletin CEE* 5/1986, p. 2.2.3.7.

28 J. Maslen (1988), op.cit., p. 563.

29 J. Maslen (1987), op. cit., p. 340.
30 cf. *Eurostat, Außenhandel, Statistisches Jahrbuch 1988-6A* and *External Trade. Monthly Statistics* 12/89, Brussels and Luxembourg, 1989.
31 In 1987 exports to the CMEA market only amounted to 3.4 per cent (1975, 7.2 per cent) and imports 3.9 per cent (1975, 4.3 per cent).
32 cf. H. Schneider 'Über Wien nach Gesamteuropa? Der KSZE-Prozeß nach dem dritten Folgetreffen' *Integration* 2 (1989), pp. 47–60.
33 On the present state of the CMEA cf. A. Aslund, 'The Soviet Union Seeks a New Role for the CMEA', *Europe and the Soviet Union. Proceedings of the CEPS Fifth Annual Conference,* Vol. II (Brussels: CEPS-Publications, 1989), pp. 53–70.
34 cf. May, op. cit., pp. 48–9.
35 cf. the analysis of A. Inotai, op. cit., pp. 51.
36 A phrase taken up by Gorbachev in his speech held at the Parliamentary Assembly of the Council of Europe, *Europe*/Documents, No. 1565,op.cit., p. 5.
37 cf. Aslund, op. cit., pp. 63ff.
38 J. Maslen (1988), op.cit., p. 567.
39 *Europe*, No. 5141, 29 November 1989.
40 cf. *Europe*, No. 5206, 3 March 1990, and M. Beise, 'Die DDR und die Europäische Gemeinschaft', *Europa-Archiv* 4 (1990), p. 149ff.
41 cf. *Europe*, No. 5164, 4 January 1990.
42 Negotiations were also complicated by criticisms of Bulgaria for violating human rights in the treatment of the Turkish minority. cf. *Europe*, No. 5049, 3/4 July 1989, p. 6 and No. 5164, 4 January 1990.
43 cf. *Europe*, No. 5159, 22 December 1989 and No. 5177, 22/23 January 1990.
44 That future East–West trade will inevitably switch from barter trade to market-based exchange and competition is recognised by Eastern economics. cf. O.T. Bogomolov (red.), op.cit., p. 249.
45 cf. *Europe*, No. 5110, 13 October 1989 and No. 5141, 29 November 1989.
46 cf. *Europe*, No. 5147, 7 December 1989.
47 See *Europe*, No. 5049, 3/4 July 1989, pp. 5–6.
48 cf. K. Schneider, op. cit.
49 cf. *Europe*, No. 5144, 2 December 1989, No. 5154, 15 December 1989 and No. 5156, 18/19 December 1989.
50 cf. *Europe*, No. 5213, 14 March 1990. The European Parliament set up a temporary Committee to review the impact of German unification on the Community. It held its constitutive meeting on 2 March 1990, cf. *Europe*, No. 5206, 3 March 1990.
51 In this context it was without precedent that Mitterrand, in chair of the EC Presidency, and Chancellor Kohl both addressed the EP on 22 November 1989 which EP President Baron Crespo called a 'historic event'. cf. *Europe*, No. 5138, 24 November 1989 and *Frankfurter Allgemeine Zeitung*, 23 November 1989.
52 cf. *Europe*, No. 4853, 16 September 1988.
53 cf. for the EPC and Eastern Europe A. Pijpers *et al.*, (eds), *European Political Cooperation in the 1980s* (Dordrecht: Martinus Nijhoff, 1988), 'Chronology'.
54 On the results of the G-7 summit cf. *Neue Zürcher Zeitung*, 18 July 1989.
55 In 1989 Polish food imports amounted to 2.5 Mrd. DM, cf. *Frankfurter Allgemeine Zeitung*, 30 September 1989.
56 cf. concerning the EP *Süddeutsche Zeitung*, 16/17 September 1989; *Süddeutsche Zeitung*, 2 November 1989.

57 cf. *Europe*, No. 5138, 24 November 1989 and No. 5153, 14 December 1989.
58 cf. *Europe*/Documents, No. 1598, 22 February 1990. The memoranda are examined in the 'light of progress towards the implementation of political and economic objectives including the rule of law, respect for human rights, the establishment of a multi-party system, free elections and the establishment of a market economy', ibid., p. 3.
59 cf. *Frankfurter Allgemeine Zeitung*, 13 November 1989 and on the so-called 'weekend of reflection', cf. *Europe*, No. 5142, 30 November 1989.
60 cf. *Süddeutsche Zeitung*, 15 November 1989 and *Frankfurter Allgemeine Zeitung* , 14 November 1989.
61 cf. *Süddeutsche Zeitung,* 20 November 1989.
62 cf. Mitterrand's proposal when addressing the EP on 25 October, *Europe*/Documents, No. 1577, 3 November 1989, p. 7.
63 cf. *Europe*, No. 5147, 7 December 1989. It is a novelty that a third country is granted a loan guaranteed of EEC budget.
64 This measure would be separately installed from the EIB, which is received with some reservations e.g. by the United Kingdom, the Netherlands and the FRG. The EIB as well as non-European third countries like America and Japan are invited to participate, cf. *Europe*, No. 5143, 1 December 1989.
65 cf. *Süddeutsche Zeitung*, 13 March 1990 and *International Herald Tribune*, 12 March 1990. The bank will hold capital of about $12 billion and offers credits for private as well as public activities. The United States will allow the Soviet Union only to borrow money from the EBRD to their paid-in capital, cf. *Financial Times,* 19 March 1990.
66 cf. *Europe*, No. 4957, 17 February 1989, pp. 5–6. In a contribution for the Soviet journal *International Affairs*, the Belgian Foreign Minister, Leo Tindemans, emphasised that for smaller countries, like Belgium, the concerted Ostpolitik within the EC/Twelve framework is of vital interest: 'The Belgian Segment of European Politics', *International Affairs*, Moscow (9) September 1989, pp. 80–6. The Belgian Foreign Minister also several times criticised the larger member states for deliberately adopting a bilateral approach and asked for 'common orientations' to guide national policies.
67 cf. *Süddeutsche Zeitung*, 21 September 1989 and 16 October 1989; and his Interview with *Die Zeit*, 'Ein Prozeß der europäischen Selbstbestimmung', Nr. 43, 20 October 1989.
68 cf. *Frankfurter Allgemeine Zeitung*, 14 October 1989; *Europe*, No. 5112, 16/17 October 1989.
69 See the dispute between the Commissioner Andriessen and Bangemann and the 'misunderstanding' between the Foreign Ministers Genscher and Hurd, *Frankfurter Allgemeine Zeitung*, 8 November 1989.
70 cf. Conclusions of the Council meeting on 8/9 Décember 1989, in *Europa-Archiv*, 1 (1990), pp. D.13f.
71 *Europe*, No. 5034, 12/13 June 1989, p. 6.
72 cf. William Wallace in *The Guardian*, 11 November 1989.
73 cf. *Frankfurter Allgemeine Zeitung*, 15 November 1989.
74 *Europe*, No. 5144, 2 December 1989; it will act in close cooperation with the CEDEFOP, headquartered in West Berlin.
75 Different perceptions of a 'European confederation', announced by Mr Mitterrand in his New Year's message has not been able to be fully reconciled between the French President and Chancellor Kohl so far. cf. *Europe*, No. 5164, 4 January 1990. cf. on the development of recent

Franco-German relations, R. Picht, 'Deutsch–französische Beziehungen nach dem Fall der Mauer: Die Achse knirscht', *Integration* 2 (1990), pp. 47ff.

76 cf. the group of four (Italy, Hungary, Yugoslavia, Austria) — initiative of de Michelis (meeting in Budapest 11/12 November 1989) esp. G. de Michelis 'Ein Ansatz für Mitteleuropa', *Die Zeit*, Nr. 46, 10 November 1989; and Andreotti on the eve of his meeting with Gorbachev prior to the Malta summit, *Europe*, No. 5140, 27/28 November 1989. cf. on the two joined declarations *Europe*, No. 5143, 1 December 1989.

77 cf. W. Kostrzewa and H. Schmieding, 'Die EFTA-Option für osteuropa: Eine Chance zur wirtschaftlichen Reintegration des Kontinents', (Kiel: Kiel Discussion Papers No. 154, 1989), esp. pp. 12–13.

78 *Europe*, No. 5055, 12 July 1989, p. 4.

79 *Europe*, No. 5060, 19 July 1989, p. 8.

80 After the special Paris summit President Delors reported to the EP that discussions on Eastern Europe still showed too rigid a division of labour by the Twelve within the framework of Political Cooperation and in what is purely Community-oriented. cf. *Europe*, No. 5141, 29 November 1989.

81 J. Maslen (1988), op. cit., p. 564.

82 *Europe*/Documents, No. 1565, op. cit., p. 5.

83 cf. *Europe*, No. 5177, 22/23 January.

84 Mr Delors before the European Parliament, 17 January 1990, cf. *Europe*, No. 5174, 18 January 1990.

85 cf. K. Schneider, op. cit. and by the same author, 'Einige Aspekte der künftigen beziehungen der Europäischen Gemeinschaft zu Osteuropa', in H.-D. Jacobsen *et al.* (eds), *Perspektiven für Sicherheit und Zusammenarbeit in Europa*, Bonn, 1988, pp. 391–405; see from the Eastern angle M. Dobroczynski and R. Lawniczak, 'RGW-Integration und internationale Wirtschaftsorganisationen', ibid., pp. 354–65.

86 *Europe*/Documents, No. 1565, op. cit.

87 cf. V. Giscard d'Estaing *et al.*, op. cit., p. 28.

88 House of Commons, 13 November, cf. *Frankfurter Allgemeine Zeitung*, 15 November 1989.

89 cf. *Europe* No. 5177, 22/23 January 1990 and before the EC Economic and Social Committee, cf. *VWD-Europa*, 2 February 1990.

90 cf. *Europe*, No. 5141, 29 November 1989.

91 The formula to discuss the 'external aspects' of German unification was invented at the NATO–Warsaw Pact open sky meeting in Ottawa (13 February 1990), cf. on 'two plus four' diplomacy *International Herald Tribune*, 10/11 March 1990.

Part III
The institutional framework: dialogue and the European actors

10 The Commission: protagonists of inter-regional cooperation

Simon Nuttall

The Commission would stress that the Community, born of its members' political will to escape from the deep divisions which had marked their history, has demonstrated that regional cooperation and regional economic integration are powerful factors for peace, stability, greater democracy and prosperity.[1]

Introduction

The Commission's policy in the field of regional cooperation is a myth: it has none. Or to be more precise, the Commission has a broad aspiration towards regional integration. Since it is a part of human nature to wish others to be like oneself, the Community seeks to export the mode it has chosen of organizing itself. This can be justified by arguments, by no means untenable, that in this mode lies the future of international relations in an increasingly multipolar world. But a study of the different cases of group-to-group dialogue shows that underlying the broad aspirations are a number of other, sometimes baser, motives. These are more political than they are economic.

A selection of theories

'Everything's got a moral, if you can only find it.'[2]

A number of explanations have been adduced for the Community's policy of group-to-group dialogue. Some apply to dialogue with third countries as much as to dialogue with groups; some are contradictory; none is wholly wrong; none is adequate in itself. The truth no doubt lies in different combinations in different cases. Here are some of the most commonly aired arguments.

The Community as civil power

The Community is an attractive partner in international relations because, while being a powerful force, it has no military dimension. It is thus safe and respectable for third countries to establish with it a relationship of dialogue in a way in which (until recently) it has not been possible to establish a relationship with the United States or the Soviet Union without coming off the fence in the confrontation between the great powers. This attraction will be all the more powerful in the case of regional groupings, which are more likely to be civilian in nature than military and hence to be interested in a 'civil power' relationship. Messages of support and appreciation from the Community have been sent to, and received by, the Summit meetings of the neutral and non-aligned countries, whose public sessions have been attended by the Ambassador of the Presidency on behalf of the Twelve. This attractiveness has been exploited by the Community in order to build up its position on the world stage, and to promote its image as a force for stability and peace.

The perception of the Community as a 'civil', almost 'neutral', grouping is the more surprising since 11 out of its 12 member states are members of the Atlantic Alliance and the Community itself has consistently supported the Western line, including statements on security questions like the INF negotiations in Geneva. It is a tribute to the institutional independence of the Community, which can be perceived to stand apart from the policies of its members either separately or collectively in other fora (NATO, WEU). Since this perception is apparently not dependent on the specific policies adopted by the Community it must arise from its institutional nature as an integrationist regional grouping.

An added attraction of the Community, comparable to its 'civil power' image, is the stability of its policies. These are not so variable as in member states, which are subject to changes in political fortunes and to more immediate response to circumstances. This is true both of European Political Cooperation and of the Community in the narrow sense. It is popularly believed that policies in EPC are conditioned by the lowest common denominator. Experience shows that this is not so; rather it is the case that EPC policies follow the median of the range of national foreign policies. While therefore capable of shifting, they vary less than national policies. In the Community *stricto sensu*, the institutional role of the Commission as both instigator and executant of policy makes for long-term stability.

A basis for equal partnership

An additional attraction of regional dialogue can be found in the way most regional groupings organize themselves. By their structure they safeguard the rights and interests of their members, regardless of the latter's relative influence and weight, and the degree to which they would otherwise be politically isolated from their partners in the grouping. This is clear in the case of the Community. The smaller countries like Ireland, Denmark, Portugal and the Benelux countries readily admit that the mechanisms of the Community both protect and enhance their interests. Similarly, regional integration in Central America is a guarantee against the political isolation of Nicaragua. SARC ought to provide a safeguard against excessive dominance by India. Other examples could be found. On the supposition that regional groupings can through dialogue mutually support each other's systems and approach, there are grounds for the smaller countries within the groupings to be particularly attracted to dialogue, in their own interests.

Paradoxically, this advantage is increased by relative institutional inadequacy. The present European institutions (of both the Community and EPC) have as their prime function mediation between national interests. Stronger institutions on more supranational lines would certainly produce stronger policies of the Community as such, but they would be less responsive to members' individual interests, whereas it is argued that one advantage of regional groupings is precisely this responsiveness.

The mirror image

The founding fathers of the Community were well aware that they were creating a new type of organization, which by pooling strategic resources (coal and steel, nuclear power) made it impossible for the participating countries to renew their former hostilities. The experiment worked: not only has war within the Community become unthinkable, but the period of growth and economic prosperity in Western Europe which followed the establishment of the Communities has been ascribed in large part to their beneficial effect.

These lessons have not been lost on other regions. The realization that most nation states are too small to sustain economic development has led many of them to study the Community as a model for their own development and therefore survival. ASEAN, the Central American countries, the Gulf Cooperation Council, have all wanted to know how the Community works. The PECC, when harbouring thoughts of a more integrated structure, quotes the European Community as a model. The Commission encourages this, in a missionary spirit: 'Go, and do thou likewise.' Imitation stops short, however, at transfer of sovereignty. In no other regional grouping have member states pooled their decision-making powers to the extent that they have in the Community. Failure to realize the importance of this step — fuelled by the idiosyncratic views held by some of the Community's member states about the organization they belong to — has led to complacency about the degree of commitment required to forge an organization of equivalent institutional strength.

A catalyst for intra-regional cooperation

Regional groupings may admire the Community as a model without having a dialogue with it. An advantage of group-to-group dialogue is that it is a potential instrument for encouraging progress towards integration in the dialogue partner; it also helps preserve equality of treatment.

The Commission tries to manipulate the financial component of group-to-group dialogue in such a way as to promote intra-regional cooperation. A sum of one billion ECU was set aside for this purpose in Lomé III; priority is given in the aid programme for Central America to projects which bridge national borders. In addition to encouraging integration, aid given on an intra-regional basis can well be more effective. The 1982 review of Lomé observed that too often the projects and schemes financed proved to be ineffective or ill adapted *because they were insufficiently integrated.*

To deal with countries in a group as members of that group, not as individuals, increases the chances of non-discriminatory treatment. All the ACP countries, if dealt with as such, must be dealt with in the same way, namely that laid down in the Lomé Convention. There is less temptation to deal with, say, Uganda (in the past) or Ethiopia in a discriminatory way than if the countries concerned were handled exclusively in the light of their own political circumstances. Similarly, Nicaragua's membership of the group of Central American countries with which the Community deals is a guarantee of non-discriminatory treatment.

The perceived advantage of membership of the group should increase its attractiveness to its members.

A paradigm of cohesion

Article 30.5 of the Single European Act provides that 'the external policies of the European Community and the policies agreed in European Political Cooperation must be consistent'. The Presidency and the Commission are responsible for seeking and maintaining this consistency. This requirement is to be seen not only in the negative sense of ensuring there is no contradiction between the policies worked out in the two frameworks, but also in the positive sense of finding opportunities for interaction between the two to produce something like an integrated European foreign policy.

Regional dialogue is a good way of doing this and is encouraged by the Commission so that its potentiality for cohesion can be exploited. As often as not, a political dialogue goes side by side with the economic dialogue. This is the case with ASEAN; in the case of Central America, the interaction between the political and economic parts of the dialogue is the prime feature of Community policy; only the inability of member states to work out a substantive policy on South Africa prevents a similar avowed approach to the dialogue with SADCC.

'Because they are there'

The Community's dialogue with other regions has increased enormously in the last decade. That is partly because so many regional groupings have come into being. It is one of the servitudes of itinerant diplomacy that diplomatic contact is the norm and the absence of it an expression of political displeasure. If a regional grouping exists, one must — so goes the general sentiment — have a dialogue with it, unless one wishes to make a gesture by refraining from doing so. It is there, so talk to it.

The Community dimension

Comprising all the motives that have been described so far, there is a general underlying feeling that in maintaining a dialogue with other regional groupings the Community is engaging in a form of diplomacy which is somehow different and more elevated than that practised by its member states. These maintain contacts with other countries, or are members of international organizations, but are too small to have a dialogue with a region. The United States and Japan, for example, both maintain a structured relationship with ASEAN (the post-Ministerial dialogue) but member states of the Community do not. That is left to the wider Community framework (Presidency and Commission).

This exclusiveness enables, or should enable, the Community to conduct a policy of a different nature and on a broader scale than the national policies of its member states, governed as they must be by bilateral considerations.

The Commission's policy

The considerations described above are of course valid for the Community and all its institutions and members, not just for the Commission alone. They are, however, felt with particular force by the Commission as the body which feels it has the primary responsibility for forging a personality for the Community and which must bear the burden of execution of Community policies. It might therefore be expected that the Community's group-to-group dialogues are particularly marked by the Commission's part in establishing and conducting them. But it is not the case, at any rate if we expect as a consequence to see primarily economic dialogues concerned with trade relations. Except for the earliest dialogues, with ACP and EFTA, the agreements are non-preferential, and in most cases the motivation appears to have been mainly political, although not always originating in EPC.

The Community's dialogue partners differ widely, as do the circumstances of each dialogue, and it is wrong to generalize. The substance of several of these dialogues is described elsewhere in the book; the purpose of this section, by separating out the predominant features of each one, is to suggest the reasons for which it was set up in the first place.

The origins of dialogue

That hardy perennial of European foreign policy, the Euro-Arab Dialogue, has never served any of the purposes for which it was intended and yet has obstinately refused to wither away. It is, on the European side, a dialogue which is economic in substance and yet political in intention while hesitating to embark on political subjects. In spite of its primarily economic nature it originated in Political Cooperation and has been largely directed from that forum.

Launched in the winter of 1973 in the aftermath of the Arab–Israeli war of the time, the purpose of the dialogue, as far as the Europeans were concerned, was to secure future oil supplies at reasonable prices and to recycle Arab capital into European industry. The Arabs, on the other hand, were looking for political support in the Middle East conflict which the Europeans were not sufficiently united in their views to give. This dichotomy has persisted to the present day, bringing to nought successive attempts to revive the dialogue. The fourth meeting of the General Commission in Athens in December 1983 ended in failure because of inability to agree on a political text. Subsequent efforts, notably under the Dutch Presidency of spring 1986, to begin a political dialogue through the Troika formula foundered on political difficulties with Syria.

The Commission's concern in the early days of the dialogue, which coincided with the early growth of Political Cooperation after enlargement, was to ensure that it was not left out especially when economic questions were being handled. This led to the particularly Byzantine structure of the dialogue apparatus on the European side, which included two coordinating groups, one in EPC and one in the Council, and a plethora of working parties, some chaired by the Commission and others, on an *ad personam* basis, by experts from member states.

After a burst of activity in the first two or three years, inspired in particular by Mr Klaus Meyer, at the time Deputy Secretary General of the Commission and thus the Commission's representative in the Political Committee, the dialogue dribbled away into the sands. Although the structures were kept in existence, and the dialogue retains its potential for group-to-group contacts with the Arab world, it has never in fact served this purpose. The Europeans' unwillingness to meld the economic and political aspects of the dialogue was one reason; another, at least as important, is the fact that the Arab countries are at least as disparate, if not more so, than the Europeans. The formal interlocutor is the Arab League, together with its member states, but the inability of that body to sow the seeds of integration in the Arab world has had its effect on the Euro-Arab Dialogue as well as more widely.

The first *Lomé Convention*, concluded in 1975, technically post-dates the Euro-Arab Dialogue, but as successor to the Yaoundé Conventions has a long previous history, which has stamped its character. Both Yaoundé and Lomé are ways of expressing in the Community the post-colonial relationship. The importance of Lomé is the immeasurably greater size and spread of the grouping with the advent of the former British colonies following enlargement, which changed the nature of the grouping. Whereas the francophone African countries had a perceivable identity of culture and interest, it can be doubted whether the Lomé ACP participants can be counted as a regional grouping at all, and thus whether the Lomé Convention should be discussed here as an example of group-to-group dialogue.

It is certainly the case that the Commission has framed the rules of the Lomé partnership, and conducted the dialogue accordingly, in such a way as to bring out some of the advantages of group dialogue mentioned above, particularly the guarantee of non-discrimination. And it may be that the existence of the structure, as the vehicle for development aid, has at least a sub-regional integrative effect through the encouragement of cross-border projects.

The Commission has also insisted on keeping the dialogue a purely economic one. Any attempt to inject a political dimension would have met with resistance from the ACP countries themselves. This was shown by the furore which greeted the Pisani idea of a 'policy dialogue' launched when Lomé III was being negotiated — it had to be explained that it meant a 'dialogue on (development) policies', not a 'political dialogue' — and by the emasculated reference to human rights which was all that could be put into Lomé III.

At the same time, the ACP countries are not sufficiently homogenous to be able to conduct a political dialogue. The only subject on which they are certain to have a common view is South Africa, and it is significant that on this question at least there is a demand for dialogue with the Twelve. The Twelve have been slow in responding, because of the difficulty of reaching a substantial consensus, but on a number of occasions the matter has at least been aired between the two parties. It has been treated more openly in the Twelve's dialogue with the Front Line States, which may be seen as the political persona of SADCC.

The dialogue with *ASEAN*, which has been taken by some to be the paradigm of all others, had a mixed parentage. The impetus began on the economic side. Contacts with the Community were initiated in 1972 by ASEAN. Discussion proceeded in the following years as ASEAN's own institutions developed. The breakthrough came following the ASEAN Summit at Bali in 1976, when the ASEAN countries sought to broaden their contacts with both the Community Institutions and the nine member states. The idea of a joint Ministerial meeting was put forward by Mr Genscher on his visit to the region in 1977 and such a meeting eventually took place in November 1978.

It was at this meeting that it was decided to negotiate a cooperation agreement, which was concluded in March 1980, dealing exclusively with economic matters. It contains no elements of a political dialogue, nor is there a separate agreement dealing with this. The practice has grown up, however, of regular Ministerial meetings at which both political and economic questions are discussed.

As in the case of Lomé, the relationship with ASEAN is economic in form but political in intent. ASEAN is not, as a grouping, of overriding economic importance for the Community. Although it is an important source of raw materials, their supply is neither more nor less secure as a result of the Cooperation Agreement. In 1981, the year after the Agreement was concluded, trade with ASEAN amounted to only 2.7 per cent of the Community's total foreign trade; it was the member states, rather than the Commission, which pressed for the Agreement and brought it about.

What, then, were the political motives for the Agreement? In his speech in Kuala Lumpur in 1974, Sir Christopher Soames, in addition to recognizing ASEAN's role in forming 'an area of peace and economic cooperation in this part of world', admitted that some countries which had had traditional exports to the United Kingdom, like Malaysia and Singapore, had been left out of the ACP club and, together with the other ASEAN members, were entitled to arrangements to obviate any unfavourable effects of the common external tariff. This obligation had been acknowledged in the Joint Declaration of intent adopted on the occasion of enlargement.

At the same time, there was a feeling on the European side that, in an area of political tension, their traditional influence had been slipping in the face of a growing Japanese and American presence. The establishment of a relationship with ASEAN would give that organization's members the choice of a 'third option' — neither Japan nor the United States, nor of course the Soviet Union.

It was also believed that, given support, ASEAN was itself a factor for stability in the region and therefore of political interest to the Europeans. This was adumbrated in Mr Genscher's speech to the ASEAN Ministers in Brussels in November 1978: 'ASEAN thus contributes to increasing stability in the whole region and to improving conditions for a lasting peace. These two factors are also of vital interest to us Europeans. We know that tensions and armed conflicts in other parts of the world risk damaging our own security interests.' Two days later, Roy Jenkins expressed a more classical approach:

The Community has always been in favour of regional cooperation because we firmly believe that such cooperation does not only contribute significantly to the economic development of the individual countries of the grouping but is an important factor for political stability and peace. From the formation of ASEAN we in the Community have always sought to treat with ASEAN as a region since we from our own experience have learnt that an external stimulus can often support internal cooperation.

The dialogue with *Central America* was a totally different kettle of fish. From the start, its motivation has been avowedly and unashamedly political. It began with the launching of the Contadora process in early 1983, which rapidly led to an expression of support from the European Council at Stuttgart in June of that year. This declaration laid particular stress on the need to find a solution for the region's tension through economic and social progress (a covert expression of support for political reform), perhaps unconsciously reflecting the 'civil power' nature of the Community and certainly providing a rationale for the second element in the Community's approach to the region, the increase of development aid.

The idea of a dialogue was pressed hard by Mr Genscher and Mr Cheysson, then Foreign Minister of France, who engaged in active diplomacy in the region. The running was made by member states rather than the Commission, which opportunistically seized on the political impetus to achieve a strengthening of the economic relationship it had been trying to bring about for some time. Whatever the motives on the European side, the Central Americans certainly found some attraction in a public relationship with a grouping which was neither the United States nor the Soviet Union. At all events, President Monge of Costa Rica invited the European Foreign Ministers to meet their Central American colleagues, including Nicaragua, in Costa Rica in September 1984. This Conference became 'San José I', the first of an annual series.

A comparison of the speeches given by Mr Genscher and Commissioner Pisani in San José is instructive. The Federal Foreign Minister's text sets out almost all the reasons for group-to-group dialogue, set in the specific context of Central America:

— only a political dialogue can open the way to cooperation among countries, based on mutual respect and trust;
— mutual respect and trusts are the conditions for regional cooperation, as no one knows better than the Europeans;
— a dialogue with the Community is only possible when the partner is a regional unit; the formation of a Community in Central America would open the way to political and economic independence;
— the Conference should lay the foundation for a regional cooperation agreement.[3]

Mr Genscher went on to set out the political conditions for a dialogue: free elections, pluralist democracy and respect for human rights. This was a warning to both extremes in the Central American troubles, and a plank of the Community's stand. It balanced the final important element in the speech, the offer of support for the diversification of the foreign relations of the Central American countries.

Mr Pisani's speech on the same occasion was pitched on a higher philosophical plane, but the same messages shone through the diaphanous periods. Great stress was laid on the Community's success, through unity in diversity, in preserving peace in its region. The Central Americans were urged to do likewise, but to ward off an external rather than an internal threat:

C'est dans la mesure où les pays d'Amérique centrale adopteront clairement et sans retour un pacte du type et de l'esprit de celui que les pays européens ont adopté entre eux que la présence de douze ministres et d'un commissaire européen doit prendre sa vraie signification. Car c'est sans doute dans le mesure où cette solidarité centro-américaine s'affirmera et s'organisera que le risque des interventions extérieures que chacun redoute sera réellement écarté.

Mr Pisani went on to develop the argument that the instability of the region stemmed from economic and social causes and urged the Central American countries to develop progressively a regional common market. The Commission was ready to encourage this effort by assistance to export promotion (tariff reductions had to be excluded because of the sensitive nature of the products on the Community market) and by increasing development aid (contrary to the Commission's hopes, the Council had not yet taken a decision on this).

The development of the dialogue continued on the broad lines set out in San José I. An economic Cooperation Agreement was accompanied by a political dialogue, instituted by a formal act but not, as the Commission would have preferred but did not formally propose, by a clause in the Agreement itself.

Both the economic and the political dialogue have served their purpose in encouraging regional integration. On the economic side, the increased aid (in the end it was doubled) was devoted as far as possible to intra-regional projects. On the political side, it was noted with appreciation by the Europeans that the very fact that political meetings with the Twelve had to be held at regular intervals coerced the Central Americans into meeting themselves beforehand, in order to present an agreed line to the Europeans. Left to themselves, they would probably not have done this; the political dialogue has made a real contribution to regional stability. Likewise, the agreement in principle to set up a directly elected Central American Parliament would probably not have been taken had it not been for pressure from Mr Cheysson, by then a Commissioner again, and from the European Parliament, which conducts its own dialogue with the region. Europe was seen to be a model it was politic to imitate.

While to all appearances economic, and couched largely in an economic framework, the dialogue with the *Gulf Cooperation Council* has strong political undertones and would not have seen the light of day without a political dialogue.

This is one of the few cases in which the initiative to propose a dialogue came overwhelmingly from the Community side. Reflection in the Commission was triggered off by the need to find a solution to the difficulties created for relations with Saudi Arabia by the repeated reimposition, early in each year, of the tariff on certain petroleum products after the GSP ceiling had been reached. The approach espoused by Mr Cheysson was to offer a free trade agreement to the region as a whole. This scheme had advantages and disadvantages: a special trading relationship ensuring the supply of petroleum and petroleum products would be to the advantage of the Community as a whole, but not to those member states with significant petrochemical industries. The compromise proposal was to offer a non-preferential trade agreement, leaving open the possibility at a later stage of a free trade area with the GCC.

In addition to the economic considerations, some additional elements were in play connected with the mechanics of integration. The GCC was a newly created regional grouping, with which the Community's relations had so far been limited to contacts on technical questions (the mechanics of regional integration) between the Commission and the GCC Secretariat. Moreover, with a few exceptions (Iraq, South Yemen, Libya), the members of the GCC were the only members of the Arab League with which the Community had no agreement; this was felt to be a gap which had to be filled.

The primary impulse, however, came from political and strategic facts, resulting from the second oil shock and the outbreak of the Iran–Iraq war. Since the Euro-Arab Dialogue was stalled, the Community saw that greater stability of oil supplies depended on placing EC–Gulf relations on a more direct and positive basis. The Iran–Iraq war, by encouraging the development of the GCC itself, helped establish the other pillar. There was consequently an interest, particularly on the part of the Federal Republic of Germany, in constructing a relationship with the new grouping on the southern shores of the Gulf.

Notwithstanding these political considerations, the discussions in the Council on the Commission's proposal were at an impasse when in September 1987 the Foreign Ministers of the Community had an EPC luncheon in New York with their GCC colleagues. A *coup de force* by Mr Genscher led to some rather startled European Ministers finding themselves committed to negotiations with the GCC within a month. In fact the negotiating directives were adopted by the Council in December and rapidly led to an agreement.

In addition to the first phase economic provisions, the dialogue also included a political element on the Central American model. This provides for annual meetings; in addition, the informal luncheons in New York continue, and an EPC Troika meeting has been held.

The dialogue with *CMEA* has followed a different pattern from those with other regional groupings for essentially political reasons. It would have been quite conceivable, following the green light given by Mr Gorbachev to the establishment of relations with the Community and the conclusion of non-sectoral agreements, for the process to have been placed squarely within the CMEA, as a corresponding regional grouping with a vocation, however imperfectly fulfilled, to regional integration. Following its own logic, the Community should have welcomed this opportunity. It did not do so. It is sometimes claimed that the absence of supranational competence on the part of the CMEA to commit its member states on economic questions makes it impossible to conclude an agreement with it. This is formally correct, but a similar situation in other cases, most notably that of ASEAN, has not prevented imaginative solutions from being found which preserve the advantages of the regional framework. A more cogent reason was the unwillingness to encourage the development in Eastern Europe of a powerful economic bloc dominated by the Soviet Union. Nor was this concern confined to the Community; it was largely shared by most of the members of the CMEA. This in itself weighed heavily with the Community in settling its own policy.

The policy of the Commission and the Community has therefore been to conclude agreements individually with the East European countries, each one adapted to the circumstances of the case. Insistence on the East European side, however, that an arrangement with the CMEA should be arrived at at least in parallel with the bilateral negotiations has meant that some attention has had to be paid to the question, resulting in a rather broad joint declaration excluding specific operational economic arrangements, to be followed up with meetings from time to time. There is no corresponding political dialogue; that is left to member states to conduct, in EPC, with the Soviet Union alone.

The dialogue with *EFTA* has been left to the last because it is in almost all ways different from all the others described so far. EFTA in its present shape is the rump of the original organization left when several of its members defected to the Community; it owed its existence in the first place to the setting up of the Community, being founded in antithesis to it; its members have few other interests or links in common and have come together for the sole purpose of dealing with the Community; yet it is more closely linked to the Community, through bilateral agreements, than any other partners; and as European neighbours of the Community sharing its commitment to Western democratic values and to economic liberalism, its members have a right to expect the closest possible relationship.

For many years the smooth functioning of the bilateral agreements seemed adequate to maintain the Community/EFTA relationship. When it became plain, however, that the Community intended to move beyond a customs union (which EFTA itself is not) to a fully integrated economic space, the alarm bells began to ring and prompted the EFTA countries to engage in thought about their future situation and relationship. The 1984 Luxembourg Declaration set a climate of opinion and a set of objectives, but not a framework for future dialogue of the intensity which will be necessary, particularly regarding fixing of standards and participation in joint R & D, let alone foreign policy questions.

The initiative made by President Delors in his speech to the European Parliament in January 1989 was an attempt to encourage reflection on the shape of this framework, so far lacking. The future framework will need to be of a kind to accommodate satisfactorily countries which, although possible future members of the Community, either do not wish or are not able to seek membership. In this it will differ totally from the Community's dialogue with any other part of the world.

Conclusions

Extraordinary how potent cheap music is[4]

As the initiator and executant of Community policy, with a standing interest in developing specific functions of the Community, the Commission of all the Community institutions can be expected to be particularly sensitive to the various motivations for group-to-group dialogue described in the early part of this chapter, political as well as economic. Yet this is difficult to document: sometimes it appears as though the Commission is concerned with an apparently minor aspect of the dialogue, such as the need to cope with the implications of enlargement for South East Asia in 1974 and the GSP problem with Saudi Arabia in the mid-1980s. These were the grains of sand around which grew the pearls of the ASEAN and GCC dialogues. And yet the Commission was fully aware of the broader geo-strategic aspects. Indeed, the case studies show that economic motives were rarely if ever primordial in the rationale of dialogue with groups (whatever may have been the case with agreements with individual countries) and certainly never exclusive. The political motivation invariably predominated.

A second point is that, although the Commission is technically the initiator of policy, the origins of policy formation are a good deal more complex and subtle than that. There is an input from member states, Parliament and public opinion; less so from the economic and social actors. Sometimes the Commission's approach is opportunistic, as in the case of Central America in which the political interest was exploited to extract more funds from the budgetary authority. The Commission's subsequent activity on dialogue with the Latin Americans in general owed much to pressure from Spain, culminating in the Spanish Presidency in the first half of 1989. The intensity of the work done on relations with Eastern Europe was largely dictated by the interest of the Federal Republic, with its special view of East–West relations, although the form of the dialogue was also partially determined by other considerations including commercial policy which the Commission was concerned to put forward. The form of the Euro-Arab Dialogue was affected by the Commission's concern to stake out Community territory in the early days of development of Political Cooperation. The political justification of Lomé has always been recognized, but the Commission's policy as executive of the EDF has been deliberately concentrated on developmental, i.e. non-political activities — which has not excluded from time to time achieving political results, an apparently growing tendency. The EFTA dialogue has throughout been part of an attempt to resolve internal difficulties, rather than a wish to have a structured relationship with a free-standing regional grouping.

In the face of the evidence for a diversity of motivations and influence, which comes out of the case studies, what weight can be attached to declarations of principle by the Commission, like the quotation which stands at the head of this chapter, but which have been a regular feature since the Commission adopted a policy of support for regional integration on the part of other groupings in April 1974? Is this just rhetoric, and the Commission's policy a myth? Perhaps so, but myths can be extraordinarily potent and by dint of repetition become reality.

It is too often thought that a European foreign policy will look something like a national foreign policy, but at the European rather than the national level. This is not only insufficiently ambitious but at the current stage of institutional development of the Community likely to fail. Regional groupings take the edge off national ambitions and homogenize policy in the good sense of making it more even and predictable. In the case of the Community, a special quality could be given its foreign policy because of its attraction as civil power.

The Single European Act recognized dialogue with regional groupings as an element of a European foreign policy (Article 30.8: the Commision was in the forefront of delegations at the Intergovernmental Conference in favour of the addition of this element). In addition, the preamble to the SEA sets out what could in itself be an agenda for a foreign policy particularly suitable to be deployed in regional dialogue:

— by acting with consistency and solidarity, protect more effectively Europe's common interests and independence;
— display the principles of democracy and compliance with the law and human rights;
— contribute to the preservation of international peace and security in accordance with undertakings under the UN Charter.

To achieve such a step forward in the formation of a European foreign policy will require foresight and determination on the part not only of the Commission but of the other actors on the European institutional stage.

Notes

1 Statement by Mr Matutes, 'The Commission welcomes moves by Arab countries on regional integration', Brussels, 20 February 1989 (IP [89] 93).
2 Lewis Carroll, *Alice in Wonderland*, Ch. 9.
3 Mr Genscher quoted the precedents of the agreements with ASEAN and with the ANDEAN Pact. Disappointing the hopes placed in it, the latter never became more than a vehicle for limited economic cooperation with the Commission, largely because of the disunion of the Pact's members.
4 Noel Coward, *Private Lives*, Act 1.

Appendix

The EC/Twelve's dialogues with other groups of states — an overview

1 REGIONAL	2 TYPE OF DIALOGUE	3 FREQUENCY	4 BASE	5 COMMUNITY PARTICIPATION	6 COMMUNITY (EPC) PREPARATION
Euro-Arab Dialogue	politico-economic	Irregular meetings of the General Committee: meetings of economic/technical working Committees and specialized groups in the intervals. Isolated Troika meetings at political level (2 so far)	only agreed base, rules of procedure of the EAD (general Committee decision 18–20 May 1976. Luxembourg)	economic/technical working committees: Member States experts and Commission: chair either *ad hoc* or (for agricultural and trade questions) Commission: General Committee: Member States and Commission at senior official level; *ad hoc* contacts: Troika meeting at Ministerial/Commissioner level: Troika meeting at level of officials	economic aspects: EAD *ad hoc* groups in the Council (Commission initiative) political aspects: EAD coordinating group in EPC coordination: EAD coordinating group and Political Committee (political): COREPER (economic/technical)
ACP countries	economic	annual meetings of Council of Ministers: regular meetings at level of Ambassadors	Lomé Convention	Commission and Member States	coordination Community and Member States in Council framework: Commission initiative
	political	irregular	*ad hoc*	Troika and Commission	EPC coordination (Africa Working Group, Political Committee)
SADCC	economic	annual meetings of SADCC with Community participation	informal	Commission and Member States	Commission Internal
Front Line States	political	Irregular	*ad hoc*, informal	Presidency (spokesman) and Member States: Commission present under EPC conditions: Ministerial level	EPC coordination (Africa Working Group, Political Committee)

1 REGIONAL	2 TYPE OF DIALOGUE	3 FREQUENCY	4 BASE	5 COMMUNITY PARTICIPATION	6 COMMUNITY (EPC) PREPARATION
ASEAN	economic and political	EC–ASEAN Joint Committee: annual at official level Ministerial Meeting; political, but increasingly dealing with broader economic issues, at approx. 18 month intervals; Post-Ministerial Conference ASEAN countries and Dialogue partners: annual	economic: EC-ASEAN Agreement (1980) political: informal post-Ministerial: Informal	Joint Committee: Commission with Member States as observers Ministerial Meetings: Presidency and Member States with Commission post-Ministerial: Troika for political and Commission for economic	Joint Committee: *ad hoc* Group in Council (Commission Initiative) Ministerial Meetings: EPC coordination with Community input for any economic questions Post-Ministerial dialogue: EPC (Asia Working Group) and Commission
SAARC	platonic	—	—	presence of Presidency and Commission diplomatic representatives as observers at public sessions	—
PECC	platonic	—	—	presence of Presidency and Commission diplomatic representatives as observers at public sessions	—
Central America	political and economic	Annual Ministerial Meetings (the San José meetings) Annual meetings of the Joint Cooperation Committee	economic: Cooperation Agreement (1985) (Implementation: 1987) political: Final Act of the Luxembourg Conference (1985)	Ministerial Meeting: Member States (Presidency spokesman) and Commission: Joint Cooperation Committee: Commission with Member States as observers	economic: *ad hoc* Group in Council (Commission initiative) political: EPC (Latin America Working Group and Political Committee) pre-discussions with Central Americans; Troika (Presidency lead for political questions. Commission lead for economic questions)
Rio Group (Contadora and Contadora support Groups)	political with economic overtones (especially debt)	semi-annual meetings at Ministerial level (Capital Presidency — margin UNGA New York)	informal	Member States and Commission	EPC (Latin America Working Group and Political Committee)
Andean Pact	economic	Joint Cooperation Committee	Cooperation Agreement (1983) (Implementation: 1987)	Commission	Commission as executant of Community policy

1 REGIONAL	2 TYPE OF DIALOGUE	3 FREQUENCY	4 BASE	5 COMMUNITY PARTICIPATION	6 COMMUNITY (EPC) PREPARATION
GCC	economic and political	economic: annual meetings of Cooperation Council political: twice yearly Ministerial meetings margin cooperation Council + luncheons UNGA New York	economic: Cooperation Agreement (1988) political: Joint Declaration in parallel with Cooperation Agreement (1988)	economic: Commission with Member States observers political: Member States and Commission	economic: Community coordination in Council political: EPC (Middle East Working Group and Political Committee)
CMEA	economic	occasional meetings at official level	joint declaration on the establishment of official relationship between EEC–CMEA 22 June 1988 Luxembourg	Commission	Commission as executant of Community policy
EFTA	economic	Irregular meetings at Ministerial level	Luxembourg Declaration (1984)	Presidency and Commission with Member States	Community coordination in Council framework
Council of Europe	political	Informal discussions on the eve of meetings of the Committee of Ministers	EPC decisions of 1983, 1986	Member States (Ministers and Political Directors)	EPC coordination in Strasbourg
	community	annual presence of community at meetings of Committee of Ministers: annual attendance of Secretary General at meeting of Ministers' Deputies: working contacts between officials: annual participation in the quadripartite meeting at Ministerial level	Act 230 EEC: exchanges of letters (most recently 1987): Council decision (1989)	Presidency and Commission Presidency and President of Commission (meeting with President of Committee of Ministers and Secretary General of Council of Europe)	*ad hoc* coordination Presidency/Commission Commission internal coordination

* the Troika always includes the Commission, following the precedent set in the Euro-Arab dialogue

11 The Council of Ministers: the constraint on action

Andreas von Stechow

The framework for Council action

Regional cooperation and inter-group dialogue involves, on the Community side, the participation of the Council of Ministers and the member states at a number of different levels. Much depends on the type of cooperation as well as the legal basis on which the agreement is set.[1] There are a number of different types of Community cooperation agreements in which the intensity of the Council's involvement and that of the member states varies considerably.

The following types of regional cooperation instruments have been developed during the Community's history.

Association agreements[2]

There are now two types of Association Agreements. The first is association leading to the establishment of a customs union in which the common customs tariff is adopted in the final stages. Examples include the agreements with Turkey, Cyprus and Malta.[3] Included in the agreement are trade matters falling under Article 113 as well as those issues that remain within the competence of the member states which require the use of Article 238. All such agreements have a financial component in the form of a Financial Protocol based again on Article 238. Association Agreements are the strongest tool of economic cooperation available to the Community. However, for various reasons, particularly the economic weakness of the Community's partners, the agreements have not evolved as envisaged. Politically, they have tended to be overtaken by less formal forms of cooperation such as the free trade arrangements with EFTA countries.

The second type of Association Agreement is represented by the Lomé Convention, the renewal of which was still under negotiation in late 1989.[4] It is a preferential trade agreement with a strong development component. Though Article 113 is involved, the Convention is based on Article 238, indicative of the particularly strong interest and concerns of the member states. This interest is especially reflected in the Convention's financial arrangements, notably the European

Development Fund, which remains outside the Community's budget, being funded by the member states.[5]

Cooperation Agreements

Again a number of different types of agreement have evolved. The classic form of the agreement is one based on Article 238 and is typified by the preferential agreements signed with the countries of the Mediterranean basin, the Maghreb and the Mashreq.[6] In addition to the trade component, the agreements have varying provisions in the industrial, agricultural and sometimes social fields as well as offering some scientific and technological cooperation. As in the Association Agreements, financial assistance for industrial development is included by means of financial protocols.

The involvement of the Council of Ministers is required in both the evolution of the agreement and its implementation. The latter, especially, highlights the role of the supreme body of the agreements, the Cooperation Council. The Councils in principle meet annually at the level of Foreign Ministers, together with the Commission and the European Investment Bank.[7]

As the GATT multilateral trading system developed, the Community in the 1970s evolved a new form of Cooperation Agreement. These were based on a non-preferential trading arrangement using Article 113 of the Treaty of Rome, complemented by a strong political element based on Article 235. The outstanding examples of these are the EC–ASEAN agreement, the EC–Central America agreement (otherwise known as the San José Dialogue or Process), and most recently the EC–Gulf Cooperation Council (GCC) agreement. The involvement of the Council and the member states is substantial as the regular group dialogue meetings at ministerial level (they are usually held annually except in the case of ASEAN when it is more often every 18 months) include political discussions, with the result that the joint communiqués have both a political and economic part.

These 'modern' agreements reflect the European Community's political evolution — an evolution later formalised within the Community in the Single European Act of 1986. But it is not only a question of the Community's growing political dimension; it is also a reflection of the increased interest of the member states in diversifying the form of their external relations and the interest of the Cooperation partners and their regional bodies in the Community. The result has been a qualitative change in the Council's participation in the agreements.

Although most regions of the world are now covered by contractual relationships, new regional approaches cannot be excluded which will have further implications for the Community and the Twelve. An example may be the newly created Union of the Maghreb.

The EC's approach to regional cooperation has remained relatively flexible; static models have been resisted. The Council has always insisted on a politically appropriate approach to specific problems. A good example of this is the Community's policy towards the CMEA or COMECON and its Eastern European member states. The twelve member states were reluctant to negotiate a substantive agreement between the Community and the CMEA because the latter's competences were so limited in comparison with those of the Community, but they recognised the political necessity of doing so. However, it was strongly felt that formal contractual relations with the individual members of the CMEA should be developed as and when possible. The formula of a 'Joint Declaration' was decided on which was flexible enough to allow for very different interpretations to be held by each side as to its institutional significance. The Declaration, adopted in Brussels in June 1988, then opened the way for a comprehensive bilateral approach towards the countries of Eastern Europe. In view of the changes that have taken place in Eastern Europe during 1989, the usefulness and appropriateness of the EC's political approach to the CMEA was confirmed even sooner than any of the negotiators on the Community side could ever have imagined.

The institutional participation of the Council and the member states

The participation of the Council of Ministers in these negotiations and discussions occurs at different stages and levels. Much depends, as has been suggested above, on the legal framework of the Agreement itself. The first decisive step in this involvement is not, as might be assumed, in the discussion of the mandate for the negotiations proposed by the European Commission. History shows that the activities of the Council and the member states begin much earlier in the process.

This is particularly well illustrated in the negotiation of both the ASEAN and San José Cooperation Agreements. As we have seen in Chapter 5, the creation of ASEAN followed considerable political tension and protracted armed conflict in the region. The approach of the Community and the Twelve was inevitably motivated by political considerations as a result. The West German Foreign Minister, Mr Genscher — considered by many to have been particularly responsible for promoting the Agreement — argued especially that regional cooperation was the best guarantee of political stability and that the Community should therefore offer its support to the new grouping as early as possible. Moreover, as the first successful example of regional economic integration after the Second World War, the Community's experience might also be valuable. Finally, the Community could contribute to economic and political stability by providing ASEAN with a partner that was not directly involved in the conflicts of South East

Asia. In proposing a dialogue, Mr Genscher believed that, far from counteracting or undermining the interests of West Germany's allied superpower, the United States, it would complement them.

Political considerations were thus predominant even if long-term economic interests were also inevitably present. Another, more complex aspect to the West German position on promoting dialogue had as much to do with the development of the Community itself as with South East Asia. Such a dialogue, through its impact on the EC and EPC, enhanced the political cohesion of the EC member states. The Single European Act, especially the inclusion of European Political Cooperation and its provision for cohesion between the Community and EPC, added a further political dimension to the Community and thus has an influence on the future development of the Community towards political union.

It is interesting to note, however, that the EC–ASEAN case is an example that, to a considerable extent, refutes the argument that cooperation policies are motivated by the naked national interests of the member states. Obviously the United Kingdom has the strongest national interests in the ASEAN region since virtually all its members are former British colonies. France, too, has had extensive interests in the region but also appeared relatively uninterested in promoting an agreement with ASEAN to begin with. Both countries today play an important role within the cooperation framework.

The history of the establishment of the San José Process is a further example of where a common political approach has been pushed in the general interest rather than in the interests of any particular member state. The negotiation of the Cooperation Agreement is analysed elsewhere (Chapter 6), but clearly it took place in a period dominated by the search for peace in Central America. As a result the political focus of the Agreement was even more evident than in the ASEAN case, although an increasing emphasis has since been placed on economic issues, especially with the introduction of the project to revitalise the Central American Common Market.

As in the ASEAN case, Mr Genscher took a leading role in promoting the Agreement, and for very much the same type of reasons. There was, for example, a major policy difference with the United States which regarded the European Community's involvement in a political dialogue with countries on its doorstep with considerable suspicion. The United States adopted a more positive approach only after East–West *détente* made a solution to the problems of the Contras more conceivable.[8] But there were no clearly defined national interests among Community members, with the partial exception of the United Kingdom.[9] West Germany, France and the Commission played the leading roles in developing the Agreement. Significantly, negotiations were opened before the 'natural ally' of the Central American states, Spain, had joined the Community. Since its accession in 1986, however, Spain has taken a particular interest in the Agreement, and the San

José V meeting in Honduras was held during Spain's Presidency of the Community in 1989.

Political change and the Council's reaction

The marked changes that have taken place in the global political and economic systems inevitably have an influence on the attitudes of the member states and the Council towards existing Cooperation Agreements and their mechanisms. The institutional structures are already under review. Since existing policies and their mechanisms have not always met the expectations of either side, they too may be open to change.

The reason why the Community's partners have been disappointed in the institutional structures of the agreements may, in part at least, simply be because of time constraints. In most cases, Cooperation and Association Councils meet at ministerial level only annually. On the Community's side, the Councils are prepared for in the framework of the General Affairs Council, made up, that is, of Community Foreign Ministers. Overloaded agendas leave little time to devote to adequate preparations and this has not gone unnoticed by ministers of the partner countries who have tended to use the period between meetings to organise more extensively and whose expectations are consequently much higher. Although thorough preparation for Cooperation and Association Councils is done by the Commission and the working groups of the Council of Ministers, there are few opportunities for more open discussion. The demands of reaching an agreed common position on which the Community can negotiate as a whole are considerable, especially when the Community cannot then deviate from it, at least not without reopening the Community negotiating package.

Moreover, as legislation forms the basis of all Community action, once negotiated an agreement leaves relatively little flexibility — nor is it intended to. Inevitably, the limits of the agreement are recognised sooner or later, particularly perhaps by the Cooperation partners who may be more vulnerable to the changes in the environment and to new demands being placed on them. Some modification of agreements may well become necessary as they reach their institutional limits. Indeed, three of the old Association partners have indicated their intention of applying to the Community for full membership and Turkey formally applied in 1987.

The Community now has to decide whether improved forms of cooperation can be developed or whether membership is the only way in which the goals of these Association agreements can be met. In addition, the other Mediterranean states with Cooperation Agreements have requested, sometimes very explicitly, a review of the cooperation structure. The Community's Mediterranean policies stem from the 1970s and need to be adapted significantly to changed circumstances, not least changes in the Community. The Commission has initiated a review process but the reactions of the member states in the Council of Ministers is as yet uncertain.

Significant though the institutional framework is, the substantive changes that have taken place and those which appear to be in train need particular attention. The existing preferences of the Community's partners may be eroded by the multilateral process of the Uruguay Round of the GATT which is scheduled to conclude at the end of 1990. Preferential treatment of trade flows in particular sectors may also be eroded by other developments, such as the dismantling of the Multi-Fibre Arrangement. But the Community and the Council will also have to review Cooperation Agreements in the light of progress towards the completion of the Internal Market by the end of 1992. Action by the Council is thus inevitable in the near future.

The non-preferential agreements, which comprise political and economic instruments, are more adaptive to a changing environment than the more structured and regulated traditional agreements. However, the Council and the member states have little time to be complacent. As the global implications of changing patterns of East–West relations are felt, new groupings are likely to arise and new political and economic challenges will be made. Nor can it be excluded that the old constellations of group-to-group dialogue will form new patterns which will force adaptation by the Community. A hint of these new patterns can perhaps be seen in the Australian initiative to convene a ministerial meeting for the Asia–Pacific Region.[10] Ostensibly, this was a trade initiative, designed primarily within the context of the Uruguay Round, and sometimes explained as a follow-up to meetings of the Cairns Group, the informal grouping particularly concerned with agricultural issues within the Uruguay Round. However, the initiative also reflects the potential for a new regional formation in the area. The Community's response, both on the part of the Commission and the member states through the Presidency, has been sluggish and the Council will have to elaborate on its attitude in the near future. As yet, the Community agreed to welcome more economic integration in the Pacific area as long as there were no moves towards the creation of new trading blocs or obstacles to the open multilateral system.

Trade flows may not be completely independent of general political changes, though they are often extremely resistant to them. The astonishing success of the newly industrialising countries (NICs) of South East Asia — often referred to as the Asian Tigers even though they prefer the image of Flying Geese[11] — must give rise to thought. So far they have been treated by the Commission and the Council essentially as a trade issue rather than as a potential regional factor.[12] Evidence suggests that economic growth eventually leads to more international responsibility. Indeed, a dialogue of some of the NICs with the OECD has begun. The NICs have also indicated a readiness to participate actively in the Uruguay Round. Political responsibility may soon follow with a strong regional dimension and the Community must develop a strategy to meet it.

Some conclusions

Regional dialogue as a political and economic instrument of policy is not static. A changing environment must lead to the adaptation of existing instruments and perhaps to new approaches and concepts. It will be priority of the Community as a whole and the Council in particular therefore to adapt to this changing environment. The Community must not concentrate on itself. It has at its disposal the most advanced and developed instruments for inter-regional dialogue and has gained broad experience in using them. The economic and political power that the EC is gaining through further integration must lead to new openings combined with increased responsibilities. Other regions can share the Community's experience and the EC should be willing to share the experience with them.

Notes

1 Legislation here refers to the EC Treaties as amended by the Single European Act of 1986 together with more specific provisions such as regulations and administrative arrangements under the Cooperation Agreements and to decisions of the Cooperation Councils as far as they apply at the national level.
2 Although the Association and Cooperation Agreements with the Mediterranean countries are not group-to-group agreements in their legal form (they have been concluded with each Mediterranean country individually), they are referred to as such here. It has also been the Community's approach to consider them on a global basis and the global Mediterranean policy was introduced in the 1970s. It is currently under review in the Council framework.
3 The Ankara Agreement with Turkey was signed in September 1963; the Association with Cyprus in December 1972; and the Association with Malta in December 1970.
4 It has been agreed that Haiti, Dominican Republic and Namibia should be included in the negotiations, increasing the number of ACP states to 69.
5 The European Development Fund (EDF) is not budgeted in the Community's own budget but agreed on by the member states who then transfer the financing required to the Commission as national contributions. This form of funding has been challenged by the Commission at each renegotiation of the Convention.
6 The Agreements include those with: Algeria, April 1976; Morocco, April 1976; Tunisia, April 1976; Jordan, January 1977; Egypt, January 1977; Lebanon, May, 1977; Israel, May 1975 and February 1977; Syria, January

1977; and Yugoslavia, a more recent type of counter-preferential agreement, April 1980.

7 The EIB participates as executive agency for the financial protocols as these include both budget-resourced and Commission-administered funds as well as loans from the EIB. In some cases only EIB loans are given under the protocols.

8 Arguably the Esquipulas I and II initiatives were Community-inspired.

9 The United Kingdom's interests were largely concentrated on Belize over which Honduras had made claims. The United Kingdom also played its traditional role as the United States's ally, often putting the US position in the Community framework.

10 The so-called Hawke Initiative on Asia Pacific Economic Cooperation (APEC).

11 They include Singapore, South Korea, Hong Kong and Taiwan. The flying geese image suggests mobility in the reallocation of capital, technology and production.

12 Though Singapore is of course already a part of ASEAN

12 The European Parliament: an emerging political role?

Karl-Heinz Neunreither

The European Parliament's role in external relations against the background of national patterns

When analysing the role of the European Parliament (EP) in the European Community's relations with other groups of states, it is useful to have a general overview of the pattern of parliamentary participation in this field. Initially, when the EP was composed of nominated members of national parliaments there was a tendency to transfer national parliamentary traditions to the European level. Since the first direct elections of the Parliament, more independent and innovative elements have evolved and can now be more clearly defined, although it must be noted that the election itself did not increase Parliament's prerogatives. It was only with the revision of the Treaty by the Single European Act (SEA) that additional powers were granted.

The increasing participation and influence of Parliament in external relations needs to be seen in the context of a more general evolution of parliamentary practices. While traditionally the prerogative of sovereigns, foreign relations gradually passed into the hands of the executive with, in more recent years, parliaments becoming increasingly dissatisfied with the restricted role allowed to them. In national systems, Parliaments have two main interests in external relations: to counterbalance the information monopoly of the executive and, as far as the minority is concerned, to enable the opposition to fulfil its control function. Within the EC, there is no parliamentary majority and no opposition; consequently the second function does not exist. However, external relations do perform an important alternative role in providing access to the international scene for new minority parties, such as the Greens, and also in allowing existing parties to improve their image internationally. An example of this was the participation of Italian communists in EP delegations to the US Congress which helped them to overcome their negative image.

The first new element in the Community context is, therefore, the replacement of the majority/opposition cluster by the more varied influence and profile of interests of the whole range of political parties. Since, within the EP, the 10 political groups and the independent members represent more than 70 national or regional party organizations, this leads to a very large variety of possible interests and representations.

The strong political party interest is one main element explaining the increased attention that the EP pays to political as opposed to economic factors in external relations. The EP is the institution which tends more than the Commission or the Council to politicize external relations, including, as a matter of course, human rights issues and questions of democracy. As far back as 1967 it was the Parliament which insisted against a hesitant Commission and a more than reluctant Council that the Association Agreement with Greece should either be cancelled or at least frozen when the Colonels took over and parliamentary democracy was abolished. When similar difficulties arose in Turkey, another Associated state, the obvious consequences were much less controversial. On numerous occasions, the Parliament has linked the procedures leading to trade or cooperation agreements with questions of democracy or human rights, or, occasionally, to more general political questions. The main example is the refusal to give assent to the Israeli trade protocols in January 1988. Questions of trade — i.e. the access of commodities from the occupied territories — were only marginally involved; the basic argument was evidently political: the EP wanted to show its dissatisfaction with Israel's handling of the political situation in these territories.

If political questions tend to dominate the EP's handling of EC/ bilateral external relations this is perhaps even more so the case in EC/group relations. By definition, in order to have such relations, regional institutions must exist on the other side. Whenever possible, the EP has shown a great interest that these institutions should not only represent governments but also parliamentary bodies. Early examples of initiatives along these lines were the establishment of a mixed parliamentary body in the Yaoundé Convention, the predecessor of the present Lomé Convention. The creation of a Latin American parliament in the early 1960s can be seen in the same context; the EP had hoped that this grouping of Latin American parliaments would become the parliamentary body of SELA. More recently, ASEAN has also established a regional parliamentary group which was encouraged by members of the EP.

As a result there is not only a clear EP interest in the political dimension of external group relations, but there is also an interest in the internal organization of these groupings themselves. EP participation in that area, as weak as it may seem if we look exclusively at its formal powers of treaty-making, contains an element of political dynamics far beyond the approach that either the Commission or Council can adopt.

The instruments of the EP in external relations

The EP has at its disposal a variety of instruments in the field of external relations. From a legal perspective, the Luns-Westerterp procedure and the new assent procedure introduced by the SEA make up the total EP role in treaty-making. However, while this remains very important as one of the major classical functions of a Parliament in external relations, the EP's possibilities go much further. We need also to look at the opportunities to ask questions of Commissioners or the Council, including the European Political Cooperation (EPC) Council, the possibility of voting on resolutions based either on initiative reports or put forward within the so-called urgency procedure as well as the direct contacts of the political groups, which to some extent formulate their own foreign policy, and the various parliamentary delegations.

The main objective of the Luns-Westerterp procedure is to ensure a certain amount of parliamentary information and participation in decision-making. This is done by providing information to the interested committees (mainly the External Economic Relations Committee) at two stages: first, early in the proceedings when a so-called mandate for the Commission for a given negotiation is worked out and agreed upon by the Council; and secondly, at the end of the negotiation when the text is ready for signature. It is important to remember that it is not primarily a plenary procedure but a procedure which involves the committees. However, there is nothing to stop the Parliament from later expressing its opinion by way of a plenary debate followed by a resolution.

The origins of the procedure go back to 1964, when the Council agreed to contacts at committee level on negotiations concerning association agreements. Commercial agreements were included from 1973 with later a distinction made between agreements of major importance and others. Finally, in June 1983 the European Council stated in its declaration on European Union, that the EP's formal opinion should be asked before the conclusion of any significant international agreement or treaty of adhesion. This closed the existing gap concerning agreements, above all based on Article 113 or 235, where the EEC Treaty had not foreseen a parliamentary participation.

Nobody is quite satisfied with the Luns-Westerterp procedure and numerous proposals have been submitted for its improvement. Many observers tend to see the only possible solution in an increase of EP's powers. Clearly the SEA was an important step in that direction for the new assent procedure requires Parliament's approval by the majority of more than 50 per cent of all its members (that is, 260 members) for association agreements and treaties of adhesion. Parliament has sought, but has not yet been given, the same powers in relation to the more important trade and cooperation agreements. The importance here is not only the veto power thus embodied in the Parliament but the perspective of a closer cooperation between the three institutions (Council, Commission and Parliament), in order to ensure that external relations develop harmoniously.

If within the Luns-Westerterp procedure the committees play the major role, direct contacts with parliaments of third countries are handled by inter-parliamentary delegations. At present there are 26 such delegations some of which are responsible for areas where groups of countries have set up regional organizations as in Central America, Southern America, the ASEAN countries and the Gulf States. There are no delegations for relations with the 'Arab countries' as such, though there are sub-regional Maghreb and Mashreq delegations, nor with the CMEA.

Delegations maintain contact with other parliaments through inter-parliamentary meetings either in the countries concerned or in the Community. Their main advantage lies in the opportunity they provide for members to following particular questions over a period of time, thus allowing for specialization. The danger of specialization leading to small groups becoming susceptible to third-country lobbying is to some extent reduced by the fact that delegations have a fixed composition and therefore represents a wide range of political groups within the Parliament. They should not be confused with so-called friendship groups that exist in some national parliaments, which are open to all members (which often leads to a rather biased composition), nor the EP's inter-groups, which are informal associations with neither a secretariat nor an identified infrastructure and whose activities are little known within the EP itself.

If the fixed composition of EP's delegations ensures contact with all political groups, the problem has not yet been resolved as to how close contacts between a delegation and, say, the Political Affairs or the External Economic Relations Committee can be assured. Only committees have access to the plenary and can introduce parliamentary reports containing draft resolutions on which the Parliament is invited to vote. Delegations do not have this access; their only recourse after an inter-parliamentary meeting is to submit a report to the Enlarged Bureau, the steering committee of the Parliament, which then usually sends it for information to the committees concerned. These committees may or may not include them in a subsequent report. What is still more awkward is the fact that the rapporteur of a committee on a given question, say on EFTA, is often not a member of the delegation, so that he or she has not participated in parliamentary meetings with the countries concerned. This is not only counter-productive within the EP itself, but leads also to confusion and irritation outside the Community.

If the above constitute the formal instruments for the EP's participation in what we may call foreign policy of the EC, informal elements should not be underestimated. Here the political groups play a predominant role: not only do they send delegations of their own to third countries on fact-finding missions or to have contacts with other political parties but there is a permanent stream of visitors to Brussels or to the plenary session in Strasbourg. These visits can sometimes cause curiosity as when an individual MEP, not backed by a political group on the issue, invited the Dalai Lama to Strasbourg, thus creating diplomatic difficulties between the EC and China. In a much more consistent way, some groups over the last few years have used this platform for advancing their own policy issues. This has been especially the case in relations with Eastern Europe where the Socialist Group, followed by the PPE group and others, initiated a series of parliamentary contacts with East European leaders. It is clear that these contacts helped to prepare the ground for the recognition of the Community by the CMEA and influenced the revision of the Soviet approach to Western European integration. Another example was the invitation from the Socialist Group to Yasser Arafat. Here also, at a crucial moment in Euro-Arab relations, and indeed, in the overall situation in the Middle East, political groups in the EP influenced the course of events.

The EP and parliamentary relations within the EEC–ACP Convention

EC–ACP relations take place in a framework which is unique in the world. Some observers might qualify it as a remnant of former historical links and therefore rather as an exception within a world dominated by global approaches. Others, however, have suggested that it might well be a forerunner or even a model for future group-to-group relations.

The parliamentary element within the EC–ACP framework reflects its unique character. As a result of major parliamentary lobbying in the early 1960s, a consultative assembly was created composed of representatives of the then non-directly elected European Parliament and of parliamentary representatives of the various associated countries. The present body, created within the Lomé III Convention is called a Joint Assembly, reflecting the fact that a number of ACP states do not have parliamentary institutions in the form of working legislative bodies as we know them. Consequently these states prefer to delegate members of the executive or senior officials, often diplomats, to the Joint Assembly in order to represent the interests of their country rather than entrusting members of their people's congress with such an important task. Thus, within the framework of the only group relationship where an institution plays an important role, its actual representative profile is rather mixed.

The Joint Assembly is composed according to strict parity: 66 members from the European Parliament and 66 members, one from each ACP country. The Assembly meets twice a year, once in an ACP country and once in the Community, with a joint bureau of the Assembly assuring continuity between sessions. The Assembly does not have standing committees but creates *ad hoc* working groups to deal with major issues such as the problems of indebtedness, the role of women, rural development and environmental protection, human rights, refugees and displaced persons and the effects of the Single Market in 1992 on ACP states. The resolutions adopted by the Assembly require a majority of both groups, thereby ensuring that neither dominates the other. Lobbying and informal contacts precede the final votes on resolutions, the latter facilitated by the fact that many of the leading members have probably known each other for many years so that personal knowledge often predominates over national, group or partisan interests. While there are clear rules of procedure, debates take place in an almost family atmosphere that is often very much more informal than the highly structured approach used in the EP.

This informality has facilitated a number of initiatives from the Assembly, for example, in the field of human rights. Respect for human rights in several ACP countries has become a major theme in the Assembly's activities. Unfortunately resolutions introduced and voted have not always brought about the desired results. The Bureau of the Assembly, therefore, established more detailed procedures on human rights issues. If, say, an MEP wishes to raise a human rights question — often inspired by documentation from one of the various international organizations active in the field like Amnesty International — he or she is first asked to get a reaction from the representative of the country concerned and to check on the validity of the accusations. Only then — that is either following an answer from the country concerned or following prolonged silence — can the case be forwarded to the Bureau and in the final stage to the Assembly itself. A second and more discreet approach has also been developed by the Bureau. On a number of occasions, personal visits by members of the Bureau, consultations and direct talks with the responsible leaders in their respective countries have been more productive in the freeing of political prisoners than the use of formal resolutions.

Other humanitarian issues of importance are food aid and refugees. Following the signing of the Lomé III Convention, the EP managed to achieve an improvement in the regulations concerning food aid. Food aid was not seen simply as a means of dumping European agricultural surpluses to developing countries but as a much more complex issue. As far as the refugees were concerned, the Assembly not only discussed the problem and adopted unanimously a resolution from its working group in plenary, but it also decided on a number of on-the-spot missions by small joint delegations which considerably increased the impact of Community assistance.

As far as other political problems are concerned (apart from the political situation in one or other ACP country), the major issue over the last few years has been South Africa. Condemnation of apartheid has been unanimous. Southern Africa and the Front Line States were another focus of major interest. Here, as could have been expected, the European side was less united on the situation in countries such as Angola or Namibia, reflecting the different views of the major political groups within the Community.

To sum up, the Joint Assembly, despite some deficiencies as to its parliamentary character, plays a major role in the group relationship between the EC and the ACP countries. The issues indicated above — to which one might add cultural cooperation — have a significant impact on the shaping of the future EC–ACP Convention. Here, clearly, the parliamentary dimension plays a role that none of the other institutions of the Community can fulfil.

When it comes to more economic questions, and notwithstanding its successful initiatives concerning STABEX, the Assembly becomes a body seeking to exercise some supervision over the Commission and the Council of the EC and the joint Council of the Association, especially via questions. Both the Commissioner responsible and the President-in-Office of the EC–ACP Council of Ministers always attend Joint Assembly meetings, make statements and answer questions. This is often rather more than the normal practice in most ACP countries. The activities of the Joint Assembly can thus be seen to constitute a lesson in democracy.

The EP's role in relations with Latin America

We have suggested that the EP had a propensity to underline political issues in external relations, especially those relating to democracy and human rights which are otherwise often dominated by economic considerations. Latin America provides an outstanding example of this, and the importance of informal relations, for several reasons. First of all, Europe is not only linked with the Latin American countries by common history and common culture but, in addition, the affinity of the political party systems in Latin America and Europe is considerable. The Christian Democratic parties and the Socialist parties are particularly close to their European counterparts, as to a lesser extent, are the Liberals. As a result, direct contacts between party leaders of the two regions are perhaps more frequent than with party leaders in other regions of the world. This is clearly an important element for an increased interest from the European Parliament.

Party interest on the European side includes an interest in a pluralistic democracy based on free elections and containing guarantees for the respect of human rights. The EP concentrated much of its endeavour on isolating non-democratic regimes which were perhaps a minority in the 1960s but threatened to become a widespread majority in Central and Latin America in the 1970s. It is an open question as to how far regional efforts, both in Latin America and in Europe (and especially the EC) have influenced the more positive evolution that took place in the 1980s.

The third factor is that regional organizations have existed or have been under discussion since the 1960s. The possibility of regional parliaments being founded in Latin America provided the EP with the motivation it needed for a political dialogue. It can be argued that, at least to some extent, the creation of the Latin American Parliament (LAP) in the 1960s was inspired by a visit from an EP delegation to a number of Latin American countries. Delegations from the two parliaments have met regularly since 1974 to discuss issues of common interest.

The EP has set up two permanent delegations for these conferences — one for Central and one for South America — totalling 50 members. Latin American participation is usually more flexible; it can be expected that 80 to 100 parliamentarians attend. The conferences are held alternately in the European Community and in Latin America. The ninth in the series took place in San José, Cost Rica in January 1989. The major subjects discussed included: human rights, external debt, trade relations, aid for development, environment and conservation of natural resources, the drug problem, the situation of women and, finally, cultural relations. Special reference was made to the Esquipulas Agreements concerning the peace process and various steps towards democratization in Central America.

If the mechanisms for dialogue exist, it must be said that the asymmetric structure between the EC and the various Latin American regional organizations and the clear difference in competences and efficiency limits the possibilities of reaching concrete results. The Latin America Parliament, the main partner for the dialogue, only received formal status in 1987. In the meantime the Andean group had created its own parliamentary body. Because of its more dynamic start, it was hoped that the Andean parliament would evolve into a more powerful partner despite its regional limitations, but these hopes were not fulfilled. We will have to see if the cooperation agreement with the Community proves to be effective and if, as planned, the Andean parliament will be directly elected.

Quite clearly, as far as sub-regional parliaments in Latin America are concerned the scheduled creation of a Central American parliament has taken interest away from the Andean parliament. Political interest has focused on the situation in Central America more than elsewhere and the EC's positive reaction to the Esquipulas plan and the various San José conferences reflect this. The institutional proposals in this context are nothing short of astonishing: relations between the five Central American states are not only marked by past conflicts (as was Europe after the last world war) but also by continuing controversies including bloodshed and organized attempts to overthrow neighbouring government and ruling élites. Yet it is proposed to elect directly a parliament which would not only have control functions over a council but would also be considered an important factor for stabilization.

Both the Commission and the EP have clearly committed themselves to bringing about the realization of this Central American parliament. The Commission, very much influenced by the EP, has put aside budgetary means in order to help prepare regional elections. The EP has agreed to contribute through its organizational expertise.

This involvement of the EC institutions must be seen in the wider context of the endeavour to find political solutions to the existing problems. In the late 1980s the EC was opposed to the Reagan administration's approach. With the Bush administration, and in view of a possible reorientation of Soviet foreign policy in Latin America and especially Central America, the overall situation is changing. But during the 1980s the EC played a political role in the area that was not too unsatisfactory and indeed exercised remarkable influence. As EC/Central American relations have been dominated by political factors rather than economic ones, the EP was likely to be stronger. On the other hand, over the Latin American sub-continent as a whole where economic interests clearly predominate, the EP's influence has tended to be much more limited.

Inter-parliamentary relations with ASEAN

Inter-parliamentary relations with the ASEAN countries are another example of the specific contribution of the EP to group-to-group relations. While from the EC's perspective these relations are clearly dominated by economic interests, the EP adds a wider dimension, in this case one that is not only focused on questions on democracy and human rights but which contains wider aspects of international relations including the overall situation in the Pacific basin.

First contacts date back to 1975 when a delegation from the EP visited the five ASEAN countries. From this arose not only the idea of permanent and regular parliamentary contacts but an interest among the ASEAN countries in creating their own regional parliamentary organization. Having inspired the Latin Americans to create a regional parliament and later on sub-regional parliaments, the idea also 'contaminated' the Pacific region. For the countries involved, interest in the regional parliament have of course not always been identical: for the Marcos regime in the Philippines, for example, it was an opportunity, among other things, of demonstrating that they actually had a parliamentary assembly. But despite this variety, regional parliamentary assemblies tend to develop a dynamic of their own. Above all, they constitute a platform for the more democratic elements, very often the minority parties, which may have only limited possibilities of parliamentary representation at home.

Once the ASEAN inter-parliamentary organization (AIPO) had been set up, the EP delegation limited its meetings to that group. The pattern is the standard one: the annual meetings alternate between ASEAN countries and the EC. Six inter-parliamentary meetings have been held so far, the last in Kuala Lumpur in parallel with the ninth General Assembly of the AIPO. This allowed the EP delegation to be involved in a major AIPO event as well as meet their counterparts for bilateral discussion. Informal meetings made it possible to raise human rights questions: in a separate meeting with an Indonesian delegation, for example, the question of East Timor was taken up; in another meeting with a Malaysian delegation the question of internments was raised; and with a delegation from Singapore, the question of press freedom. These informal approaches are effective; if such an issue were put formally on the agenda in the presence of other ASEAN representatives, a national delegation might feel that it would lose face and it would thus be counter-productive. Parliamentary agendas, in other words, cannot be the same all over the world; in Latin America, for example, it is quite customary for human rights or other awkward questions to be discussed publicly in formal meetings.

Political questions concerning the Pacific region and East Asia also usually form a focus of interest, not least the situation in Kampuchea and Vietnam as well as problems like the proposal for a Pacific nuclear-free zone. Other political concerns do not always find their way easily on a parliamentary agenda. Because of their history and geographical location, many of the ASEAN countries feel (not without some justification) that they are the object of a struggle for influence among the world powers, especially China, the Soviet Union, Japan and the United States. The EC has very limited direct political power in the region but its interest and its overall world position does perhaps provide some potential to influence the balance between the traditional powers in the region. With considerations of this kind, some of them real, some of a more speculative nature, a wide field for informal inter-parliamentary contacts is open.

Cooperation with the Gulf States

The EP's delegation for relations with the Gulf States has not been the most active of delegations. So far (i.e. to the end of 1989) only one parliamentary visit has taken place, in February 1988. Of course, there is considerable interest in the Gulf region both economically and politically but, against this, there is practically no parliamentary counterpart; only Oman has a consultative assembly and its 55 members are appointed by the Sultan rather than elected. Political discussions during the 1988 visit focused mainly on the Iran–Iraq war and the situation in the occupied territories. On the economic side, the dialogue concentrated on the EC/GCC Agreement which was still under negotiation. The agreement itself was something of a disappointment for the EP in that, despite its efforts to base it not only on Article 113 and 235 of the EC Treaty but also on Article 238 (which would have given the Parliament more influence), neither the Commission nor the Council changed the legal base. The EP had no major objections to the agreement itself.

The EP and relations with Arab countries

There is no formal dialogue between the EP and parliamentary representatives of the Arab League. The Parliament has three delegations dealing with relations with sub-regions in the Arab world: one for the Mashreq countries, the second for the Maghreb and the third, that for the Gulf states.

The Maghreb delegation reveals the typical problems of relations with states which do not possess a corresponding sub-regional organization. In practical terms, the Maghreb delegation was largely a delegation for bilateral meetings with Tunisia, Algeria and Morocco. Meetings have been held in each of these three countries and in the Community. Economic questions centred around the adaptation of the association agreements following enlargement of the Community by Spain and Portugal which much affected the economies of the southern littoral of the Mediterranean. Political issues have included the situation in the Western Sahara, of very great importance of course for Morocco, the situation in the Middle East and questions of human rights. As far as the situation in the occupied territories is concerned, the North African partners looked with satisfaction at EP's handling of the Israeli protocols in 1988.

In its meetings, the EP delegation stressed its desire to see Parliamentary cooperation develop between the three Maghreb countries and suggested that the three delegations should come jointly to Brussels or Strasbourg. This initiative was accepted with interest. A new element was introduced with the move towards closer cooperation between the five Maghreb countries (that is including Libya and Mauritania) formalized in the treaty signed in Marrakesh in February 1989. A few months later a Consultative Assembly was established. This may create the necessary conditions for a group-to-group dialogue with this sub-region.

On the Mashreq side the situation has been somewhat similar. Bilateral contacts took place with Egypt, Syria and Jordan. In February 1989, a Council for Arab Cooperation (CAC) was created between Egypt, Iraq, Jordan and North Yemen. In its first phase the aim of the CAC is economic cooperation. The grouping was established soon after the creation of Maghreb Union and could also lead to group-to-group dialogue with the EP.

Why is there no overall regional dialogue with the Arab League? The answer is political. The Arab League, which has a quite active parliamentary representation, contacted the EP on several occasions in order to establish direct relations between the two organizations. This was turned down for a number of reasons. First, the Arab League is an organization which does not easily fit in a classical pattern. In addition, the exclusion of Egypt after the Camp David accords strengthened the arguments of those in the EP who did not want direct contacts with the Arabs.

The non-existence of formal links did not prevent informal contacts. The Euro-Arab parliamentary intergroup (i.e. one of the informal associations of parliamentarians from various political groups on specific subjects) is quite active within the EP and meets Arab parliamentarians regularly. The visit of Yasser Arafat to Strasbourg in 1988 on the invitation of the Socialist Group is a good example of informal contacts. In retrospect, it can be considered a major step in the process of recognition of the PLO, not only within the Community but also more widely.

The EP and relations with EFTA

The Community's relations with EFTA and its member countries are quite clearly dominated by economic interests. The political approach preferred by the EP that has marked its relations elsewhere does not prevail here. The fact that the party systems are similar and could provide an interesting infrastructure for such a role has so far been largely irrelevant.

As far as the organization of the Parliament is concerned, there are no less than four inter-parliamentary delegations following relations with EFTA countries: the delegation for relations with Northern Europe (Sweden, Finland, Iceland and the Nordic Council); a second delegation for relations with Norway; another one for relations with Austria composed of 10 members each; and finally, one for relations with Switzerland composed of eight members. Obviously, their structure reflects a predominance of a group/bilateral pattern. As for Norway, it should be noted that it has been 'associated' with EPC since 1982 via a renewable agreement with the Council Presidency which allows it to be kept informed and to give its opinion on certain issues. Political elements also play a role in the possibilities of a future membership. The same must be said of Austria, which has formally applied. The internal Austrian discussion of eventual membership has politicized the relationship.

To some extent, the interest of group-to-group relations is reduced by the existence of these group/bilateral peculiarities. The delegations for relations with Northern Europe was not only responsible for relations on a bilateral basis but also followed relations with the Nordic Council as well, which is a mixed executive/parliamentary body. In addition, the delegation used to follow relations with the EFTA parliamentary group. However, after the enlarged Bureau of the Parliament claimed that MEPs were travelling too often, the EP's Committee for External Economic Relations is now directly competent for the EFTA parliamentary group.

In a report adopted by the External Economic Affairs Committee (Galuzzi — Doc. A2-0032/89), the Parliament noted the excellent functioning of the free trade agreements in force between the EC and EFTA and underlined the high degree of homogeneity and interdependence between the communities of Western Europe. It stressed that cooperation should develop further but within a pragmatic approach which did not affect the autonomy of Community decision-making. To that end, the EP called for a consultative body for organizing and managing EC–EFTA relations. Finally the Commission was asked to study the possibility of a new association agreement under Article 238 of the EEC Treaty. The European Parliament's position on how to improve existing relations short of adhesion has been equally positive and open but not very precise.

The predominance of the economic dimension in the EC–EFTA relationship has not contributed to an enhanced profile for the EP. Parliamentary contacts have been useful but it is not always easy to see where any specific contribution has been made. One could even maintain that as far as global issues are concerned the Commission plays a greater role as a think-tank in forwarding long-term policy options than the Parliament itself. This should be noted because it is more often the other way round.

EC relations with Eastern European countries

EC relations with Eastern European countries cannot easily be classified as group-to-group relations. This has been due to a number of political, economic and organizational factors, and especially the non-recognition of the Community by Eastern European countries under the influence of post-war Soviet foreign policy, and the different interests of the member states (see Chapter 9). In addition, during the 1970s, the Soviets pursued the idea of stepping up the competences of the CMEA in trade — in part in view of a possible recognition of the EC. After a period of stalemate, events moved quickly with the arrival of Mr Gorbachev and with the emergence of 'new thinking' in Moscow. A declaration was signed between the CMEA and the EC in Luxembourg in June 1988 which was followed by formal diplomatic recognition from various East European states. But the group-to-group declaration was little more than a framework or a letter of intent to begin talks between the two organizations on a number of issues. The main interest of the declaration was elsewhere, in the negotiation of full-scale trade and economic cooperation agreements with individual Eastern European countries.

Where does the EP come in? First, there are a large number of EP resolutions on issues of human rights, on security, on peace, on the political situation in various East European countries, and on international questions such as Afghanistan. Secondly, there have been attempts to bring about a more structural dialogue as in, for example, the report by Mr Seeler in 1987 on the relations with the CMEA (Doc. A2-187/86) and by Mr Hansch in 1988 (Doc. A2-0155/88) on the political relationship with the Soviet Union. The former provided a well-balanced assessment of the situation but was not very outspoken on the political choice which should have been obvious between pursing multilateral or EC–bilateral contacts.

A major influence of the EP in EC–East European relations was clearly due to the initiative of the various political groups. The Socialist Group above all under the chairmanship of Rudi Arndt was particularly active, but also the PPE chaired by Mr Egon Klepsch showed a clear interest. Delegations of the various groups visited Eastern Europe and had contact at high levels while delegations from Eastern Europe visited Strasbourg during plenary sessions. These contacts are officially classified as informal but the borderline is not very clearly marked and the political effect is almost the same. In any case, during a period when official contacts were completely banned political parties had a unique opportunity and they used it fully.

On the formal side, the EP had established delegations for relations with Eastern Europe as early as 1979. These were completely inactive as far as interparliamentary meetings were concerned. Only after formal recognition of the Community had followed the Luxembourg Declaration of June 1988 were formal interparliamentary contacts established. At present (in 1989) there is one delegation of 22 members for relations with the Soviet Union. The other Eastern European countries are now covered by two delegations, composed of 19 members in total. Again, there is an EC–national pattern: one group handles bilateral relatioɪs with the GDR, Poland and Czechoslovakia, the other, relations with Hungary, Bulgaria and, once the political difficulties are overcome, with Romania. In the meantime the various delegations have visited the Soviet Union, Poland, the GDR, Hungary and Bulgaria. The Czech government postponed a visit planned for 1988; an invitation for June 1989 was not accepted.

What is the political echo from these parliamentary contacts? The prevailing impression is that each country concentrates on its own problems. Quite evidently neither Poland nor Hungary are very interested at present in introducing aspects of group-to-group relations in a parliamentary dialogue. Other countries are more discreet: the GDR, for example, has pursued their system. Here, of course, the future of the special relationship of the GDR with the EC once the Single Market has come into force is a question of additional concern. Since the CMEA does not have a parliamentary body, despite some recent initiatives, the EP does not have a regional parliamentary partner in Eastern Europe. As a result, and particularly because the headquarters of CMEA are in Moscow, the parliamentary delegation maintaining relations with the Soviet Union has also included contacts with that organization. The CMEA secretariat has shown almost euphoria as far as the possibilities of a great variety of contacts and future relationships from group to group are concerned — realism has not been a characteristic.

To sum up, one could say that the EP has not been a totally negligible element on the political side over the past few years in the evolving relationship between the EC and Eastern Europe. The relationship is now dominated by the process of internal reforms in all the countries of Eastern Europe. As a consequence, Eastern Europe does not present itself as a group, and group-to-group relations are rather secondary.

EP and the Council of Europe

The EP does not have an easy relationship with the Council of Europe. This goes back to the origins of the Community when the parliament of the then Coal and Steel Community came into existence. At least initially it was considered by the Council a sub-organization of the Council of Europe itself. The new parliament moved away from Strasbourg to Luxembourg, to the seat of the High Authority, in order to assure organizational independence. Before 1979, during the period of the non-elected EP all members had a double mandate — a national and a European one — and many of them were delegated from their national parliament to both the Council of Europe Assembly and the European Parliament. Formal annual meetings were held of the two bodies to discuss matters of common interest.

Direct elections changed the position radically. Not only have double mandates between the Council of Europe and the European Parliament disappeared but the EP mandate has also become a full-time job and only a very small number of members have been able to keep a seat in a national parliament. Contacts between the institutions themselves are limited to annual meetings with rather small delegations, usually chaired from the EP side by a vice-president and composed of five or six members. Meetings between committees of the two assemblies are practically non-existent.

As a result, relations of the EP with parliamentarians from non-member states who are represented in the Council of Europe take place on a bilateral and *ad hoc* basis within the respective delegations. Relations with the EFTA countries are of course the main example. The question is whether this situation, which reflects the more dynamic character and evolution of the EP over the last 10 years and which has accelerated since the coming into force of the SEA, will continue. One might speculate that the Council of Europe will gain a new role inspired by the changing situation in Eastern Europe. If a European 'house' were constructed providing 'rooms' or 'apartments' for each European nation, the Council of Europe might well provide a better 'building site' than any other existing organization. President Gorbachev visited Strasbourg in July 1989 in order to address the Council of Europe assembly, not the European Parliament. This was, perhaps, due to some bad timing since the EP was not operational so shortly after its election. But the message remains: there is an increased interest from Eastern Europe in the Council of Europe and it may well be that this will influence the future of relations between the EP and the Council of Europe Assembly as well.

Conclusions: the EP in group-to-group relations and its potential for development

The EP's formal powers in treaty-making are still limited despite the assent procedure concerning adhesion treaties and association agreements. The Luns-Westerterp procedure, largely confirmed by the SEA, provides for a certain amount of information which should not be underestimated — it may well be as much or even more than received by parliaments from their national governments. The EP has requested the extension of the assent procedure to the more important trade and cooperation agreements. The SEA was clear on that and did not include it in Article 113 and 235 procedures where the weak form of a mere parliamentary opinion is maintained. An extension of the EP's powers would require that the legal base be broadened and Article 238, relating to association agreements, be included. In the 1970s and early 1980s the Commission was fairly generous with the use of this article for political reasons: 'association agreement' sounds much more meaningful than a mere 'trade' or 'cooperation agreement'. It is now, however, possible that a more purist line will be reintroduced and that Article 238 will be strictly limited in order to minimize the EP's direct participation in treaty-making.

It is an open question whether the Luns-Westerterp procedure could still be improved or whether the EP, over the next few years, should endeavour to win a revision of the treaties to obtain more powers. The basic difficulties lie, in any case, in the nature of the Community institutional system itself. The EC does not have a parliamentary government where the executive is directly responsible to the legislature and in addition has many links to its majority. The close interplay between a parliamentary majority and the executive does not exist in the Community. That is why, on the one hand, formal powers are perhaps more important than in national systems and why, on the other hand, more informal and disparate elements like direct party interests evolve very strongly. In that respect the examples we have given show that the EP has not lacked imagination. The combination of informal political group activities and more formal contacts provides opportunities which the other institutions do not possess. Moreover, the possibility of new institutional formula are emerging: the presence of an EP delegation in the ministerial meeting of San José V was one of the possible schemes that should be further elaborated on. The independent functioning of the EP when compared with national Parliaments may, in this context, prove to be an advantage.

The EP has clearly added to the political nature of the Community in external relations in so far as its activities tend to politicize issues, especially perhaps because of its concern for democracy and human rights. The contents of most trade and cooperation agreements are either extremely technical, listing one commodity after another, or contain vague general clauses for economic cooperation. The political dimension often comes from the Parliament and this is not unimportant. An issue such as the indebtedness of the Third World can be approached either from the banker's point of view or within the context of north–south relations. In order to find a balanced answer, the political arguments need to be put forward and the Parliament is better equipped and traditionally a more appropriate arena than an executive body.

The EP has also advocated regional or sub-regional cooperation wherever possible, including the setting up of parliamentary cooperation. Parliamentary contacts have become a tradition with Latin America, but not only with the Latin American parliament for there are links also with the Andean Parliament and the forthcoming Central American Parliament. The ASEAN group is a second example of good working relationships. Where parliaments do not exist at all or only marginally as in the Gulf States, or where national parliaments do not cooperate among themselves as in the Maghreb and the Mashreq regions, this aspect does not of course play a role, and parliamentary contacts lack an important dimension.

As for the parliamentary situation in Europe, relations with non-member countries continue to be largely on a bilateral basis and we will have to see whether the relations with the EFTA parliamentary group will be strengthened. The same is true for relations with the Council of Europe assembly where we can only speculate for the time being whether the rather low-profile relationship will change in the future. Parliamentary relations with the CMEA countries clearly follow a group–bilateral pattern.

Certainly during the immediate future the EP will continue to express its concern for democracy and the respect of human rights. It has become almost a moral conscience of the EC. Its esteem outside the Community is often much greater than within it, where its lack of formal powers is often misinterpreted as ineffectiveness. The Parliament is likely therefore to strengthen its role as the moral watchdog of the Community, even it if needs to be careful not to overdo it and to express an opinion on every minor issue of perhaps only news value. In one year alone, the Parliament voted 37 resolutions on questions concerning Latin America, not all of them of major importance. The EP should be selective in its approach and should concentrate its efforts on the main issues, while not forgetting that the imprisonment of an individual in a country may be a major issue.

The various instruments at the disposal of the Parliament, from formal committees or parliamentary delegations to the activities of the various political groups and beyond to the rather informal inter-groups, provide a wide and differentiated scope for the EP's activities in external relations. This scope should certainly not be reduced but some internal harmonization, where it is necessary and useful, would increase its effectiveness. This might include a closer interaction between the various competent parliamentary committees and the delegations. But these are matters for internal organization which do not put into question the broad orientations as they have emerged over the last 10 years since the first direct elections and will certainly be strengthened and further developed during the present third legislature.

Annex

Parliamentary delegations of the European Parliament

	No of members
A. *Europe*	
- Northern Europe	10
- Norway	10
- Switzerland	8
- Austria	10
- Yugoslavia	10
- The countries of Eastern Europe working in two groups	19
- The Union of Soviet Socialist Republics	22
- Malta	8
- Cyprus	10
- Turkey	18
- Poland	11
- Hungary	11
B. *North Africa/The Middle East*	
- The Maghreb countries (Algeria, Morocco and Tunisia)	12
- The Mashrek countries (Egypt, Jordan, Lebanon and Syria)	11
- Israel	13
- The Gulf States	10
C. *The Americas*	
- The United States	26
- Canada	13
- Latin America (Latin American Parliament, Andean Parliament) working in two specialized groups:	
(a) for the countries of Central America	25
(b) for the countries of South America	25
D. *Asia and Australia*	
- The countries of South Asia	14
- The Member States of ASEAN and the ASEAN Interparliamentary Organization (AIPO) and the Republic of Korea	20
- The People's Republic of China	18
- Japan	18
- Australia and New Zealand	14
E. *International Organizations*	
- United Nations	9

13 European Political Cooperation: concerted diplomacy in an inter-regional context

Peter von Jagow

At a time when European Political Cooperation was still a relatively new field of common action, the Foreign Ministers of the Community member states predicted in their London Report of 1981 that:

As European Political Cooperation intensifies and broadens, the Ten as such will appear as significant interlocutors. Third countries will increasingly express the desire to enter into more or less regular contacts with them. It is important that the Ten should be able to respond effectively to these demands.[1]

This line was confirmed by the Solemn Declaration of Stuttgart in 1983[2] and by the Single European Act of 1986, which stipulates that 'The High Contracting Parties shall organize a political dialogue with third countries and regional groupings whenever they deem it necessary'.[3]

The London Report has proved to be a correct prediction of the further development of EPC. In its practical work, i.e. the 'endeavour jointly to formulate and implement a European foreign policy',[4] contacts with third countries have considerably increased in number and importance. Political dialogue with regional groupings are special cases in this general framework.

A broad variety of different ways of conducting dialogue has emerged over the years. While the principle remains intact that requests for dialogue must be adequately responded to, practical implementation has led to problems of capacity. Contacts have therefore to be organized efficiently within the limits of timetables and logistics.

The policy pursued by the Twelve has been driven by strong motives. As early as 1970, in their first ministerial report on EPC, the member states envisaged 'the time when Europe will be able to speak with one voice'.[5] Two decades later, remarkable progress has been made towards this goal. On an increasing number of issues and occasions, the Twelve do present a joint position, thus enhancing the effectiveness of their common endeavour, strengthening their influence in the world and reinforcing the European identity.

Political dialogues of the Twelve with other regional groupings are more than just a useful combination of contacts with individual third countries, convenient for reasons of time and logistics as it may be. The conceptual approach is more ambitious. It was spelled out by Federal

German Minister for Foreign Affairs, Mr Genscher, speaking as President-in-Office of the EC and EPC at the General Assembly of the United Nations in 1978:

This Europe of the Nine wants to be a centre of cooperation in the world, and it sees itself on the side of those who seek to create an order for that cooperation founded on equality and partnership ... The European Community is founded on respect for the equality of all its members and on the principle of joint decision making. On the strength of these qualities and principles it can serve as an example for a global order giving all States, big and small, the same right and the same opportunity to play a part in the shaping of their common future. It can also serve as an example of the countries of a region forming an association and combining their efforts so as to accomplish the task at hand and to strengthen the independence, the political stability and the economic growth of that region. We are glad to see that the idea of regional association among States with equal rights is gaining ground in all parts of the world and we support this trend.[6]

In November 1978, when opening the first Foreign Ministers Conference of EC and ASEAN, Mr Genscher, again speaking as President-in-Office, stressed the political significance of the event in similar terms. He said:

The Community and ASEAN are voluntary groupings that have formed themselves on the basis of equality. Both have set themselves the aim of furthering the economic and social well-being of their Member States. Both are, in their respective regions, major and recognized factors of stability and peace. With this conference we are adding to the regional and inter-regional dimension. The first meeting at ministerial level is a testimony to the firm will of both organizations to join each other as partners in the work of building the one world whose main characteristics are interdependence and cooperation.[7]

Inter-regional cooperation and political dialogue, two sides of the same coin, have remained preferred strategies of the EC and the EPC ever since, repeatedly applied and with notable success. In this sense, the relationship built up between the EC and its member states and the Association of South-East Asian Nations (ASEAN) presents itself as a classic case. Economic cooperation and political dialogue with this group of states has become an example of steadiness and maturity. It is an important contribution to international stability and development. To the Community, this dialogue offers a welcome opportunity to raise the European voice in the Asian–Pacific region.

Seven meetings at Foreign Minister level have been held since 1978, alternatively in Asia and in Europe. The meeting convened in Dusseldorf in May 1988 was one of the highlights of EPC under the German Presidency. As the final communiqué of the Düsseldorf meeting put it, the Foreign Ministers 'confirmed that EC and ASEAN [had] developed a working relationship which matured into an enhanced and broad mutual understanding in all fields'.[8] They found it be in the best interests of both sides to strengthen this relationship in its political as well as its economic elements. The list of regional and international issues covered in the dialogue stretched from Kampuchea to the INF Treaty; it is a dialogue that deserves its name. The European Council of Madrid endorsed this policy welcoming 'that political dialogue and economic cooperation with ASEAN have proved effective and will further be developed at the forthcoming meetings'.[9]

Parallel to this group-to-group dialogue the Community participates in a unique form of conference diplomacy in the same area but in a larger circle. Connected to the annual ASEAN Ministeral Conferences, high-level meetings are held between ASEAN and its 'dialogue partners' from the Pacific: Australia, Canada, Japan, New Zealand and the United States. Since 1982 the Community has taken part in these, represented by the Troika and the Commission. Brunei hosted the meeting in July 1989.

The pattern established by the EC–ASEAN conferences was, as seen in Chapter 6, later applied to the relationship with a region in crisis, Central America. In inaugurating political dialogue and economic cooperation in San José in 1984, the Twelve did not seek the role of a mediator. It was a group of Latin American neighbours acting as the 'Contadora Group' who sought to bring about a political solution to the Central American crisis that had developed out of the civil wars in Nicaragua and El Salvador. The aim of the Twelve was to encourage and support a solution emerging from the region itself. On the political side, this idea was pushed by opening a forum for political dialogue with Central America, the Contadora states being present.[10] In a parallel approach, the EC and its member states offered the five Central American states and Panama the possibility of economic cooperation based on the inter-regional agreement signed in Luxembourg in 1985.[11]

The Ministers participating in the first of the 'San José conferences' characterized the undertaking as a 'new structure of political and economic dialogue between Europe and Central America'. They stated their conviction in the following terms:

that this dialogue, and the increased practical cooperation that it will engender, will reinforce the efforts of the countries of Central America themselves, with the support of the Contadora States, to bring an end to violence and instability in Central America and to promote social justice, economic development and respect for human rights and democratic liberties in that region.[12]

The initiative of 1984 has developed into a steady process which both sides want to continue. At the time of writing (December 1989), the sixth San José conference is being prepared and will be held in Dublin under the Irish Presidency. The achievements and possible setbacks in the Central American peace process will be evaluated as well as, on a parallel track, the record of economic cooperation and its further possibilities. The political commitment of the Twelve to the Central American question was reiterated by the European Council of Madrid.[13] In September 1989, Roland Dumas, Foreign Minister of France, speaking on behalf of the Twelve in the UN General Assembly, paid tribute to the spirit of moderation and concertation of the Central American Heads of State inspired by the 'breeze' of democracy. Referring to the San José V conference held in Honduras he added that: 'La Conférence de San Pedro Sula en février 1989 a illustré la volonté de la communauté européenne et des pays du groupe de Contadora d'appuyer le processus de négociation et d'interrogation économique que les gouvernements centraméricains se sont fixés comme objectifs.'[14]

The political dialogue with the Group of Eight is of more recent origin since informal talks of the Twelve with the Foreign Ministers of Argentina, Brazil, Colombia, Mexico, Panama, Peru, Uruguay and Venezuela were inaugurated in the margins of the 42nd UN–General Assembly in New York only in September 1987. In February of 1988 the Group, also known as 'Rio Group', suspended the participation of Panama. Taking advantage of the San José IV conference, the second meeting with the Group of Eight was arranged in Hamburg in March 1988.[15] The meeting stretched over an afternoon conference and a working dinner, thus offering more time than in New York. The informal character of the exchange of views was maintained with no fixed agenda or joint communiqué. However, in order to avoid a sequence of repetitive general statements, the debate was structured with alternating introductions of subjects by ministers from both sides. The same pattern was followed a year later in Grenada, where Spain hosted a morning and lunch meeting, before the informal or 'Gymnich type' ministerial weekend of the Twelve Community Foreign Ministers.[16]

The informal character of the dialogue has enabled participants to discuss subjects such as the economic crisis in Latin America and especially the problem of foreign debts which could not be formally negotiated in this forum. The value of the dialogue lies in the direct and frank exchange of views on questions of common concern, thus preparing the ground for solutions that have to be worked out in other circles. In contrast to the case of Central America, the dialogue with the Eight was not intended to focus on one main subject. The list of subjects to be discussed included in principle all major questions of international politics, European developments, East–West relations as well as Latin American issues. However, in practice the trend has been to concentrate on critical developments in Latin America. Apart from the debt problem, one of the major subjects discussed was the fight against drugs.

For the Twelve, these meetings with the representatives of 330 million Latin Americans have been opportunities to get a better feeling for the basic concerns of the partners and to express their continued support for the development of democracy in Latin America. This aspect found its public expression in the conclusions of the European Council of Madrid which called for the continued development of political and other contacts with Latin America.[17] As in the case of the Central American dialogue, Ireland will be host to the next meeting.

If these examples are in many ways classical cases of group-to-group political dialogue, the remaining cases are of a somewhat different nature. The dialogue with the Gulf Cooperation Council (GCC), for example, has included political issues of special interest to that region, but it is evidently a collateral exercise beside the economic cooperation between the EC and the GCC based on the Cooperation Agreement of July 1988. The habit of meeting in the margins of the UN General Assembly was established in 1986. On 27 September 1989 the Foreign Ministers of both groups met in New York for their fourth working luncheon. In addition, two meetings under the troika formula were held in June 1987 and June 1988.

The Euro-Arab Dialogue (EAD) initiated in 1974 was designed as a broad exercise in improving relations in general, including the economic, technical and cultural fields. It was equipped with a substantial institutional mechanism. As an instrument of comprehensive multilateral consultations it was meant to have positive effects on the key political problem of that region, i.e. the Israeli–Arab conflict. However, the EAD was not to serve as the forum for negotiations on that conflict, a position which itself caused the EAD to come to a standstill in 1983. Various efforts to revive it have been undertaken since 1986. Under the German Presidency, for example, the 'Troika' of both sides met on 24 June 1988 and reached agreement that the dialogue should be revived and that the General Commission composed of Ambassadors should be convened again. This has not yet taken place.

On 25 October 1989, President Mitterrand took a new initiative by inviting both sides to a ministerial conference to be held in Paris. The initiative was confirmed by the European Council of Strasbourg — under the French Presidency — in the following statement:

The European Council expresses its desire to make closer the ties which unite the Twelve to the Arab world from one side of the Mediterranean to the other. It is in the spirit that a Conference has been organised which will meet in Paris on 21 and 22 December and whose purpose will be to give a new impetus to the Euro-Arab Dialogue in order to strengthen and develop their cooperation.[18]

The issues of Southern Africa are the core of the two other sets of political group-to-group dialogues: in 1986 a ministerial dialogue was taken up with the six Front Line States (FLS), using the opportunity of the Non-Aligned summit of Lusaka. The Six and the Twelve met again three years later, this time on the margins of a European event, i.e. the Seventy-fourth EPC Ministerial Meeting in Luxembourg. It was considered a useful exchange of views.

The other case involves the oldest region-to-region relationship undertaken by the EC, to which the element of political dialogue was added relatively late, the Group of African, Caribbean and Pacific states (ACP). Again, Southern Africa was the main issue which led to the desire of the 66 ACP states to add political consultations to their long-standing institutionalized relation with the EC. In 1988, under the German Presidency a formula of representation of both sides was developed for the purpose: the Troika and Commission on the European and thirteen states on the ACP side. A second meeting of the European Troika and the ACP 'Thirteen' followed in Brussels in November 1989.

The list of dialogue partners of the Twelve usually includes the Council of Europe and the EFTA states. In both directions political dialogue does take place, but not really in a group-to-group manner. Regarding the Council of Europe, it seems more appropriate to speak of a dialogue in it rather than with it. The Twelve, who are all members of this larger circle, use the Strasbourg forum to exchange views with the eleven states that do not belong to the EC.

In 1983 it was agreed to set aside an informal part of the semi-annual ministerial meeting in Strasbourg, normally half a day for such an exchange. In this framework the minister holding the EC Presidency reports on the activities of the past six months. Not surprisingly, developments in Central and Eastern Europe have been at the centre of more recent debates. As a result of the debate, the Council decided to build a new bridge towards the reforming countries in Central and Eastern Europe offering them the forum of the Council for political dialogue, and inviting Poland and Hungary to accede to the cultural convention and others.

This dialogue within the Council of Europe is held on three levels. Beside Ministers, Political Directors of the member states meet in the margins of the Committee of Ministers for complementary consultations. In practice, the exercise seems to be suffering from the lack of time available to Political Directors. At the working level, experts from capitals together with permanent representatives hold semi-annual consultations on United Nations and CSCE matters.

On 11 July 1989 a first 'quadripartite meeting' was held in Paris, assembling the President-in-Office of both the EC and the Council of Europe, as well as the Secretary General of the latter and the President of the EC Commission. This does not contradict the view that political dialogue does not take place between the two organizations but rather within the Council of Europe. The meeting was not an EPC matter but fell under the competence of the EC as such and it dealt with practical questions of coordinating the activities of both institutions.

As far as the EFTA states are concerned, the current intensification of relations between EC and EFTA has not yet led to a change of the established forms of political dialogue with those states. The Twelve maintain close political contacts with EFTA states at all levels but they do so with every EFTA state individually and within the Council of Europe.

As contacts of the Twelve with third countries and regional groupings increase, problems of coordinating the schedules of twelve ministers and the Commission grow. In outlining his Government's programme to the European Parliament, the French Foreign Minister, M. Dumas, as

President-in-Office of the EC and EPC declared: 'J'observe avec intérêt ce besoin de dialogue avec les Douze, qui s'exprime partout dans le monde, de manière de plus en plus pressante au point que cela finit par poser de sérieux problèmes de calendrier.'[19] Given the heavy commitments of the EC and EPC calendars, ministers have difficulty in finding time for further meetings. However, in view of the declared political will to have such meetings, the logistical problems have to be solved, which is a matter of prudently deploying limited resources. Conducting political dialogue with regional groupings instead of individual third countries represents in itself a way of economizing on scarce time. There is a large variety of further possibilities that can be adapted to the individual situation involving level, participation, frequency and form.

With regard to level, the opportunity of delegating the dialogue to Political Directors is already frequently taken in contacts with individual states. However, the ministerial level has remained the general rule with regional groupings. For all five San José conferences held so far with Central America, ministerial participation has been maintained. But the formal commitment, undertaken by both sides in the Luxembourg Final Act, is somewhat cautious: the political dialogue was institutionalized 'in particular by the holding of annual meetings, in principle at ministerial level'.[20]

As far as participation is concerned, this usually involves the Twelve as a whole and the Troika and the Commission, rather than the Presidency alone. Some meetings have been limited to the 'troika formula' (EAD, ACP) while a mixed pattern has been applied in other cases such as ASEAN, Central America and GCC. The Central American states meet the full Twelve in annual San José conferences and the Troika during the UN General Assembly in New York.

As for frequency, meetings of the Twelve and ASEAN follow each other roughly every 18 months, a rule that has been followed over seven conferences since 1978. With Central America the more ambitious annual rhythm was introduced. With the exception of 1986, one San José conference has been held every year and it seems that this rhythm will continue. The dialogue with both groupings is completed by meetings with the Troika using the opportunity of ministerial presence at other events (such as the UN General Assembly and the ASEAN Ministerial Conferences). The frequency of meetings with the Group of Eight seems to have been even shorter. Since the Autumn of 1987 both sides have in fact met twice a year. But in all cases, the opportunity of another forum was used: the opening week of the UN General Assembly has allowed for regular meetings with the Gulf States since 1986. They are held in the form of a luncheon meeting. The logistic advantage of the United Nations is clear. In 1989, within a single week, a total of eight meetings were organized in the framework of EPC, three of them with regional and five with individual states. But even in New York there is no exception to the rule of 24 hours to a day.

As has been indicated, meetings can take place in varying forms. As far as modalities are concerned, there is some room for manoeuvre. Combining meetings with others seems to render especially good results in efficiency, reducing time and workloads for everybody. Another way of alleviating the burden is to keep meetings informal. Working over meals has become a familiar procedure. It is often combined with restriction of attendance to a minimum, a formula which allows ministers to have eye-to-eye contact with their colleagues, but which makes life difficult for advisers and note-takers.

At the other end of the scale of formality, there are conferences that stretch over two days, which conclude with a joint political declaration or communiqué and which are combined with talks on economic cooperation. These cases require considerably more preparation, including preparatory meetings of experts. ASEAN and Central America are such cases.

The preparatory work for all such meetings is clearly considerable. The work of ministers is of course most visible to the public. Decisions taken by the European Council and by Foreign Ministers meeting in political cooperation are published and are usually well covered by the press. Much less visible in the political dialogues with other regional groupings is the work undertaken by Political Directors and the experts groups.

It needs to be remembered that, in the EPC framework, there are no standing bodies in Brussels comparable to those in the EC. EPC is a network directly linking actors in foreign ministries in their respective capitals. They remain in daily contact via a special telex system (COREU) and, of course, by telephone. At regular and frequent intervals they leave their desks in their ministries and assemble either in Brussels in the premises of the EPC Secretariat (experts) or in the capital of the Presidency (Political Committee and European Correspondents).

It must also be remembered that EPC works without an organ comparable to the EC Commission. The EPC Secretariat is comparable in nature to the Secretariat of the EC Council. Its tasks are defined in the Single European Act: '[it] shall assist the Presidency in preparing and implementing the activities of European Political Cooperation and in administrative matters. It shall carry out its duties under the authority of the Presidency.'

'Assisting the Presidency' includes the work that has to be done to prepare, carry through and follow up dialogues with regional groupings. Just as the Secretariat in general has become an increasingly useful instrument of the Presidency, so its role in organizing regional dialogues is of considerable importance. On the occasion of the signing of the Single European Act (28 February 1986), ministers agreed that the Secretariat should 'assist the Presidency, where appropriate, in contacts with third countries'. On this basis, and under the guidance of the different presidencies, the Secretariat has developed to become a solid pillar in the construction.

One of the five officials accompanies the relevant working group, and especially its chairman, through the whole process of organizing political dialogue meetings with a regional grouping. Seconded to the Secretariat for a period covering five presidencies, these officials are able to develop considerable experience over their two and a half years. This personal experience, combined with the 'memory' of the Secretariat archives, provides valuable bases of their work. In several cases members of the Secretariat have drawn up the first draft of joint political declarations and followed their development through the discussions among the Twelve and with the other side in the dialogue. Just as valuable is their assistance to the Presidency in drawing up conclusions of meetings and of elements for the information of partners' capitals through the COREU network. The head of the Secretariat has an important function in supervising the work of the five officials and in his liaison with political directors and at all ministerial levels. The mandate of the Secretariat will be among the questions to be reviewed in due course. For the time being it can be said that the political dialogue with regional groupings could not be conducted without it.

A general conclusion could simply be that the work done by EPC bodies in this field has proved to be useful and should be pursued. There is little doubt that it will, the number of events being organized under the Irish Presidency being indicative of that. Yet the tide of political interest may seem to be running against this form of dialogue. Certainly, the dynamic development of the relations with Central and Eastern European countries does not follow the group-to-group pattern for evident reasons. But even if some of the energy of the Twelve may at present be absorbed by East–West relations, the Twelve can hardly allow themselves to be distracted from their other fields of activity where they must also meet their responsibilities and honour their commitments.

For the Twelve, group-to-group dialogue has become one of their main ways of taking action, i.e. for 'implementing a European foreign policy'. It offers valuable opportunities to strengthen the political principles commonly agreed upon. That means essentially that for the Twelve their dialogue with other regional groupings is one of the ways of contributing to a peaceful, just and stable world. The echo received over the years from their dialogue partners seems to indicate that these basic and general motives are being shared by their partners in all parts of the world. All this makes group-to-group dialogue a worthy cause and satisfying to work for.

Notes

1 Report on European Political Cooperation issued by the Foreign Ministers of the Ten on 13 October 1981 (London Report), para. 7.
2 Solemn Declaration on European Union (Stuttgart, 19 June 1983), para. 3.2.
3 Single European Act (Luxembourg, 17 February 1986 and The Hague, 28 February 1986), Art. 30 para. 8.
4 ibid., Art. 30 para. 1
5 First Report of the Foreign Ministers to the Heads of State and Government of the Member States of the European Community of 27 October 1970 (Luxembourg Report), Part 1 para. 8
6 Speech at the 33rd UN General Assembly (New York, 26 September 1978)
7 Opening statement at the EC–ASEAN Foreign Ministers Conference (Brussels, 20 November 1978).
8 Final Communiqué Düsseldorf, 2–3 May 1988. The date of the next meeting is still open (December 1989).
9 European Council (Madrid, 26–27 June 1989), conclusions Part II, para. 6.
10 Conferences between the EC and its Member States, Spain and Portugal and the States of Central America and of the Contadora Group, San José de Costa Rica, 28–29 September 1984, and Luxembourg, 11–12 November 1985, *Bulletin of the EC* 9-1984 and *Bulletin* 11-1985.
11 Cooperation Agreement, Luxembourg, 12 November 1985, *Official Journal of the EC*, No. L 172, 30.06 1986.
12 Joint Communiqué of San José, 29 September 1984, para. 3.
13 European Council (Madrid, 26–27 June 1989), conclusions, part II para 5.
14 Speech at the 44th UN General Assembly (New York, 26 September 1989).
15 Hamburg, 1 March 1988.
16 15 April 1989.
17 See note 14.
18 European Council (Strasbourg, 8–9 December 1989).
19 R. Dumas, President-in-Office of the EC and EPC, Foreign Minister of France, speech held at the European Parliament (Strasbourg, 27 July 1989).
20 Final Act of the Luxembourg Conference, see note 11.

Part IV
Conclusions: the dialogue and its place in the European and international systems

14 The relevance of theory to group-to-group dialogue

Geoffrey Edwards[1]

The academic as a purveyor of fashion is not a new phenomenon. The social scientist has often been charged with being particularly prone to chasing the latest fad, some commentators speaking in terms of 'pack scholarship', the herd instinct as applied to academics.[2] Regionalism as an area of study has suffered along with others; it has swept in, and out, of fashion. Its heyday was the late 1960s/early 1970s, its nadir its public condemnation as obsolescent in 1976.[3] However, regional organization now appears to be making something of a comeback, at least empirically, and with it, inter-regional dialogue. Academic theorists have yet to catch up. There is, so far, no clearly discernible regionalist bandwagon on the move within the International Relations discipline, merely isolated commentaries.

If the 'pack scholarship' criticism is justified, it is of course merely a matter of time before regionalism becomes once again the object of extensive study. However, the jibe of faddishness needs an extra comment or two. IR as a discipline is perhaps beset by problems of fashion more than others in the social sciences; if the subject matter is war and peace, conflict and cooperation, it is not particularly surprising that immediate political issues and new ways of trying to deal with them affect those involved in their study. It is not that fashion is necessarily a 'bad thing'; it is rather that what has been left by the fashionable may be unrelated to what has gone before, that, to change the metaphor, there are too many 'islands of theory' within the discipline. The concerns of the discipline have too rarely been those of incrementalism and of synthesis rather than revolutions and 'paradigm shifts'.[4]

The issue becomes important if, in part at least, criticisms which imply an excess of superficiality rest on a lack of appreciation (or perhaps too great an appreciation!) of some of the fundamental problems of epistemology — after all, the 'laboratory' of international relations is decidedly deficient in the extent to which it allows for experimentation and validation. History may well be a rich quarry for model-building and theorizing but it requires a decidedly positivist commitment to hold that what information is now available on an historical event was all that was 'real' then, or that general explanations can hold good over time and space, or that 'facts' can be happily if not easily divorced from values. But this is not an essay in epistemology. Rather it is a discussion set at a more mundane level; it seeks to explore the extent to which a discipline moved largely by a desire to solve 'problems' can assist us in understanding the growth of regional organization and can offer guidelines or suggest future tendencies in the international system.

Yet one of the difficulties involved in such a venture is of course the question of the separability of the theorist from either his/her environment or time. In terms of environment, there may well be a debate over the question of the decline of American hegemony within the international system, but the emphasis placed on, and, of perhaps even greater moment, the resources devoted to, International Relations theory in the United States has created its own hegemony. As Steve Smith has pointed out,[5] all the major debates in the discipline have for the most part been confined to the United States, whether idealism versus realism, realism versus behaviouralism or behaviouralism versus post-behaviouralism. Moreover it has not simply been domination of the debate over differing approaches, it has also extended to determining the subjects 'fit' for theorizing.

America's global leadership has not unnaturally led to a great deal of theorizing about global 'order'; or as Kratchwill and Ruggie put it: 'The substantive core around which the various theoretical approaches have clustered is the problem of international governance.'[6] A strongly normative element has been characteristic of that approach even if sometimes only implicit (and sometimes even hotly denied in favour of 'hard-nosed' realism). But it is also not surprising that an essential component and a vital determinant of those approaches has been the role of the United States in that international governance. Clearly the need for the United States, its administration and its political and economic processes and structures to come to terms with its position in the global system required both moral and intellectual explanation and legitimation. That it should achieve such leadership within a post-war system which was markedly different from the multi-polar, balance-of-power system that had preceded it reinforced the need. The fact that its own breadth of knowledge and cultural diversity had been further extended by many scientists from a multitude of disciplines who had suffered because of the weaknesses of liberal democracy perhaps inevitably led to rigorous innovation, debate and conflict.

America's relative decline — or the rise or resurgence of others, most notably, of course, Japan and Western Europe — and loss of hegemony has caused a recurrence of inward preoccupation. The popular success of Kennedy's *The Rise and Fall of the Great Powers*[7] clearly reflected prevailing concerns. For others, the loss of hegemony has raised wider issues, particularly the role of American leadership in creating and maintaining international stability. The implication is sometimes somewhat obvious, that the world is in for a period of instability, that the United States maintained observance of rules and had thereby upheld and encouraged expectations and confidence in continued stability through the various international regimes and organizations set up since 1945. Such preoccupations should not have been unexpected, nor are the findings without value. What, however, is sadly lacking in the US academic debate — from admittedly a non-American perspective — is the limited awareness of what the rest of the world has been doing over the last 20 years. American academics may have been theorizing about the role of the state in a world of complex interdependence, but somehow the model always seemed to be the United States. For their part, too, US political leaders have sometimes appeared to be doing their best to ignore or at least avoid the consequences of interdependence. Elsewhere, practitioners as well as academics have been obliged to come to terms with it. However, such criticisms are perhaps another aspect of the hegemon's dilemma: when it leads it is criticized for leadership (because, of course, it is not leading in the 'required' direction); when it hesitates it is criticized for lacking the qualities of leadership.

The rise and fall and rise again of regionalism

What has been absent from the agenda of all too many international relations theorists has been a discussion of regionalism. Paul Taylor in a recent paper[8] suggested that up to five different approaches to the concept of regionalism had been discernible in the 1970s and none had really survived into the latter part of the same decade, except perhaps for what was becoming their historical interest. Their range was wide and encompassed a number of different behaviouralist approaches.[9] By the late 1970s, all, including neofunctionalism, had been damned as passé, victims either to methodological criticism (either for lacking rigour or for being over-rigorous), the inability of the European Community to conform to patterns and predictions, or the greater salience of more global issues.

Yet it is clear from the evidence — not least that presented by Taylor using the *Yearbook of International Organization* — that regionalism has been on the increase and, similarly, inter-regional arrangements. That American academics have not returned to the fray is, of course, in part due to particular American preoccupations suggested above. Moreover, regionalism does not easily 'fit' into debates on global interdependence; indeed it may detract from holistic approaches (which have themselves been criticized for being reductionist in the sense that they are ultimately dependent on the nature and the role of states, not least of the United States). Nor is regionalism necessarily compatible with more sectoral 'regime' theories. It is probably irrelevant to 'critical theory'.

But those involved in establishing regional groups have themselves remained largely silent. With, of course, some notable exceptions, Europeans often appear loath to theorize.[10] It has been suggested that this is due to recent analysts pursuing an inductive strategy which, in

terms at least of the West European 'region', leaves such a vast array of
sometimes contradictory variables that an orderly theoretical
framework becomes impossible.[11] Ifestos has been cited to make the
point,[12] for he appears to suggest that the interplay of intra-regional and
extra-regional variables establishes such a multi-dimensional network
of inter-relationships and interactions that it becomes almost
impossible to include them all in any single model. Weaving a clear path
through such complexities becomes an impossibility — unless, of course,
one is prepared to simplify, to forgo richness for parsimony, to
systematize, to generalize — on a more overt and rather more rigorous
basis than simply intuitive induction.

   If so, one is inevitably forced back on to the old maxim that what one
sees is determined by where one stands — or sits. Sitting in the
Berlaymont will give one a rather different perspective from that
provided by a seat in a national cabinet; the Mediterranean takes on a
completely different dimension depending on whether one depends on it
for one's livelihood or uses it simply for a two-week holiday. Examples
can be multiplied *ad infinitum*; the point is perhaps too obvious. The
International Relations discipline has a multitude of different
approaches, of grand theories and sub- and pre-theories, some focusing
on political economy issues, others on security studies and so on. Their
evolution need not detain us; the point is that by the end of the 1970s,
divisions within the discipline were manifold. In an effort to understand
and explain what was going on and to provide some element of focus,
several scholars sought to bring together the variety of bits and pieces
within three main approaches or paradigms,[13] each a relatively
coherent set of values, principles, beliefs and logical patterns, each in
competition in its attempts to explain. The most common categories are
known as the realist or state centric, the pluralist or liberal and the
structuralist or socialist/neo-Marxist.

   This competing paradigm approach has not won universal
acceptance, whether in the social sciences or as an explanation of the
revolutions in the natural sciences. For our purposes, it does not need to.
It serves here in order to point to and give weight to different factors
within relatively coherent frameworks. What follows therefore is an
effort to explore some elements of the 'inter-paradigm debate' which
may explain the growth of regional organizations and the objectives of
their various members and which, in addition, may offer some
indication of how those organizations inter-relate with each other
within the international system.

   In view of the inter-governmental nature of EPC and all the other
regional groupings discussed in this volume, a realist approach might
well be considered the most appropriate point of departure.[14] Some
might also argue — as Ifestos appears sometimes to do — that given the
central position of the Council of Ministers in the Community decision-
making process, the role of the member states is maintained and
realism reinforced. Moreover, it is clear that neither EPC nor the

external relationships of the Community exhaust the external interactions of the member states; bilateral relations are still of the utmost importance. However, as becomes clear, the concept of group-to-group dialogue suggests alternative views. It implies, for example, that we are dealing on the European side not simply with EPC or the Community but with both in what Flaesch-Mougin describes as a 'global dialogue' (Chapter 2) in which the 'political' and 'economic' aspects are intimately inter-related. A purely political explanation of the Community and, it is suggested, of other regional organizations becomes inadequate; just as economics is too serious a business to be left to economists, so political intercourse and exchange cannot be left to political scientists. In other words, maintaining the artificial division between EPC and the Community is inappropriate and misleading; 'Real life allows no such distinction', as Douglas Hurd once put it (when Minister of State at the Foreign and Commonwealth Office).[15] For all the subtleties of the Single European Act, the Community and EPC are more appropriately to be seen as the manifestation of similar underlying forces or, rather, as parts of an overall response to a variety of pressures which emanate from both within the member states and from the international system. Moreover, there are comparable pressures at work in other regional organizations, which may determine or influence the way they interact with the Community/Twelve. Structures and systems may differ; they are after all the result of unique configurations of historical processes, but they frequently remain comparable at a level which has meaning and insight.

The realist approach

The realist approach has dominated International Relations since the Second World War. It has sustained a number of challenges (particularly over methodology between traditionalists and behaviouralists) and has even witnessed the evolution of a sub-species, 'neo-realism', when it retained those seemingly moving more towards a structural theory of International Relations[16] and enticed back into its ample fold some who had appeared to stray towards a more pluralistic, transnational approach during the 1970s.[17] The basic assumptions and goals remain very largely those enunciated by Carr, Morgenthau and others[18] which, put simply, add up to the following: the primary unit in the international system is the state; the domestic character of the state is very largely taken as a given, the essential influence on a state's behaviour being its participation in the international system; the international system itself is anarchical in sharp contrast to the domestic system within the state; and thus the over-riding goal and national interest of the state is the pursuit of power, with security provided best by means of a balance of power.

If the maintenance of such a system of nation states is fundamental, regional groupings are, logically, only voluntary exercises in cooperation or 'convergent whims' to use a phrase of Puchala;[19] the state is merely adapting to different circumstances. Even though its sovereign independence may be more circumscribed than in the past, or at least circumscribed by new factors, states still take the final decisions. In principle, at least, it retains the right to secede from any organization — on the basis, that is, of a rational assessment of the national interest. Cooperation, as Calleo has suggested, may even have been sought in order to gain greater control over the national economic environment; 'Cooperation has increased rather than diminished national sovereignty'.[20] It is certainly clear from many of the chapters in this volume that many states have sought to achieve a better negotiating position *vis à vis* the Community by means of cooperative group activity.

If cooperation can better protect sovereignty against 'external' challenges, in so far as it extends a national capability in the international system, then 'supranationalism' becomes illogical, a mere rhetorical flourish. Regional groupings such as the European Community remain essentially concerts of states.[21] European states may, perhaps, slough off their 'national' labels — they after all are of relatively recent vintage — but they remain a collectivity of states pursuing state interests in a still anarchical international environment. The implications for group-to-group relations thus become clear; relations are essentially a reflection of state interests born of the inherently unstable inter-state system, even if bounded by a general predisposition to seek peace and order in the system (so better to maintain security and prosperity), and determined by each state's appreciation of it of the maximum bargaining pay-off.

Cooperation in the conditions of anarchy presented by the realists can thus be seen as a rational outcome. This is especially so, according to some games theoreticians, in circumstances of continuous negotiation, repeated playing of the Prisoners' Dilemma game being particularly illustrative of such an option.[22] But the applicability of the game — and indeed some others — to the interaction of states is questionable and even more so in the case of the interaction of groups of states. The internal rationalization of an individual's behaviour is a poor substitute for the decision-making processes of the state subject as they are to domestic constraints and pressures as well as the pull and push of the international environment — a line of argument which, together with the whole foreign policy analysis approach, poses a challenge to or at least stretches the realist's concept of the state as a monolithic and rational actor. But the interaction of groups of states complicates the issue even further, both in terms of the structure of the international system and its processes.

The pluralist approach

While perhaps not as clear and coherent (simplistic?) as the realist approach, the pluralist 'paradigm' has none the less sought to view 'reality' on the basis of some consistency. In essence, it accepts that individuals, organizations and international institutions are international actors alongside states and that they can have a role in modifying the interests of states.[23] To some, it is essentially a question of liberalism in the sense of freedom either in a pure or 'compensatory' form,[24] that is, freedom from government or from restraint as far as is possible. There is, as in the realist approach, a normative element, but whereas the realist might believe that a balance of power, however fundamentally precarious, is in the interests of long-term peace and security, the pluralist tends to hold that cooperation in the interests of maximizing benefits is an end in itself. The goal of free, or at least freer trade, for example, increases trade and thereby interdependence which brings about both greater opportunities for and the necessity of cooperation which thus engenders peace.

The pluralist approach received considerable stimulus from the work of the transnationalists such as Keohane and Nye in the early 1970s[25] and the 'world society' approach of scholars such as Burton.[26] Their re-emphasis on individual needs and values, on the role of trade, on the implications of the size and resources of multinational corporations and the role of international institutions all pointed to a marked shift in the traditional role of the state. To some extent their enthusiasm may have led them to exaggerate the demise of the state (and the decline of the United States). However, the debate they launched on the changed role of the state in an inter-dependent international system continues.

To some extent, the debate may appear to be over whether the glass is half full or half empty. What is significant to some are the powers and instruments of power retained by the member states of EPC.[27] To the pluralist, the question concerns more what the states have given up. Clearly the member states have not given EPC a supranational dimension, nor have they extended it beyond cooperation in foreign policy to encompass a defence identity; defence has remained a national responsibility although (with the exception of Ireland) each is heavily committed to NATO or, at least, the Atlantic Alliance. NATO to the realist is assumed to be a traditional alliance; the question of whose thumb is on which button — and the issue of the 'independence' of Britain's nuclear deterrence taxes even some British Conservatives — is largely ignored.

In a similar way, the Community is not as yet (and *pace* Mrs Thatcher) responsible for monetary policy. On the other hand, the British Chancellor of the Exchequer, or even the President of the Bundesbank, would probably welcome an international monetary system in which they could exercise effective control over their own currencies.

Speculators may make fewer profits under the EMS; they have not yet disappeared from the monetary scene. Moreover, the debate over the relationship between governments — and, indeed, the Community — and capital continues; states may often work through large enterprises and multinational corporations; they do not always control their future investment patterns, as many governments have found to their cost.

A pluralist approach does not necessarily deny sovereignty and autonomy of action to the state. It posits, however, that sovereignty in its traditional sense of the ultimate political authority in a political community that is not subject to another ultimate authority elsewhere is no longer wholly appropriate in absolute terms and that state action can be modified by other non-state actors. Thus the Community is not reduced to the sum of its parts but is an independent variable, which has influence and authority in its own right. Its actions may be determined by national interest groups working together at the European level, especially through the European Commission, with final decisions being taken by the Council of Ministers but its authority is ultimately, perhaps, manifested in its institutions, not least, of course, the Court of Justice.

The implications of a pluralist approach for group-to-group relations are almost perversely confusing. Since there is a strong focus on processes and interactions, the suggestion that individuals and their needs, along with organizations and their demands, are to be taken into account at the same time as those of states and governments and international institutions may indeed lead us back to the untidy, multivariate networks that baffled, say, Ifestos. Certainly the approach creates innumerable 'boundary' issues since it suggests that inter-group relations take place on a multitude of levels, including those below and beyond the regional groups themselves. It is, in other words, in marked contrast to the realists' neat division between the domestic and international environments. The pluralists deliberately conflate the two. It is the distinction between the 'billiard ball' approach of the realists and the 'cobwebs' of the pluralists.[28] For some, it is a richer picture of reality with consequently greater explanatory and possibly even predictive qualities; for others it is an unscientific confusion.

But as a result, the agenda of the pluralists differs. What is significant is the existence and strength of various ties that can bind groups, within, that is, an overall framework that does not assume anarchy and potential hostility but potential cooperation and conflict resolution. The emphasis has been less on issues of war and peace, but rather on trade and, in its broadest sense, the opportunities for 'management' in the international system. Clearly there is considerable overlap between the paradigms — many realists including Bull worked within a conception of international society and order. Realists, too, in so far as they examine ways of avoiding war, look at trade and aid policies, just as those looking for cooperative ventures inevitably come up against innumerable cases of competition and conflict. Yet the assumptions are different and hence the stress is different.

The structuralist approach

If, for some pluralists, the global system can be reduced to individual needs, it is the whole that concerns the structuralist. Structuralists 'assume that human behaviour cannot be understood simply by examining individual motivation and intention because, when aggregated, human behaviour precipitates structures of which the individuals may be unaware'.[29] Nor have all realists been impervious to the influence exerted on state behaviour by the existence of an international system even if one made up of states. Waltz, for example, stresses in particular the influence of the structure of the system.[30] At the same time, since states continue to exist, a number of Marxists or neo-Marxists have attributed to it some autonomy, even if within the overall global capitalist system.[31] The hallmark, as it were, of the structural approach is both its holistic nature and its conviction that structure is an autonomous independent variable.

Clearly a good deal of structuralist thinking owes much to Marx and interpretations of Marxism even if the analysts are not themselves Marxists.[32] It has, as a result perhaps, rarely been at the centre of the American International Relations debate, except perhaps briefly in the late 1960s as part of the reaction to war in Vietnam. A primary preoccupation, which owed much to the writings of Lenin and others on imperialism, has been the inequality derived from the international division of labour. The basis of the international system is economic, with capitalism as its predominant form and with inter-state relations constrained by both factors.

Much of the post-Second World War structuralist work was inspired by continued under-development, particularly in Latin America. The stages of development through which the developed North progressed were regarded as inapplicable to the still under-developed South when tied in to a system dominated by international capitalism. Autonomous 'national' development had little meaning, regardless of the World Bank and the IMF, if trade and investment remained largely under the control or direction of the former Imperial powers and the United States. The theme of a centre–periphery or metropolitan–satellite divide is frequently used.[33] The general thesis is that the centre exploits the periphery in order to retain the surplus value for its own development.

While perhaps inspired by the circumstances of Latin America, a number of studies have been done with a neo-Marxist or structuralist paradigm which relate to the European Community and its external relations. The Community itself has sometimes been·regarded as a willing tool of American capitalism in order that indigenous capitalism should be strengthened.[34] For Cox, the Community offers a case of 'intensive internationalization', not simply in the sense that they have become more closely integrated but also in the sense that 'as a group they become more responsive to world-economy pressures', within an overall framework provided by 'pax Americana'.[35] Others have regarded the Community as, whether inevitably or not, perpetuating neo-colonialist relationships.[36]

The implication of the structuralist paradigm for group-to-group relations is that it is both logical and necessary for the Community to sign agreements with its former imperial possessions (imperial here applying to both to formal and informal forms of control) in order to retain as great a control as possible over traditional trading patterns. The inevitable competition from other advanced industrialized states, especially the United States and, increasingly, Japan, reinforce that need. It is equally in the interests of those former possessions to attempt change. Regional organization may be an answer, although the overthrow of global capitalism is no small challenge. Moreover, the capitalist system has according to several structuralists more than subtle ways of undermining opposition. Galtung, for example, points to the interlinkage between élites within the states of the centre and the periphery, where the peripheral élites are, to put it crudely, bought off.[37] Wallerstein suggests that there is an intermediary group of states making up a semi-periphery, dependent on the core, which manipulates it in its own interests, but in a privileged position *vis à vis* the periphery.[38] The basic core–periphery conflict however is for Wallerstein overlaid with the more conventional Marxist struggle between the bourgeoisie and the proletariat.

Beyond the paradigm

The purpose of this paradigmatic excursion has been to suggest some of the over-arching theoretical considerations and approaches that exist in the International Relations discipline. The growth of regional organization and the growing range of ties between such groupings has not as yet been a focus of attention within them. Each approach may explain something of the phenomenon but fuller explanations are lacking. If one accepts the Kuhnian proposition, then the question to be considered is whether regionalism and, consequently, inter-regional dialogue, provides the anomaly that the paradigm cannot contain and which therefore demands a paradigm shift. Hill in his 1988 paper, 'Research into EPC: Tasks for the Future'[39] suggested that EPC is 'too specific and too dependent a variable to entail *in itself* a paradigm shift'. But the growth of regional organization epitomized by the Community/ EPC nexus is rather different. And, as Hill himself suggests, EPC — or rather perhaps the Community and EPC — has to some extent acted as a pressure on other regions 'to get their own acts together in order to be able to deal effectively with the EC'.[40]

However, it is clear that at least some within the International Relations discipline have experienced a distinct wish, even while adhering to the general precepts of Kuhn's approach, to synthesize, to modify some elements within one paradigm in the light of principles emphasized in another. Those claiming to be neo-realists are a case in point. Does, for example, the realist concept of national sovereignty any longer adequately account for the nature of statehood in the contemporary international system given the extent and range of international intercourse? Does regional organization give rise to new international actors that are in a significant sense autonomous even if, in other ways, they are dependent on their member states? Is, on the other hand, the growth of regional organization in its many different forms only a temporary response to deeper pressures within the global system, whether due to capitalist production patterns, the dictates of finance capital or the speed and significance of technological change? Moreover, even if they are only temporary manifestations in their present shape, will the range of relationships entered into by existing regional organizations establish patterns or forms that will persist?

Although Regelsberger (in Chapter 1) pointed to the supplementary character of group-to-group dialogues, that is, supplementary to the bilateral relationships established by the member states of the different groups, she none the less held that the dialogues are important in their own right. One of the themes suggested by both Regelsberger and Flaesch-Mougin (Chapter 2) is the growing 'globalization' of group-to-group dialogues in the sense that the political and economic aspects of the dialogues have become increasingly integrated and consistent. Many of the chapters in this volume point to the myriad of contacts between the groups at different levels — inter-group, inter-state, inter-institutional, inter-interest and even inter-personal. It might be logical in such circumstances to conclude that a realist approach lacks many explanatory insights into the phenomenon, and that, clearly, the pluralist approach offers greater scope. Alternatively, one might conclude that in view of the asymmetries in the relationships established by the EC/Twelve a structuralist approach might elicit even richer rewards.

Clearly, whatever the assumptions made, group-to-group relations can raise interesting and highly relevant questions about the nature of international relations and not least about the role of the state in the international system.

If group-to-group relations are supplementary to bilateral relations, let us assume that the member states of the Community pursue national interests (however determined)[41] in their bilateral relationships with other states, including members of other regional groups. These interests, if one follows the realist path, will lead to rational policies, with a clear ranking of preferences.

At the same time, however, the member states participate in EPC to coordinate their foreign policies. While decisions are ultimately taken on the basis of unanimity, it is clear that there is a strong disposition to agree among the EPC member states. There is, indeed, continuous pressure to do so, not least because of the frequency of contacts at all levels of EPC. There is also the moral pressure exercised by the SEA to consult and to agree on common positions. As a result, it is now news when member states do not agree and break ranks. As Nuttall points out (Chapter 10), experience shows that a median line is usually followed. None the less, one might still argue that EPC is a collection of states pursuing 'state' interests even if on an increasingly coordinated basis.

But these national interests need to be reconciled with the demands of membership of the EC. After all, the Community's competence extends to nearly all trade issues and into aid matters. Moreover, under the SEA, each member state is committed to making their agreed positions in EPC consistent with the policies of the EC. The Community's policies are initiated (formally at least) by the European Commission after considerable discussion with various interested parties and decided on by the member states in the Council of Ministers. The Council — or rather the member states there represented — prefer to reach decisions by consensus, but member states are under even greater pressure than in EPC to concur with the majority view — and on an increasing range of issues it is now a treaty requirement to do so. On some agreements, including Association agreements, the European Parliament, which as Neunreither has shown (Chapter 12) has its own sources of information as well as authority, has also to be consulted.

The question then arises of the extent to which participation in the EC/Twelve significantly modifies national policies. Participation inevitably carries with it the possibility of compromise; standing out against consensus may not carry with it the ultimate threat of being left out (at least so far in the Community's history, though it is sometimes a useful negotiating ploy against more peripheral states — including the United Kingdom), but there is a considerable degree of 'log-rolling','back-scratching' or 'tit for tat' (and similar bargaining ideas) which suggests that standing out too often can be costly. Moreover, as Scharpf has pointed out,[42] standing out against a new decision may simply mean the continuation of existing policies; it does not at this stage in the Community's history necessarily mean a return to unconstrained national action. Existing policies are likely to include elements of common action, which, since there were incentives to negotiate a new agreement, it may be neither rational nor efficient to continue.

Scharpf, as Regelsberger noted in Chapter 1, goes on to suggest that there may, indeed, be a 'joint decision trap', 'an institutional arrangement whose policy outcomes have an inherent (non-accidental) tendency to be sub-optimal'.[43] His suggestion is useful, less perhaps for its implied structural determinism, than simply for revealing the impact of process on participants. At the more general level, Putnam in his 1988 article[44] is less concerned with decision-making as such than with understanding how diplomacy and domestic policies interact. His conclusions provide some useful insights into how, for example, domestic cleavage may foster international cooperation or how policy possibilities previously beyond domestic control can be created by the reverberation at the domestic level of international negotiations.[45] Clearly, negotiators need to take account of entanglements between the two levels at all times, and, equally clearly, the relationship is a symbiotic one and neither level is dependent on the other.

But Putnam recognizes the possible dangers of oversimplification of the relationship when using only two levels (the international and the domestic) and that further levels are possible though with, inevitably, greater complexity involved as a result. If Putnam's model was applied to the 'international' negotiations within the Council of Ministers or among Foreign Ministers in EPC, then clearly a further level is necessary, as the EC/Twelve then negotiate with others. But at that level there is a further complication for although the EC/Twelve negotiate in an increasingly 'globalized' dialogue, individual member states continue to be involved in pursuing their national interests. There are in a sense two interlocking sets of international/domestic negotiations in play.

This obviously has a number of consequences not least a tendency towards immobilism. Given the difficulties of reaching an agreed mandate or position, very little leeway is left to the EC/Twelve when they come to negotiate with third parties, including other groups. If, as would be more than likely, the partner group also had problems in modifying its common position, there will be a tendency towards stalemate that can only be avoided by a reopening of the intra-group negotiations. Minor adjustments might be possible (through, for example, the agreement of the Commission and the Article 113 Committee which is made up of officials from the member states) but they are likely to be minor. If more significant changes are required, it means renewed bargaining among the member states, a bargain that guarantees no greater protection or promotion for any one member state's interests.

Indeed, if, as Scharpf has suggested, the EC/Twelve mandate will be sub-optimal for individual member states, it is possible that the agreement with the partner group will be even less optimal. In such circumstances, one perhaps needs to remember that there was reason to enter into a dialogue. But given the possibility, the member states will face a dilemma between endorsing the EC/Twelve line in their bilateral contacts or attempting to persuade the partner group to stick to a line that might lead to a more optimal outcome, if such an outcome were feasible. One of the more significant factors militating against the temptation to defect from the common position will be the possible consequences for national interests in the continuous bargaining process that now characterizes the EC/Twelve.

But to some the question of whether or not bargaining in the EC/
Twelve and with other groups modifies national aims and objectives
(and the means available to pursue them) is of less interest than the
direction in which those aims are modified; it might, indeed, be
considered somewhat obvious. Is it still a question, as Bull and
Galtung[46] suggested, from radically different perspectives, that the
EC/Twelve is still a state writ large pursuing 'state' objectives? Nuttall
and others have pointed to the attractiveness of the concept of the
EC/Twelve as a Civilian Power even if aware that it may be a notion
once described by Duchene in 1972 as 'soggy with good intentions'.[47]
That a community of hitherto sovereign states determine to resolve
their disputes peacefully among themselves is one thing; it does not
necessarily mean that they wish to resolve external conflicts in the
same way. Moreover, their example may provide an important model for
others to emulate, but perhaps only for their intra-group disputes.

Yet the model would be far less attractive if, in its external relations,
the EC/Twelve merely pursued narrow self-interests — though, of
course, other states might be led to emulate it and to group themselves
together in order to counter its strength. But many of the chapters
collected here point to the significance of other, indigenous factors
involved in regional integration as well as a 'positive' and a 'negative'
role for the EC/Twelve. And, in addition, there are a number of factors
which suggest that self-interest in the traditional sense has not been the
basic EC/Twelve motive. First, the integration process within the
Community has been of profound political and legal significance for its
member states; the pooling of sovereignty over an ever-growing range of
issues that increasingly affect basic economic welfare cannot be ignored
as an influence on the Community's external relations. It has been both
a symptom of complex inter-dependence as well as being a catalyst for
others to come to grips with the phenomenon. Secondly, the process of
integration has spawned, as we have seen, a vast range of interlinking
contacts and relationships, a network that has to be taken into account
whether or not there is any agreement on the extent to which it
determines inter-governmental relations. Thirdly, the EC/Twelve have
eschewed the adoption of the traditional trappings of the state, i.e. a
common defence identity. The fact that the member states have rejected
a common defence structure necessarily restricts the EC/Twelve to a
civilian role in the international system. There is though perhaps an
element of disingenuousness here for not all third parties fully
appreciate the subtleties that divorce the EC from EPC and its
considerations of only the political and economic aspects of security,
from Western European Union, the Independent European Programme
Group and even NATO; all such bodies are a reflection of Western
Europe's 'power' whatever the chains of command or differences of
membership. On the other hand, it has become almost commonplace to
point out that in a tightly interdependent world, military power is no
longer necessarily the most efficient instrument of policy and that

other, civil means can be very much more persuasive. In that case, one is left, however, with the question of the extent to which means influence ends.

Such arguments may or may not reflect underlying assumptions that are justified. The conclusion that the EC/Twelve is a different kind of actor from that of the traditional state with different aims and objectives is convincing. The implications are that the EC/Twelve pursue policies and positions that may be sub-optimal in terms of its individual members but they are policies that are at least acceptable to all as in the 'general' interest. At the same time, of course, those policies cause additional problems in terms of negotiations, especially with other groups of states.

But if there is such a shift in terms of priorities and interactions, it would suggest that the phenomenon of group-to-group relations needs to be taken seriously. This is especially so if the move towards regional groupings is a lasting one, which the evidence suggests that it is. If so, further studies would be relevant not only to the International Relations discipline in moving it beyond the state- and US-centric approaches that have tended to characterize it so far but would also be to the benefit of policy-makers who, of necessity, are working in a radically changed and changing environment.

Notes

1 The author would like to thank Randolph Kent and Paul Taylor for their comments on an earlier draft of this chapter.
2 J. M. Rochester, 'The Rise and Fall of International Organization as a field of study' *International Organization* (1986), Vol. 40, 777–813. See also S. Strange, 'Cave Hic Dragones: A Critique of Regime Analysis', for a telling criticism of regime theory as creating precisely such a bandwagon in S. Krasner (ed.), *International Regimes* (Ithaca and London: Cornell University Press, 1983).
3 Ernst Haas, 'Turbulent Fields and the Theory of Regional Integration' *International Organization* (1976), Vol. 30, 173–212.
4 The influence of Thomas Kuhn has clearly been of the utmost importance. See his *The Structure of Scientific Revolutions* (Chicago and London: University of Chicago Press, 1962).
5 In his edited volume, *International Relations: British and American Perspectives* (Oxford: Basil Blackwell, 1985).
6 F. Kratchwill and J. G. Ruggie, 'International Organization: a state of the Art or an Art of the State', *International Organization* (1986), Vol. 40, 753–75.
7 P. Kennedy, *The Rise and Fall of the Great Powers: Economic Change and Military Conflict from 1500–2000*, (London: Unwin Hyman, 1988).
8 'Regionalism Reconsidered: A Critical Theory for the 1980s', in A. J. R. Groom and P. Taylor, *Frameworks for International Cooperation* (London: Frances Pinter, 1989).

9 The categories identified by Taylor include: (i) the approach that sought to measure the coincidence of economic, social, cultural and political indicators epitomized in the work of Bruce Russett, and which was seen as methodologically complicated and possibly not worth the effort — see Bruce M. Russett, *International Regions and the International System* (Chicago: Rand McNally, 1967); (ii) a description of the dynamics of integration — including of course the concept of 'spill-over' — in the work of those known as the neo-functionalists — see Ernst B. Haas, *Beyond the Nation State* (Stanford, University Press, 1964, and L. Lindberg and S. Scheingold, *Regional Integration* (Cambridge, Mass., Harvard University Press, 1971); (iii) the analysis of primarily the motives of élites and their interpretation of the costs and benefits of regional organization which led, for example, Joseph Nye to conclude that it was unlikely that new political actors were evolving that would overturn the existing character of the system — see J. Nye 'Regional Institutions', in Cyril E. Black and R. Falk, *The Structure of the International Environment* (Princeton University Press, 1972); (iv) an approach that was preoccupied more with prediction and prescription, not least structuralists such as André Gunder Frank, and the need for South–South cooperation — see A. G. Frank, 'The Development of Under-development', *Monthly Review* (Sept. 1966, pp. 17–30); (v) lastly a group preoccupied with multipolarity in the international system and the possibilities for stability in a multi-block system, well illustrated in the work of Roger Masters, 'A Multi-bloc Model of the International System *APSR* (1961) Vol. 55, No. 4, 780–98.

10 See for example Weiler and Wessels 'EPC and the Challenge of Theory', in A. Pijpers *et al. European Political Cooperation in the 1980s* (Dordrecht: Martinus Nijhoff, 1989).

11 See Alfred Pijpers, 'European Political Cooperation and the Realist Paradigm', as yet unpublished paper presented to the European Community Studies Association, George Mason University, May 1989.

12 P. Ifestos, *European Political Cooperation: Towards a Framework of Supranational Diplomacy* (Aldershot: Avebury, 1987).

13 Again the influence of Thomas Kuhn (op. cit.) is clear. For a discussion of the evolution of International Relations theory see K. J. Holsti, *The Dividing Discipline*, London (Allen & Unwin: 1985), or Michael Banks *Conflict in World Society,* (Brighton: Wheatsheaf, 1984).

14 This is in fact what Pijpers plumps for in his paper, op. cit.

15 Douglas Hurd, 'Political Co-operation', *International Affairs* (1981) Vol. 57, 383–93.

16 For example K. N. Waltz, *Theory of International Relations* (London and Reading, Mass.: Addison Wesley, 1979).

17 See R. Keohane (ed.), *Neo-Realism and its Critics* (New York: Columbia University Press, 1985).

18 E. H. Carr, *The Twenty Years Crisis 1919–39* London (Macmillan: 1946); H. J. Morganthau, *Politics Among Nations* (New York: A. Knopf, 1972).

19 D. Puchala, 'Of Blind Men, Elephants and International Integration', *Journal of Common Market Studies* (1972), Vol. 10, 267–84.

20 D. P. Calleo, *Beyond American Hegemony* (Brighton: Wheatsheaf, 1987).

21 See Hedley Bull, *The Anarchical Society* (London: Macmillan, 1977), p. 265.

22 Robert Axelrod and Robert Keohane, 'Achieving Cooperation under Anarchy', *World Politics* (1985), Vol. XXXVIII, No. 1, 226–54.

23 For an application of the inter-paradigm debate to international organizations which suggests these distinctions see P. Taylor, 'Prescribing for the Reform of International Organization' *Review of International Studies* (1987), Vol. 13, 19–38.

24 See R. D. McKinlay and R. Little, *Global Problems and World Order* (London: Frances Pinter, 1986).

25 Robert Keohane and Joseph Nye Jr (eds), *Transnational Relations and World Politics* (Cambridge, Mass. and London: Harvard University Press, 1971).

26 J. W. Burton, *World Society* (London: Cambridge University Press, 1972).

27 The concern, for example, of Pijpers, op. cit.

28 Although the analogy at least of the cobweb is decidedly misleading in that it presupposes some sort of creator and maintainer, perhaps even a Hobbesian Leviathan!

29 Richard Little, 'Structuralism and Neo-Realism', in M. Light and A. J. R. Groom, (eds), *International Relations: A Handbook of Current Theory* (London: Frances Pinter, 1985), p. 76. That is not to say that all structuralists or at least all neo-Marxists deny any role to the individual. Little goes on to note the criticism made by E. P. Thomson that structuralists dehumanizse history where 'systems and sub-systems, elements and structures are drilled up and down the page pretending to be people'.

30 See R. Keohane, *Neo-Realism and its Critics*, op. cit.

31 See, for example, Bob Jessop, *The Capitalist State* (Oxford: Martin Robertson, 1982).

32 For example, Robert Cox, *Production, Power and World Order* (New York: Columbia University Press, 1987) who forsakes 'the actors-interactions paradigm that has been so influential in social science, in favour of one grounded in historical structures'. It is the latter which give a framework for action and form the actors, p. 395.

33 See for example André Gunder Frank, *Capitalism and Underdevelopment in Latin America* (Harmondsworth Penguin, 1971).

34 See for example E. Mandel, *Late Capitalism* (London: Verso, 1978).

35 Robert Cox, *Production, Power and World Order,* op. cit. p. 259.

36 See for example Timothy Shaw 'EEC–ACP Interactions and Images as Redefinitions of EurAfrica ...', *Journal of Common Market Studies* (1979) Vol. XVII, 135–58.

37 J. Galtung, *The True Worlds* (New York: Free Press, 1980).

38 I. Wallerstein, *The Politics of the World Economy* (Cambridge: Cambridge University Press, 1984).

39 In Pijpers *et al., op. cit.,* p. 211.

40 ibid., p. 212.

41 The suggestion is meant to defuse arguments over how interests are determined and the freedom of manoeuvre that 'the state' might have among competing interests, etc.

42 Fritz W. Scharpf, 'The Joint Decision Trap: Lessons from German Federalism and European Integration', *Public Administration* (1988) Vol. 66, 239–78, see especially p. 257.

43 ibid., p. 271.

44 Robert D. Putnam, 'Diplomacy and Domestic Politics: The Logic of Two-level Games', *International Organization* (1988), Vol. 42, 427–60.

45 Putnam, *ibid.*, p. 447, where this is termed *synergistic linkage*.

46 Bull, op. cit.; J. Galtung, *The European Community: A Super-Power in the Making* (London: Allen & Unwin, 1973).
47 François Duchêne, 'Europe's Role in World Peace', in Richard Mayne, *Europe Tomorrow* (London: Fontana/Collins Chatham House: PEP 1972, p. 43. See also Christopher Hill, 'European Foreign Policy: Power Bloc, Civilian Model — or Flop?', in Reinhardt Rummel *et al.* (eds), *Konferenzbericht betr: Die Europäische Gemeinschaft zwischen nationaler Interessenbefriedigung und weltweiter Mitverantwortung*, Ebenhausen, 1987.

Selected Bibliography

The bibliography that follows includes some of the basic documents relating to both the EC's external relations and European Political Cooperation (EPC), together with some of the more recent works by both academics and diplomats, on the making of a 'European Foreign Policy'.

Documents

Auswärtiges Amt (ed.): *Europäische Politische Zusammenarbeit (EPZ)*: *Dokumentation*, 8th edition, Bonn, 1987.
Bulletin of the European Communities (sections on the EC's external relations and EPC).
Commission of the European Communities (ed.): *Annual Report on the Activities of the EC* (sections on the EC's external relations and EPC).
Department of Foreign Affairs (ed.): *European Political Cooperation*: *Statements* 1989, Dublin, 1990.
European University Institute and Institut für Europäische Politik (eds): *European Political Cooperation Documentation Bulletin 1985*, Luxembourg, 1987 onwards (biannual reporting on all official EPC documents).
Ministerio de Asuntos Exteriores (ed.): *European Political Cooperation*: *Statements* 1988, Madrid, 1989.
Official Journal of the European Communities (publication of all legal agreements).

Monographs/Articles

Bassompierre, Guy de, *Changing the Guard in Brussels: An Insider's View of the EC Presidency*, Washington, 1989.
Froment-Meurice, Henri and Ludlow, Peter: *Towards a European Foreign Policy*, Centre for European Policy Studies, CEPS Sixth Annual Conference 1989, Brussels, 1989.
Gerard, Yannick, 'La coopération politique européenne: Méthodes et resultats', *Revue du Marché Commun* (1987) Vol. 309.

Januzzi, Giovanni, 'European Political Cooperation and the Single European Act', in Panos Tsakaloyannis (ed.): *Western European Security in a Changing World: From the Reactivation of the WEU to the Single European Act*, Maastricht, 1988.

Nuttall, Simon, 'European Political Cooperation', in Jacobs, Francis G. (ed.): *Yearbook of European Law*, Oxford, 1982, 1983 et seq.

Pijpers, Alfred, Regelsberger, Elfriede and Wessels, Wolfgang (eds): *European Political Cooperation in the 1980s: Towards a Foreign Policy for Western Europe*, Dordrecht, Boston, London, 1988. (dt: Die Europäische Politische Zusammenarbeit in den achtziger Jahren. Eine gemeinsame Aussenpolitik für Westeuropa? Europäische Schriften des instituts für Europäische Politik, Band GS, Bonn, 1989.

Regelsberger, Elfriede, 'Die Europäische Politische Zusammenarbeit', in Weidenfeld, Werner and Wessels, Wolfgang (eds): *Jahrbuch der Europäischen Integration*, Bonn, 1986, 1987 et seq.

Rummel, Reinhardt *EPZ: Erfolgsformel für gemeinsame westeuropäische Aussenpolitik?* Ebenhausen, 1987.

Schoutheete, Philippe de, *La coopération politique européene*. 2nd edition, Brussels, 1986.

Index

(NOTE: This index is compiled in word-by-word order. Page numbers printed in italics indicate Tables. The word *passim* indicates that the subject so annotated is referred to in scattered passages throughout the pages indicated.)